LUTHER'S FAITH

The Cause of the Gospel in the Church

by

DANIEL OLIVIER

Translated by

JOHN TONKIN

Concordia

Publishing House

To the teachers and students of the
Institut Protestant de Théologie
for one hundred years of service
in the cause of the Gospel (1877-1977)

To Françoise Fourès, Pierre, and Céline

Cover: Luther preaching the Gospel from the stone pulpit of the Castle Church in Torgau. Detail from the *Predella* of the Altarpiece by Lucas Cranach the Elder, 1547.

Photograph appeared in *From Luther to 1580: A Pictorial Account*, copyright © 1977 by Concordia Publishing House, St, Louis.

Most Scripture quotations are from the Revised Standard Version of the Bible, copyrighted 1946, 1952, © 1971, 1973.

When possible, quotations from Luther's writings are from *Luthers' Works*, American Edition, © Concordia Publishing House, St. Louis, Mo., and Fortress Press, Philadelphia, Pa. Used by permission.

Copyright © 1978 Beauchesne Editeur
72 rue des Saints-Pères
75007 PARIS, FRANCE

English translation first published 1982
by Concordia Publishing House
3558 South Jefferson Avenue
St. Louis, Missouri 63118

Manufactured in the United States of America

Library of Congress Cataloging in Publication Data

Olivier, Daniel.
    Luther's faith.

    Translation of: La foi de Luther.
    1. Luther, Martin, 1483-1546. I. Title.
BR333.3.04413   1982   284.1′092′4   82-8298
ISBN 0-570-03868-5

---

1 2 3 4 5 6 7 8 9 10

Contents

Foreword

The publication in English of Daniel Olivier's *La Foi de Luther* is an event of great ecumenical importance. It is a book of tremendous significance to the *una sancta*, the whole Christian church on earth. Why so?

Luther once said that when it comes to theology—*es gehört eine gewisse Bescheidenheit dazu.* Yes, theology calls for a good deal of humility, for only God really knows. In a way, only Roman Catholics can really understand what bothered Luther and what the evangelical cause was all about, not fatuous though very educated liberals and not ingenuous undereducated moral majority types. What a book you now hold in your hands!

Following the often mindless polemics between Catholic and Lutheran scholars of the past and present centuries, we now have yet another more ecumenical approach to Luther's faith. Professor Olivier is a pioneer in ecumenicity. He was a student of Yves Congar in Paris and a senior fellow at the Institute for European History in Mainz, where he encountered the formidable brilliance and ecumenical approach of the sainted Prof. Dr. Joseph Lortz. Professor Lortz in his pioneering volumes on the Reformation and his many published lectures told all the world that Luther was a good and well-intended man. Luther had his shortcomings, was *nicht vollhörend*, not attentive to the whole counsel of God. But, Lortz maintained, he was a godsend to the Catholic Church in redirecting it to its religious mission and would someday be rewarded with sainthood. Professor Lortz's students and colleagues have moved on to examine Luther's theology more closely. Professor Olivier, as befits a French intellectual, has always followed an independent course.

This book, which is a sequel to Olivier's quite remarkable earlier work, *The Trial of Luther* (Concordia, 1978), takes for its major thesis that Luther's chief contribution to the religious life of the Reformation was his rediscovery of the Gospel with its

5

liberating message that faith or trust in Jesus Christ as Savior is the all-sufficient means for man's salvation. It is a gift of the loving God, not dependent upon adherence to the old law, a mediatory priesthood, a prior state of humility, or the performance of good works as a contribution to one's own salvation.

Olivier's method is effective and reminds us that the French "explication du texte" or, as Olivier terms it, "la lecture integrale," is an unbeatable technique for an exegetical approach to theology. In this very exciting volume every major facet of Luther's theology is attested by the inclusion of extended texts drawn from his early, middle, and mature years. They are followed by Olivier's learned and relentless explanation of their meaning in the light of Roman practice and German experience. Olivier's admiration for Luther as a theologian, his assertion of his catholicity, his focus on the *theologia crucis*, and his feeling that the Church's rejection of Luther's theology was a net loss represent a bold step forward in the ecumenical rapprochement of Protestants and Roman Catholics.

The reader is fortunate to have in hand John Tonkin's felicitous translation of the French text into English. Those of you who know Luther's open letter *On Translating* will savor again his moving sentences:

> I have constantly tried, in translating, to produce a pure and clear German, and it has often happened that for two or three or four weeks we have searched and inquired for a single word and sometimes not found it even then. In translating Job, Master Philip [Melanchthon], [Matthew] Aurogallus, and I labored so, that sometimes we scarcely handled three lines in four days. Now that it is translated and finished, everybody can read and criticize it. One now runs his eyes over three or four pages and does not stumble once—without realizing what boulders and clods had once lain there where he now goes along as over a smoothly planed board. We had to sweat and toil there before we got those boulders and clods out of the way, so that one could go along so nicely. The ploughing goes well when the field is cleared. But rooting out the woods and stumps, and getting the field ready—this is a job nobody wants. There is no such thing as earning the world's thanks.

Nevertheless, Professor Tonkin, we thank you for translating both *The Trial of Luther* and this volume on Luther's faith into English.

When an impudent fellow once asked Luther why he did not

"leave the ivory tower" and enter the "front trenches," in the parish, Luther responded with, "I send forth my books into all the world!" It was a typical answer of the intellectual. This book of Daniel Olivier has a special charm, for it not only has precious points to make for the scholar but, above all, it speaks to everyone.

Lewis W. Spitz
William R. Kenan Professor
of History
Stanford University

Translator's Preface

English-language readers who gave Daniel Olivier's previous book such a warm reception will be pleased to see this sequel appear in translation, though they will find it in some respects a very different book from *The Trial of Luther*. Its careful and subtle theological analysis at first seems a far cry from the dramatic and racy narrative of the earlier work. The reader who in that book was thrust imaginatively into the midst of the vivid drama of Luther's trial is here invited to join the author in a search for the "real" Luther by grappling closely with some of the Reformer's writings in which he lays bare his innermost thoughts and convictions. Yet for all the differences in style and approach, the Luther who emerges from the pages of this book is the same "Man of the Gospel" whom we met earlier, now etched in sharper detail.

This is a Luther who will challenge readers of all backgrounds and persuasions. Catholic readers who have been taught by two generations of their own scholars to come to terms again with Luther will find something fresh in these pages. By the same token, Protestants will find no opportunity for self-congratulation, for this picture is far from the realms of pious hagiography, and it shows us a man whose challenge is directed today as much to his followers and heirs as to those who rejected and denounced him. As for those who would forsake the theological questions of this period of history for purely secularist perspectives, a telling warning is given that to abandon those issues which drove Luther in his search and caused so many to flock to his cause is to falsify history.

This is a book in principle for everyone, yet it is obviously directed towards French readers, and sometimes those very features which do most to enliven it for the French audience pose problems for another audience and for the translator who tries to mediate between the author and his readers. This is especially true of the translations of Luther's writings, which bear Olivier's distinctive stamp, though they are often based on standard French versions. The Luther who emerges from this process is a Luther who speaks especially to the French, and Olivier deftly justifies this by appealing to the analogy of Luther's own defense of his German translation of the Psalms:

> Whoever would speak German must not use Hebrew style. Rather he must see to it—once he understands the Hebrew author—that he concentrates on the sense of the text, asking himself, "Pray, tell, what do the Germans say in such a situation?' Once he has the German words to serve the purpose, let him drop the Hebrew words and express the meaning freely in the best German he knows (LW 35, pp. 213—14).

By the same principles, what the English version needed was clearly not an English translation of Olivier's French Luther texts but something that would perform a parallel function for English readers. Since most of these writings were readily available in excellent modern English in the American Edition of *Luther's Works*, I have chosen to use this edition, while retaining the subheadings which Olivier has provided for the guidance of his readers. In those cases where the texts were not available in the American Edition, I have translated directly from the Weimar Edition, attempting as far as possible to preserve the particular nuances of the author's French versions. Six long excerpts have been put into italic type.

Other significant changes in this edition include relocation of the chronology and bibliography in keeping with usual English conventions, and modifications of the footnotes. Some notes of interest only to French readers have been eliminated, while other notes have been combined or condensed, and a few have even found their way back into the text. The aim was not to reduce the bulk of the notes as an end in itself, but to make them more accessible and useful to English-language readers, while preserving everything that was necessary from a scholarly point of view. Accordingly, citations and references have been given to accessible English versions wherever possible. On the other hand, there has been no attempt to eliminate foreign-language sources simply because they were not available in translation. A notable feature of Olivier's work is his use of the great French interpreters of the Reformation—so often bypassed in the English-language sources, which tend to be more attuned to German literature—and I have considered it important to preserve much of this material both in the text and in the notes. Identical considerations have governed the recasting of the bibliography.

Among those whom I wish to thank especially for their help, without relinquishing my responsibility for the final product, are Heather Vose, a postgraduate student in the Department of History at the University of Western Australia, who functioned as my critic for the entire translation; my colleagues in the Department of French Studies, especially Graeme Lord and Brian Willis, who were most helpful in sorting out difficult linguistic problems; my wife Barbara, who made many useful suggestions about English style; and the author, Daniel Olivier, who showed keen interest in the problem from the very beginning and was willing as before to clarify the residual problems of a translator anxious to interpret him faithfully to his English readers.

John Tonkin
History Department
University of Western Australia
November 1981

Chronological Landmarks

Luther's faith is presented in this book on the basis of the history of the Church since the Avignon papacy, through the 30 years of the Reformation crisis and the centuries of confessional struggles down to our own time. This historical tableau reveals the permanent character of the problem of the Gospel in the Church. The condemnation of Luther only scratched the surface of most of the questions which his advent and his success posed to the Western Church. That condemnation belongs to the past. But the call for the conversion of the Church to the Gospel remains at the heart of the dynamic of the ecumenical movement. Paul VI's visit to Geneva is in continuity with Luther's coming to Worms.

Before Luther

1305—78	Avignon papacy. Development of the Roman system of benefices, taxes, indulgences, etc.
1349	Death of William of Occam, the English Franciscan who was the founder of "Nominalist" theology. This "modern way" defined things by their own names and preferred logical evidence to abstraction. It took its place within theology alongside the "old way" (Thomas, Bonaventura). Occam was an opponent of papal power.
1350—1450	Hundred Years' War. Great Plague. In England John Wyclif criticizes indulgences and preaches a return to the Bible.
1378—1417	Great Schism. Two, or even three, popes at the same time.
1414—17	Council of Constance. End of the schism, by the election of Martin V.

1415	Execution of John Hus, Czech preacher against indulgences, supporter of a return to Scripture and Communion in both kinds (Wyclif's influence).
1419—34	Hussite wars. Bohemian schism.
1434—48	Council of Basel. An anti-pope and another schism.
1450—55	Beginnings of printing; first printed Bible. The spiritual movement of the "new devotion," the *Imitation of Christ* and the *German Theology*.

Luther's Catholic Period (1483—1517)

1483	Luther's birth.
1492—1503	Alexander VI (Borgia). Discovery of America.
1497	Death of Gabriel Biel, a nominalist and "last of the scholastics," one of the first authors studied by Luther (on the Mass).
1498	Execution of Savonarola.
1501—05	Luther at the University of Erfurt.
1503—13	Julius II.
1505	Luther with the Erfurt Augustinians. Erasmus: *Praise of Folly* and *Enchiridion*.
1507	Indulgence for rebuilding St. Peter's in Rome.
1510—11	Luther's journey to Rome. During this period occurred the schismatic Council of Pisa, supported by France.
1512—17	Fifth "Ecumenical" Council (Lateran). Leo X (1513—21).
1512—18	Luther, doctor of theology. Lectures on Holy Scripture in Wittenberg.
1516	Erasmus: Edition of the Greek New Testament.
1517 (April)	Carlstadt's *151 Theses* at Wittenberg, on indulgences.
1517 (4 Sept.)	Luther's *97 Theses Against Scholastic Theology*.

The Beginnings of the Reformation (1517—21)

1517 (31 Oct.)	Luther's *95 Theses* on the value of indulgences.
1518 (April)	Heidelberg: Meeting of the Chapter, and Disputation.
1518 (June)	Opening of proceedings by Rome against Luther.
1518 (Aug.)	Melanchthon becomes professor at the University of Wittenberg.
1518 (Oct.)	Luther appears at Augsburg before Cajetan, the papal legate. He refuses to retract, and appeals to the pope and to the next council.
1519 (28 June)	Charles V, Holy Roman Emperor.
1519 (July)	Leipzig Debate, with John Eck. Luther takes up a position against the infallibility of popes and councils, and against papal primacy by divine right.
1520 (15 June)	Bull *Exsurge Domine* "against the errors of Martin Luther and his followers."
1520 (June)	*On the Papacy at Rome.*
1520 (Aug.-Nov.)	The Reformation writings: *Appeal to the Christian Nobility, The Babylonian Captivity, The Freedom of a Christian.*
1520 (Oct.)	Henry VIII of England, *Defense of the Seven Sacraments* against Luther.
1520 (10 Dec.)	Luther publicly burns the papal bull.
1521 (3 Jan.)	Luther's excommunication.
1521 (17—18 April)	Luther at Worms. Another refusal to retract.
1521 (4 May)—	
1522 (1 March)	Luther at the Wartburg.
1521 (26 May)	Edict of Worms. Luther put under the imperial ban. Proceedings against his supporters and his works.

Protestantism

1521—22	Luther's Writings at the Wartburg: *Commentary on the Magnificat, On Monastic Vows, Sermons, Translation of the New Testament*, reply to Henry VIII, etc.

1521—22 (Winter)	Troubles at Wittenberg, with Carlstadt and Münzer. Zurich: Zwingli's Reformation, from 1519. France: the evangelical circle at Meaux.
1521 (Dec.)	Melanchthon's *Loci communes* (an attempt to systematize Luther's doctrine).
1522	Luther takes Wittenberg in hand, through his preaching.
1523	Reform of Gustavus Vasa in Sweden. The Anabaptists.
1524—1525	The Peasant's War, in Alsace and Saxony.
1525 (13 June)	Luther's marriage.
1525 (Dec.)	Treatise *On the Bondage of the Will*, against Erasmus. Reformation in Prussia, Denmark, and at Basel.
1529	Marburg Colloquy: Luther in disagreement with the other Reformers on the Real Presence. *Large Catechism* and *Small Catechism*. Diet of Speyer: first appearance of the term "Protestant," after the protestation addressed to the emperor by the German princes and cities (including Strasbourg).
1530	Diet of Augsburg and Augsburg Confession.
1531	Zwingli's death at Cappel, in the war against the Catholic cantons. Smalcaldic League between the German Lutheran states. *Commentary on Galatians*.
1534	Appearance of the German translation of the Bible.
1534	Henry VIII's schism. In France the Affair of the Placards.
1536	Calvin (b. 1509), *Institutes of the Christian Religion*, published at Basel. Crushing of the Anabaptists at Münster.
1537	Smalcald Articles.
1539—41	Colloquies at Hagenau, Worms, Ratisbon, to reestablish religious unity.
1543	Calvin at Geneva.
1545	Luther: *Against the Papacy at Rome, an Institution of the Devil*.

1545 (13 Dec.) Opening of the Council of Trent. Beginnings of the Counter-Reformation.

1546 (18 Feb.) Luther's Death.

After Luther

1545—63 Council of Trent. St. Pius V.

1555 Peace of Augsburg: recognition of the legality of Lutheranism within the Empire. The principle *cuius regio eius religio* (each should observe the religion of his country).

1560 Wars of Religion in France. Massacre of St. Bartholomew (1572). Conversion of the Protestant Henry IV to Catholicism.

1598 Edict of Nantes: recognition of the legality of Protestantism within France.

1618—48 Thirty Years' War.

1620 Arrival of the English Puritans (Pilgrim Fathers) in the New World.

1648 Treaty of Westphalia: definitive victory of Protestantism in Germany.

1685 Revocation of the Edict of Nantes (Louis XIV).

18th Century War of the Camisards in the Cavennes. Age of Enlightenment. Influence of the Protestant Jean-Jacques Rousseau. 1787 Edict of Toleration in France, in favor of Protestantism.

19th Century Bonaparte: freedom of worship. Protestant awakenings in Europe. Kant, Hegel, Marx, Schleiermacher. Liberal Protestantism.

20th Century Ecumenical Movement. Bultmann, Barth, Tillich, Bonhoeffer. World Council of Churches, at Geneva. Protestants at the Second Vatican Council (1962—1965). Paul VI at Geneva (1969).

Abbreviations

ARG   *Archiv für Reformationsgeschichte* (Gütersloh, 1903—)
CR   *Corpus Reformatorum* (Halle/Braunschweig, 1834—1900)
Lj   *Lutherjahrbuch* (1919—41, 1957—)
LW   *Luther's Works* (American Edition), ed. J. Pelikan and H. Lehmann (Philadelphia and St. Louis, 1957—76)
MPL   J. P. Migne (ed.), *Patrologia Latina* (Paris, 1844—90)
NRTh   *Nouvelle Revue Théologique* (Tournai; 1868—)
PL   *Positions Lutheriennes* (Paris, 1953—)
RSPT   *Revue des Sciences Philosophiques et Théologiques* (Paris, 1907—)
WA   *D. Martin Luthers Werke: Kritische Gesamtausgabe* (Weimar, 1883—)
WA TR   *D. Martin Luthers Werke: Tischreden* (Weimar, 1912—)

Introduction

In 1983 the 500th anniversary of the birth of Martin Luther (1483—1546) will be celebrated. This event will not pass without due recognition; indeed, very little time ever goes by without some mention of the name of a man who symbolizes the greatest crisis in the history of Christianity, and the only one which has resisted all attempts to solve it. That crisis was the Reformation, which brought about the division between Catholics and Protestants over the question of the place or the role of the pope in the Church of Jesus Christ.

What should we think of Luther today? His name was brought up again in relation to the Lefebvre affair.[1] The conflict between Rome and a prelate who made himself the guarantor of faith and tradition against the pope evoked memories of the beginnings of the Reformation. But the new dissidence struggles against the "Luther-Mass" and the "protestantization" of Catholicism since the Second Vatican Council (1962—65). It puts itself forward as the last plank of salvation for those who do not want to die as Protestants.

The question of the "protestantization" of the Church of Rome will necessarily be the great issue of this book, though it was conceived quite independently of that quarrel. Lefebvre's movement brought pressure to bear on Rome and on Church opinion by reducing the question of conciliar reform to a simple alternative: whether to stand for the Council of Trent and St. Pius V or to deviate, with Vatican II and Paul VI, into Communism, Freemasonry, and Protestantism. Can a study of Luther's faith by a priest specializing in Luther studies be anything other than a new trial for the Catholic faith?

Looking coldly at the facts, the assertion that the changes within the Church since the Council[2] tend to bring Catholicism into line with Protestant views is at best only a hypothesis. Confusion is always possible, and the risks are not to be underestimated. But that should not be allowed to prevent the study of problems which Lefebvre's movement alone wants to ignore, against the feelings of the universal Church and the clear evidence of recent years.

The starting point of the changes criticized was the impulse given by the Council. The Catholic faith holds that the bishops assembled in Council are inspired by the Holy Spirit. Now fraternization with Protestants began precisely at the Council, by the admission of observers invited by Pope John XXIII to the sessions of Vatican II. That presence had been wanting at the Council of Trent (1545—63), which condemned the Reformation. The consequence then had been the development of an anti-Protestant Catholicism, precisely what Lefebvre's movement is attempting to perpetuate in the name of the faith.

But no one should take lightly the efforts of a large social institution such as the Catholic Church to try to remedy a catastrophic decision within its own past—catastrophic not in the sense that Trent might have been mistaken about the true nature of Catholicism, but because the Counter-Reformation failed to overcome the schism, leaving Christianity lamentably divided. The solution brought to the crisis was a mistaken one, and the new attitude which appeared at Vatican II was really only the outcome of a reasoned decision no longer to be blindly anti-Protestant because that attitude has brought no solution and is no longer necessary.

The Council of Trent tried to defend a Catholicism whose existence was threatened by the progress of Protestantism. The urgency of the moment explains why it had to condemn a movement which turned away from Rome a growing number of the faithful. But this problem of the survival of Catholicism in the face of Protestant expansion is no longer present. The world now faces the Church with challenges formidable in other ways. At the Vatican Council, Catholicism was able to contemplate with composure the existence of other ecclesial communities and the necessity of dialog with them. In so doing, it became itself again.

Is the price to be paid for this thaw the inevitable infiltration of Roman dogma by Protestant ideas, as the purists noisily claim? Their interpretation of the Council of Trent is that every rapprochement with the Protestants amounts to a pact with heresy. They imagine that they see this menace taking shape in the reform of the Mass, which, they claim, has become "Luther's Mass."

Certainly it did seem for a long time that the Church could not modify the position which prevailed from the Council of Trent until Pius XII, who died in 1958. But can there be any doubt that the evolution of Catholicism since Vatican II has been in conformity with its fundamental principles? Was not the constitution on the liturgy, which was the first act of conciliar reform, a response to the clear necessity of adapting the ancient rites and evangelizing the people by the Word of God?

At that time I had already begun to study Luther. I was struck by the fact that this gathering of bishops from all over the world granted to the Church, in matters of worship and the celebration of the Mass, justifiable changes which the Reformer had sought in vain four centuries earlier. This led me to another conception of the problems inherited from the 16th century. The dogmatism and ritualism of St. Pius V (the pope at the end of the Council of Trent) amounted in the end to a process of impoverishment in that the development of Church life was arrested at a particular stage of its history. The measures of the reign of Pius XII could not be Rome's last words on ecumenism, or on so many other contemporary problems, for that would have been to push to absurd lengths the denial of facts which could no longer be ignored. Would Catholicism, under the pretext of fidelity to the letter of Trent (certainly not to its spirit) renounce indefinitely the freedom to take necessary steps for the well-being of the Church and of the faithful, just in case such measures could be called "Protestant"?

What is presented in this book is the result of research stimulated by reflections like these. It is apparent that the real Protestants are not always those who appear to be so. It is one thing to protest one's faith and another thing altogether to be more papist than the pope. My aim here is to put to rest once and for all the idea of the "protestantization" of the Church. What is at stake is not washing conciliar Catholicism clean of the reproach of compromise with heresy or issuing a certificate of orthodoxy to Protestantism. What matters is to help every Christian of goodwill to take the measure of the development in which he is actor as well as spectator, and which is only the long-delayed fulfillment of what the Council of Trent would have been able to do had the moment been right.

This work was in hand before Lefebvre's first ordinations. In keeping with the nature of this series,[3] its aim was to make a point on a subject still of present importance for the Church. Luther's topicality scarcely has to be demonstrated, for Luther studies are being pursued at the rate of many hundreds of publications every year.[4] The result of all this endeavor is considerable, though little known to the public. Problems of history and doctrine are being more effectively mastered. The debate about Luther himself is becoming clearer than it was, though it remains difficult to agree about him. In any case, it is no longer the Luther of the past who matters to us, but the lasting value of his work. Rome's condemnations of his errors are maintained without change. But we have seen brought to birth a Catholic Luther research which has standing among Protestants and which led the Holy See to recognize in 1970 that Luther had been a sincere Christian, and devoted to the Gospel.[5] Our task is to sketch an outline of those researches and the knowledge now acquired, within the limits of the space available to us.

As far as Luther studies are concerned, religious significance matters every bit as much as scientific results. Research, in fact, is always driven back to the debate about Luther's faith. That faith is the source of a dogmatic antagonism which has a continued impact on the study of Luther's life and thought. The real point of the Luther problem is thus to show what point the discussion on faith, which lies at the basis of the Reformation, has reached.

The nub of the conflict is Catholic opposition to Protestantism's characteristic ideas: the authority of the Word of God, justification by faith, and the universal priesthood. Catholics have their own perspective on these ideas, which leads them to define a large number of Protestant doctrines and practices as heretical. Roman intransigence in the face of Protestantism today constitutes the insurmountable obstacle to an agreement about Luther's faith, so much are the past and the present bound together in this debate which concerns at its highest point the image which Christianity would like to give of itself.

The discussion entered on a new path by virtue of the "discovery"[6] of Luther by a number of 20th-century Catholic historians and theologians. This word "discovery" is not too strong, for in its eagerness to identify Luther from the start as the man to condemn, Catholicism through the centuries has "ignored" him in every sense of the term. In their incomparable zeal for cataloguing the Reformer's heresies,[7] the defenders of Catholic truth have, without exception, passed by obvious facts recognized today by the community of historians.

Now it is readily admitted that Luther was improperly condemned and that the rigid attitude of refusing any association with Protestants, taken once and for all after Luther's excommunication in 1521 and at the Council of Trent, was not without injury to the Church. But what is really significant is the growing feeling that Luther's reformation was not a pointless event, that it was and is of positive significance for the Catholic faith. Joseph Lortz saw it as "nothing short of the uncovering of the Church's own deepest treasures, but in a one-sided and hence objectively false presentation," and he had no hesitation in envisaging the "reintroduction into the Catholic Church of Luther's riches."[8] The same point was made by one of the leading Catholic Luther experts, O. H. Pesch: "Luther is today for Catholic theology a witness to the common faith, for the past as well as for the future; he is our 'common master,' as Cardinal Willebrands said in 1970 at Evian."[9]

I shall have to speak in more detail of this Catholic change of direction in relation to Luther, about which recent books and specialized reviews allow us to be readily informed. It has engendered a sense of euphoria which has led to an unsuccessful request to Rome for a lifting of Luther's excommunication.[10] But we are not on the point of "rehabilitating" Luther, and this book itself has not been written with that aim in mind. Too many obstacles are set in the path of a Catholic reception of Luther's faith. Roman orthodoxy has its vigilant guardians, for whom wanting to make Luther Catholic is tantamount to becoming Lutheran oneself.[11]

Nevertheless, the Catholic revaluation of Luther is not a passing fashion. It is too recent a phenomenon for all the new problems which it raises to have been brought out into the open. But it is based on solid historical and doctrinal studies. It certainly seems to be marking time, to the point of raising fears about a retreat, and needs to find a way through that will allow it to arrive at a clear vision of what many sense intuitively without being able to formulate.

The change of direction in thinking already achieved in essentials came first of all from scholarly questioning of the fact that the official Church never showed any inclination to listen to the young monk who made himself from 1517 the advocate of the

Gospel. The Council of Trent, moreover, with an amazing insensitivity, ignored the significance of the attachment of Luther's disciples to the Word of God. The problem of Luther is connected, in the first place, to this insensitivity of Catholicism, ever since Luther's time, to what was responsible for Protestantism's vitality—the ceaseless struggle to maintain the Gospel as a living challenge within the Church. That is where the real debate lies. The Protestants, in the last analysis, expected from Rome a response to Luther's evangelical claims—claims whose implications are drawn out by the other Reformation ideas—but that response was always put off. The Roman attitude has always been to condemn as a whole without any desire to listen. The proper response is to begin listening, to recognize, from the point of view of the Catholic faith, what Luther brought to Christianity when he first appeared in the life of the Church.

Catholic publications show how difficult it is to listen to Luther. Everything authentic that is found in him counts for less than his faults and errors, and discussion is cut short. What is needed is the ability to forget the controversies for a moment and concern ourselves with Luther's message itself, so that it can be perceived in a Church which should not have been divided on his account. At the present stage of the discussion this still seems to be a utopian proposal. Nevertheless, my own work is oriented in this direction, and this is my point of departure.

Luther appears to me as one of the great theologians of the faith. He stands at the beginning of the modern history of Christianity. He penetrates many problems more profoundly than the Catholic theologians, who have not always had the freedom to do so, yet he still knows everything which Protestant theology has since forgotten. His career unfolded within a Church badly in need of reform, and he was the first victim of this context of crisis. Not everything he says can be accepted without question, yet rushing in to charge him with heresy is inappropriate, for in the situation of conflict which governed his thought, he could not avoid a collision with orthodoxy. Obsession with his real or supposed errors leads Catholics to wall themselves up in the ghetto of sectarianism, surliness, and self-glorification. It is too bad that Luther has not been treated with the breadth of understanding which has benefited so many authors of doctrinally debatable textbooks inflicted on theology students.

I came to the study of Luther under the influence of three of the most eminent teachers of the new Catholic interpretation of Luther: Father Yves Congar, Joseph Lortz, and Paul Vignaux, [12] and after a thorough initiation into the Church fathers and the history of theology. I saw in Luther, to begin with, a Christian writer: I read his works, as I had done those of the tradition, concerning myself with his thought as it unfolded through his writings.

Considered independently of the struggles of the 16th century and the controversies between the Churches, Luther's teaching is no different in nature from that of the authors included in Migne's *Patrologia*, some of whom, moreover, are "heretics." It is theology, and in this case very powerful theology. It is not really a question of "Protestantism." The best proof of this is that there are few of Luther's ideas on which the Protestants are absolutely unanimous. Everything rather points to the fact that, in coming to grips as he does so vigorously with the fundamental problems of the faith, Luther plays the role of the impartial scholar reflecting on Christian truth rather than the advocate of partisan interests. He tries to put us on the track of a renewed faith, and it is not so difficult to make allowances for a historical situation which was in every way so turbulent and volatile.

This impression of a Luther "transformed within himself by the eternity of his work" has never left me. [13] If we did not have his writings, we would perhaps have to admit that Luther had been the disturbing person that polemics has made of him. But the fact that these writings, in our context so different from the context of crisis which provoked the break, still have so much significance speaks volumes about the true drama of Luther. The tragedy is not that he was condemned by a hasty procedure but that the magisterium of the Church found nothing positive to draw from a teaching which still profoundly touches the man of faith, whatever his background. Those who attend my lectures or ecumenical conferences are not always very knowledgeable about Reformation history and the questions which divide their Churches. But they find Luther's plea on behalf of the cause of the Gospel in the Church irresistible. What really strikes them in Luther's writings is not so much his more or less orthodox ideas as his way of speaking about faith which is inspired by the Scriptures and is able in turn to open the understanding to a deeper and more fruitful encounter with their message.

We know today that Luther disregarded many of the problems

of the political and social order, even though the Reformation was
also a revolution, full of all the conflicts of a new age coming to
birth. Luther's discourse about faith develops according to an
inward plan and does not avoid the philosophical, psychological,
or linguistic ambiguities which are analyzed these days by the
human sciences. It is true that we can understand the course of
faith as Luther never knew how to. But such limitations detract
nothing from the value of his Christian discourse, which is
resonant with the Biblical message and often more effective than
the official discourse of the Church.

A balance sheet of Luther studies runs the risk of losing itself in
countless questions, lists of authors and their works. This
information does not interest everyone, and it will suffice to
indicate the works where it may be found. For the same reason it
would be better to resist the desire to dwell on the details and heap
up analyses. While all these materials should not be disregarded,
they should be put at the service of the principal task, the
examination for its own sake of Luther's discourse about faith,
with the help of the texts—all this without prejudice to discussions
under way or to the demands which the Catholic faith maintains
in relation to other communions. This is only an aspect of a much
broader debate, but it is the main one, and the fact that it has been
so much neglected fully justifies giving it definite priority.

My usual method is to read Luther's writings with my hearers.
This procedure has great advantages, and I shall try to apply it
here, for it is the best way to capture the true character of Luther's
discourse. This book, therefore, takes the form of a collection of
texts, presented in a way intended to assist judgment in the light of
actual knowledge. Luther's faith appears in the context of the
Reformation and of the Reformer's life, and of what matters for
him: the Gospel, the righteousness of God, Christ, the Church.
This explicitly theological and religious approach to questions
often treated today in a very "materialistic," if not profane, spirit
could seem like a step backwards. It is a response to the necessity of
taking the debate back to its source. The great discussions of
international research will be mentioned, but it will be above all a
matter of letting Luther speak for himself.

1
The Eternal Faith

Martin Luther is among those great figures of history who live in human memory because their thought and work has shaped the destiny of individuals and nations over a long period of time. Hasty attempts to make Luther into a "hero" should be regarded with suspicion. But concern for objectivity should not blind us to the exceptional character of the man and his life. How can we fail to be amazed at the place still held today by one who left us so long ago?[1]

The Reformation was a turning point in the history of Western Christianity. So much is sure. What is less sure, but appears to be the case, is that this development has not been the disaster which the opponents of Luther and of Protestantism wanted to see in it. For those of us who see these realities from a perspective different from those who took part in them, the crisis of the Reformation appears to have brought in its train genuine progress—painful progress, indeed, like a birth—but progress nevertheless, in the proclamation of the apostolic message. Faith is now better understood thanks to the Reformation, and primarily to Luther.

Thus Luther belongs inseparably with the proclamation and understanding of faith—a concern fundamental to Christianity in all ages but posed in each epoch in its own way. Luther claimed that he was responding to the questions of his contemporaries, and we should take the trouble to see what he found to say to them and what persuaded a great number of his fellows to follow his lead.

On the broad canvas of Luther's intervention in the history of faith there are, to be sure, many things which are obscure. We must take account of the objections raised against Luther, just as we note the side effects of certain medicines. But the full story of his "heresies" has been told, and I will not be speaking of them except to further our grasp of the fundamental issue.

Luther's primary importance was his role in the origins of the Reformation. He is, more than any other, the man of the

Reformation, which is not necessarily to say the man of the schism—another issue altogether. Without in any way distorting the historical reality of the 16th century, we should see how important it is to search out the meaning of the resultant split into Protestantism and Tridentine Catholicism. From the very beginning there has been much misunderstanding of this question of our common, historic faith during one of the most profound crises in its history.

1. The Reformation: A Struggle for Faith

The idea of the Reformation to which we are commonly accustomed is still dominated by the memory of events which have struck the popular imagination: Luther's "revolt," the massacre of St. Bartholomew (24 August 1572), the wars of religion, etc., and by the "distressing separation"[2] between Catholics and Protestants.

Yet historical studies invite us to look more deeply. A recent study of the religious crisis of the 16th century has aptly described it as a peak in Christian history, a decisive moment disclosing Christianity's true nature.[3] In any event, it is too narrow a view to reduce the Reformation to the disorder created by a "fallen monk"[4] or a general slackening of religious fervor.[5] That crisis was a fundamental change in the papal Church, which had become inevitable well before Luther's appearance on the scene.[6] It was a change which miscarried; instead of being a renovation of the one Church, it ended in the Church's division.

This phenomenon, in which Rome could see only the lapse of Luther and his associates into heresy, was nonetheless, when things are viewed in a way more detached from earlier passions, a leap of faith—the common impulse of a whole generation which was reacting against a "process of non-Christianization": the people of the Christian West "had not been deeply touched by the message of Jesus," the faithful "aware of their faith" were only "a minority, which the two reformations, Protestant and Catholic, allowed to grow."[7] The break itself and the permanent division arose out of a fundamental disagreement about the higher interests of the faith.[8] The extent of the developments brought about by such a debate took the world by surprise. Having tried, ever since the 16th century, to recover unity by any means, including force of arms, war-weary Christians entrenched themselves in antagonistic positions which hardened in the fires of controversy.

It was to Luther's merit that he provoked this immense struggle. Perhaps "merit" is too strong a word. It would take a great deal of discussion to decide whether or not the Reformation was for the good of the church, or whether the church would not have found itself in a better position deprived of the services of such a "reformer." But the fact is that when Luther issued his theses on indulgences, six months after the conclusion of an ecumenical *reform* council which had sat for five years without much result, it was to his voice that the church awakened. "On 31 Oct. 1517," René Esnault said to me one day,[9] "the Luther of the indulgences was the true voice of the Catholic conscience." The disappointing result of the movement which he had initiated has never been able to wipe out the profound significance of his point of departure.

Luther was born on 10 Nov. 1483 at Eisleben in Thuringia, in a Christian environment,[10] into a young peasant household which had been obliged by the laws of succession to rural property to leave the family farm and earn a living from mining. He was successful in his studies and gained his master of arts degree at the University of Erfurt in 1505. Soon after, he entered the monastery of the Eremite order of St. Augustine in Erfurt. Then followed his religious profession, priestly ordination (Easter 1507), and theological studies. A doctor in theology in 1512, he took up teaching at the University of Wittenberg, in Saxony. From 1513 to 1518 he expounded Holy Scripture: the Psalms, the epistles to the Romans, the Galatians, and the Hebrews.[11]

On 31 Oct. 1517 his *95 Theses* "on the power and efficacy of indulgences" brought him to public notice[12] and set in motion the process of the Reformation. From 1518 to 1521, as he made known his views on one subject after another, he came under attack in a Roman legal action[13] which brought about his excommunication, followed by his appearance at Worms before the Imperial diet. Commanded to recant, he asked 24 hours to reflect—then refused on 17—18 April 1521. The Edict of Worms put him under the Imperial ban, in May, when he had taken refuge at the Wartburg. In March 1522 he returned to Wittenberg and took up his former position.

He had become "the Reformer" and, to begin with, he had to struggle with the extremists who were trying to radicalize his movement, his colleague Andrew Carlstadt, and Thomas Muentzer. The year 1525 saw him engaged with the problem of the

Peasants' War. After the crushing of the revolutionaries, which he had called for with his prayers in a pamphlet *Against the Robbing and Murdering Hordes of Peasants*,[14] he married an ex-nun, Katharine von Bora, by whom he was to have six children.[15] In December of the same year he published his treatise *On the Bondage of the Will* (LW 33) against Erasmus. Two further dates worthy of note are 1530, the Augsburg Confession, the first official confession of the Lutheran faith; and 1534, the appearance of Luther's translation of the Bible into German. Luther died at Eisleben on 18 Feb. 1546.

His was clearly an active life but not very eventful, and with few changes of scene: a journey to Rome in 1510—11, to Heidelberg in April 1518 for an Augustinian chapter meeting, to Augsburg in October for an interview with the papal legate Cajetan, and the escapade at Worms.[16]

Luther did not amass great wealth and refused every political role of the first rank. His background did not presage an exceptional career.[17] His theological genius would not have delivered him from the oblivion which overcame even a Cajetan, "prince of theologians" and one of Luther's principal adversaries. But the Reformation came—after 34 years of "Catholic" living, more than half of his entire life! That—and his own prodigious oratorical and literary productivity—preserved his name.

For Christians at the beginning of the 16th century the question of the reform of the Church was as commonplace as discussions of the Council are for us. There was a revival among religious orders, of which the brief revolution of the Dominican Savonarola, burned at the stake in Florence in 1498, was a sign.[18] The humanists, enemies of the monks, had taken issue with the obscurantism of the theologians and the superstition of religious practices. Bursting with erudition and a "return to the sources," they accustomed the men of intellect to ideas which promised a great future: the study of the Bible and the Fathers, and concern with the person of Jesus Christ. But their ambitions scarcely went any further at all than the search for a reordering or updating of the Church among men of refinement.[19] The papacy at last brought together the Lateran Council (1512—17), which responded only feebly to Christendom's expectations. Six months later, with the indulgences affair, reform very quickly found its character, its objectives, its style, its soul, and its prophet.

What had happened? Imbart de la Tour defined Luther's

"novelty" in these terms: "It is no longer the humanist critique, the vague appeal of the mystics to an inward religion, the attitude of the men of letters who spiritualize the forms or the formulas which they preserve. It is a positive theology which aspires to direct, console, and raise up the soul."[20] It was, therefore, a conception of reform which went beyond the preoccupations of the diverse reforming currents already taking shape. Luther's "reforming" stance appeared to be universal, popular, and dynamic.

The indulgence affair was only the issue which revealed the real problems on the basis of which the crisis was going to develop. "Real abuses," wrote F. X. Kiefl, "gave Luther the occasion for pushing to extremes an idea fundamentally religious and justified at the outset. By the prodigious tenacity with which he exploited this idea, he plunged the Church into a battle for the very basis of its existence."[21] This was, indeed, Luther's particular function, as the new Reformer of the Church: to show that the reform which everyone felt to be necessary was focusing on a point which was eclipsing familiar problems and defying all administrative and doctrinal practices—that of knowing where the Church stood in relation to its faith. From the time that question was posed, and unhappily in most unfavorable circumstances,[22] everyone knew it would have to be answered. Rome immediately instituted proceedings against Luther, and the Wittenberg monk aroused interest on all sides.

The succession of events is well known. But the complexity of the phenomenon of the Reformation, the multiplicity of factors which must be taken into account, in particular the individual actions of other Reformers who, each in his own way, developed the ideas and themes on which Luther had focused attention—all that should not allow us to lose from view the central thread of what was the struggle of a whole generation for its faith, at Luther's summons. Only the issue of faith had the power to change the course of events in that century.

The Rijksmuseum in Amsterdam displays a Dutch painting from the 17th century which shows the great Reformers—from Wyclif and John Hus to Theodore Beza, but above all Luther and Calvin—grouped around a table on which is placed a simple candlestick with a lighted candle. The Sermon on the Mount comes to mind: "Nor do men light a lamp and put it under a bushel, but on a stand, and it gives light to all in the house" (Matt.

5:15). The Reformers' work amounted to one simple achievement: They unveiled the flame of the Gospel after a long eclipse and gave to the Christian world the benefit of its light.

The first "Protestants" had the feeling of having recovered, thanks to Luther and those who modeled themselves on him, the preaching of the pure Word of God. The break with Rome was in their eyes not a departure from the Church but the consequence of its restoration on the basis of evangelical faith—all this was directed against a papacy which was accused of having concealed that message beneath human doctrines and which was persecuting the new followers of the Gospel. The "Reformation" appeared to them as a miraculously successful enterprise, a favor of divine mercy: They had rediscovered the true faith and rid themselves of an ecclesiastical system in which only superstition, idolatry, and tyranny were to be seen.

Western Christians—Catholics and Protestants—still wonder about the strange fate which in the course of those few decades of the Reformation drove their fathers into a corner where they had to choose between a fixed conception of the Church and a new perception of the Gospel.

Luther stands at the beginning of the polarization which ended in such a dilemma. For a long time his role in the crisis of the Reformation was conceived in terms of the rival ideologies of the separated churches. To Protestants, who piously held to the memory of the "new St. Paul," Catholics held up the image of the impious destroyer of the Church and her unity. Both were concerned less with historical truth than with making points against a confessional adversary.

It was only at the beginning of the 20th century that the debate began to take the direction that we now know. In 1904 a learned Dominican, Father Heinrich Denifle, thought that he had discovered the means of making the Catholic view triumph and of alienating Protestants from Luther. The discovery, then recent,[23] of Luther's lectures on Romans (1515—16) had furnished him with the materials for a study of the origins of the Lutheran "heresy." Denifle showed that Luther was the product of a decadent theology corrupted by nominalism and of a decline in monastic life. The Reformer's often scandalous teaching revealed an astonishing ignorance and complete dishonesty. His conclusion was: "Luther, there is nothing divine in you.—Leave Luther, then, and return to the Church."[24]

The explosion backfired. Its unexpected effect was to focus attention for a long time on a Luther who had never been known, the "catholic" Luther prior to the indulgence theses, the "young" Luther. A new picture of things asserted itself in opposition to Denifle. Already in 1911—12 Fr. Grisar, S. J., had mitigated the standpoint of his Dominican colleague.[25] But Kiefl opened up a pathway which went further, in affirming that the young Luther had only "pushed to an extreme an idea fundamentally religious, and justified at the outset."[26]

This change led little by little to justice for Luther, which he thoroughly deserved.[27] Without seeking a priori to minimize the "errors" which continued to divide the Church, or to stop speaking of Luther's active part in the unfortunate development of the Reformation conflict, it would be as well to take account of the historico-doctrinal context in which he suddenly appeared and which ensured that his evangelical claims would be misunderstood in the worst possible way.[28] The questions he raised were far from being as clear as they can be today.[29] There was a real merit in posing them and attempting to find a solution. Moreover, one can no longer doubt that in putting forth the ideas which were supposed to defuse the crisis, Luther had sincerely sought the regeneration of the people's faith through a preaching inspired by Scripture.

Lortz had acknowledged urbi et orbi that Luther was a profoundly religious man. "If in Luther we find a false interpretation of revelation," he wrote, "this resulted not from laxity and lack of depth, but from an exaggerated seriousness and too much zeal. . . . It is a poor interpretation of history which says that a superficial mind lacking religious depth was sufficient to deal the colossal blows which rent the Church."[30] There is, in fact, no understanding of Luther and the problems posed by this subject, as long as the role of faith in his life is misconstrued.

Luther studies, since the Catholic discovery of the Reformer and a new interest in the young Luther, accent the analysis of the documents which have preserved for us the feel of the debates of Reformation times. This development, insofar as it concerns Luther, is the fruit of the publication of the Weimar Edition, from 1883 on.

Luther's complete works began to be edited during his lifetime. But for a long time Catholics searched in them only for arguments against Protestants,[31] who interpreted the texts as dogmas of their respective churches. These Protestant orthodoxies were fixed after Luther's death, as a result of many influences other than his, and they only referred to him in order to claim him more effectively for themselves. They did it so well that it is only within the course of the 20th century that Luther has been read without a confessional prejudice. For that to take place, complete texts are required, in a suitable and truly "critical" edition (notwithstanding the imperfections which must be remedied). Protestantism, moreover, must discover that the Gospel did not begin with Luther and that he is in the mainstream of the life of the medieval Church; while Catholics, for their part, cannot read Luther profitably unless they are prepared to recognize the validity of looking further back than the Council of Trent. In Denifle's time this combination of circumstances simply did not exist.

Now we may discover the enduring value of a work which remains the first witness of this particularly critical moment in the history of the Western Church's understanding of the faith, which we call the "Reformation." Luther's questioning of the doctrine of the Roman Church is a revelation of Catholicism's weak points, in the 16th century as now. He put his finger on real deviations within the Roman tradition, and looked to the remedy of Holy Scripture, presented as the Word of God which appeals to faith. Along these lines he analyzed question after question and offered pertinent critiques that have flowed into the life of the Church to our own day. He revealed problems not suspected before him. He found there the way out of the impasse into which he himself had been led by the Catholicism inculcated in him—an impasse resulting from a development which the papal ministry had undergone every bit as much as it controlled it.

Luther's work deserved something better than the partisan exploitation it has received in the past.[32] It was a response to questions that have arisen again in the present experience of the Church. It allows us to understand how the traditional faith could be put into a state of conflict by ideas simply taken from the Bible: the sovereign authority of the Word of God, justification by faith, the theology of the Cross, the common priesthood of the baptized. Luther's reflection clarifies the techniques which govern the transmission of the faith in an epoch of change. It shows how the debates of the present often raise not merely transitory difficulties but the permanent problems of the Christian faith.

It also appears that Protestantism and Catholicism do not have the answer to the problem of a common reform of the Church by the proclamation of the Word of God. Luther has a broader perspective on this problem than the Church divided after him.[33] The unique character of his work is that it reflects the initial form of the Reformation debate as it disclosed itself within the undivided Church, in the name of the Gospel.

This is what ecumenism tries, more or less, to rediscover today. The search for the young Luther is also a step in this direction. The revision of received ideas about Luther cannot, therefore, be content with his history or his person. One should go as far as to take into consideration his lasting contribution to our understanding of faith. We must recognize in Luther what made him "Luther" in the eyes of his contemporaries; that is, his initiation of a discourse about faith, destined for the Church and echoed by the other Reformers. This discourse is only "Protestant" by accident. The Church could learn it, and go on from there to talk about faith in the terms which made the preaching of the apostles such a success. The Weimar Edition gives us some idea of the place Luther held in the Reformation of the 16th century, and attests that he has lost nothing of his attraction. Yet these days he is scarcely known.

I have indicated in the preface the reasons which seem to me to draw us to center the present point of Luther studies, as I propose to do, on the examination of this discourse about faith. But that does not dispense with the need for speaking about the wider context.

The chronology near the beginning of this book sets out this historical framework and should serve to locate the events to which I can make only brief allusions.

2. Luther: From Faith to Faith

The predilection for trying to find fault with Luther has prevented Catholics from perceiving what is probably the most damaging point against the papal case—that Luther lived only for faith, that nothing else in his life mattered.

His lectures and his writing are nothing but a sustained teaching about faith, less marred by polemic than some have claimed. Even when he lets loose against the pope, imitating on occasion the rough example of the prophets (indeed, surpassing them!), Luther does not allow us to overlook the concern which animates him.[34] At least he did not seek ecclesiastical benefices or temporal power! He drew neither wealth nor honors from his success. He wanted to be the man of the Gospel. It is all very well for each of us to cast the first stone at this Christian whom the church in other times would have had no hesitation in holding up as an example.

Some of his actions tellingly illustrate this lifelong attitude. The first of these really unveils the kind of Christian Luther was, that is, his sudden decision at the age of 22 years to interrupt his studies in law to become a monk in the strictest branch of the Augustinian order. This religious commitment, the motives behind which remain matters of debate,[35] was to take an unexpected change of direction, but was not to be reversed. It was as an Augustinian monk that Luther became Reformer of the Church. At the climax of his trial at Worms, the crucial moment of his life, it was again the surrender to faith which asserted itself in his obstinate refusal to retract: "Unless I am convinced by the testimony of the Scriptures or by clear reason (for I do not trust either in the pope or in councils alone, since it is well-known that they have often erred and contradicted themselves), I am bound by the Scriptures I have quoted and my conscience is captive to the Word of God. I cannot and I will not retract anything, since it is neither safe nor right to go against conscience. I cannot do otherwise, here I stand, may God help me, Amen" (LW 32, 112—13).

About 10 years later, glancing back over his work, he wrote:

> I would willingly accept that all my books should perish, for my only aim has been to bring the Holy Scripture and divine truth to the light of day. Now, God be praised, they shine so clearly and powerfully that people can do without books like mine. . . . They can still, however, be useful for learning the story of what happened; how the precious Word of God came to me, what had to be suffered from so many great enemies in these last 15 years, before it came into its own. And how it increased, and how I advanced further and higher in it from day to day and from year to year. For the first books show how I conceded too much and gave too much honor to the papacy, but the later ones deal purely with Christ alone (WA 38, 133—34 [1533]).

In this picture we may even include the last witness of the dying Christian, convinced that he was to appear before God. The accounts of Luther's agony report that those who attended the dying man tried to obtain from him a final declaration of his faith.

"Venerable father," they said to him, "do you wish to die leaning on your Lord Jesus Christ, confessing the doctrine which you have taught in his name?" A weak "yes" was the reply. That was also Luther's last word. About 20 minutes later he expired. All this happened at Eisleben, in the early hours of 18 Feb. 1546.[36]

Twenty-five years earlier pope Leo X had excommunicated the Wittenberg monk for heresy. Luther had never submitted. The faith in which he died was not that of the Church which had baptized him, on 11 Nov. 1483, the day after his birth, in this same little town of Eisleben. Was that faith still the common faith, the faith of the apostles? Luther's life turns on that question, to which centuries of battles in the four corners of Europe would bring no answer.

We have seen that Catholicism today has recognized that Luther was really a man of faith. But the objection raised against the Reformer since the 16th century remains unchanged: In the light of Catholic truth, Luther lost the true faith and foundered into heresy.[37] His sincerity and his piety do not justify his teaching against the doctrine of the Church. History cannot turn back the clock, and the evidence of the texts is there.

This matter of Luther's heresies, however, by no means exhausts the debate. His deviation in regard to the official line of the Church was not error pure and simple. It is not even necessary to discuss the distortions which Catholic books have made of his thought to prove the point.

The ideas for which Luther stood accused arose out of a stance which Rome wanted nothing to do with, but which was not heretical. They were, therefore, largely a consequence of the extremities to which a man of Luther's passionate character was driven in the situation created by Roman hostility. What he was proposing, from the theses on indulgences on, was to purify Catholicism of its nonevangelical characteristics and lead it back to the historic faith. "The true treasure of the church is the most holy gospel of the glory and grace of God." Indulgences are "the most insignificant graces when compared with the grace of God and the piety of the cross."[38] It was not illegitimate to raise such a problem. The anomaly is rather that the papacy in this period considered itself beyond any challenge.

A theologian by profession, Luther was only doing his job in showing where the true need for a reformation of the Church lay. His stand of conscience at Worms must give cause for reflection.

His faith, in which he wished to die, was a matter of turning from himself more and more towards Christ, as his favorite author, Paul, had done before him. Luther owed to the apostle the idea that the Christian life is a continual growth, "from faith to faith" (Rom. 1:17), from the faith formed in a rather lackluster period of the Church's history to the purity of the eternal faith. The justice of such a struggle did not escape spiritually minded men, weary of scandals and abuses; the humanists, who were discovering the clarity of the Biblical texts; the theologians, conscious of the decadence of studies; the people, starved for good preaching. This struggle should have been taken up by the leaders of the Church. But they had other things on their mind than proclaiming the Word of God. They were incapable of seeing that many preferred the freedom of the Gospel to a submission which too often corresponded to nothing, so unequal were the clergy to their task.

Today Catholicism has discovered the value of what it previously rejected. Lortz made himself the spokesman of a renewal of the Church through the assimilation of the religious riches abandoned by Rome to the churches of the Reformation.[39] Tridentine Catholicism has no equivalent of the evangelical explosion which aroused a whole epoch and continues to bear its fruit in Protestantism. No saint since Trent has possessed the secret of Luther's way of speaking about faith, which has the capacity to influence the entire Church.

The way to restore to the Church what was suppressed at Trent is not to try to show that Luther was less heretical than has been suggested. It does not matter much that his excommunication might appear to some more justified than ever.[40] We have his writings; it is simply a matter of reading them. They show the breadth of Luther's attempt to think through the entire Christian faith. In what follows we shall see how to rediscover in some of his works Luther's teaching about faith, which so captivated his contemporaries and still has the power to lead every Christian on—from faith to faith.

3. Bringing to Life Luther's Discourse About Faith

For a long time Luther was denied any voice in the Church. The first official reply to his message was: "Do you wish to retract, yes or no?" After his death his writings remained forbidden to Catholics, and Protestants often thought they knew enough without him.

A common problem today is that we know about Luther only what his interpreters want to let him say. Luther research abounds with learned discussions in which Luther is made to talk with any number of citations. But in reproducing only the "interesting" passages, what is sacrificed is the process of discourse, the living thought, which is something more than a mosaic of particular propositions. Luther did not assert himself through his particular ideas, most of which were not absolutely new. Those who followed him were often incapable of grasping theological subtleties. What drew them was a particular way of speaking about faith. Luther was trying to promote within the Church a new style of preaching, and he set the example himself.

The Library of Congress holds a great number of anthologies of texts of Luther in all languages. Great care has been taken to allow anyone to understand Luther independently of the learned editions. But these old—sometimes obscure—documents cannot be read easily, even in translation, without some training. Anthologies of texts are certainly not the answer to the problem of bringing Luther's discourse about faith to life again.

The necessities of teaching have led me to institute the practice of a complete reading, with my students, of significant texts of Luther on the same question. This method allows us to perceive how Luther was thinking, speaking, and writing, and to discover what books produced by other methods scarcely allow us to recognize: the precise reason for the stances he took, the way he constructs his argument, the real motives behind his critique of the Church. It is impossible to overlook how much his reflections were dominated by Scripture, how full they are of Biblical quotations, so often, alas, passed over. Luther would never have had so many indefensible notions attributed to him if his sentences had been left in the Biblical context which establishes their meaning. The editors of the bull *Exsurge Domine* had culled out assertions of Luther which were "heretical, scandalous, false, unseemly, seductive of simple souls, and contrary to the Catholic faith." If problems were going to be solved in this way with scissors and paste, why not pick out some sentences from the many to be used as examples in this book?

I propose to explore Luther's faith through some writings chosen from among those in which he tries most deliberately to show what faith means. I shall present those texts in their entirety, as Luther conceived them, without any of their content omitted.[41]

Many of Luther's writings offer the material needed for such an enterprise: the *Commentary on the Lord's Prayer* (1519) the *Treatise on Christian Liberty* (1520), the *Commentary on the Magnificat* (1521), the *Catechism* (1529). But it is desirable that, without excluding the possibility of resorting to extracts, the essential material be put together from complete pieces, i.e., with texts of a length suitable for a work which does not aim to be a substitute for the full edition. Hence my choice of the following works:

(1) The *Brief Instruction* (1522)
(2) The *Preface to the Epistle to the Romans,* and
(3) The 1528 *Confession of Faith.*

Such a selection gives Luther a good chance to speak for himself. Other authors readily put together weighty dossiers of his writings, but without relying on texts of comparable length. This means that the impression which becomes clear from my choice has every chance of being the closest to reality.

The texts selected explain Luther's thought on many of the points which I cannot treat elsewhere. Thus we can apprehend directly from him what he is really saying. A brief restatement here and there will allow us to show the significance of a remark which should not be let pass.

To give over a chapter to a whole text could appear cumbersome. However, the material cited is scarcely any more extensive than one finds in the notes of some works. The advantage of laying out the continuity of thought as Luther intended compensates for any inconvenience. It is by such development and in the form found here that Luther was able to offer his contemporaries something authentic to hope for.

2

The Gospel (1522)

Luther's doctrine does not appear at first sight as a harmonious whole, unified around a single idea. He was not a man for syntheses, and left no work which was truly "systematic." Nevertheless, it is possible to establish, through reading his writings, a genuine unity of thought which corresponds to what history tells us about the continuity of his studies and his activity. He hardly ever deviated from his path, except on points that make no difference to the overall picture. He produced writing after writing throughout his life on the basis of the same essential conviction. The whole point of this book is to find a way of bringing to the fore this central belief which gives form and significance to everything else.

It is tempting to take as the main thread one or other of the great Lutheran themes: justification by faith, Law and Gospel, the Word of God, the theology of the Cross, or faith in Christ. But the example of the first Lutheran theologians, beginning with Melanchthon, shows that each of Luther's great principles, taken in isolation, led to the elaboration of theories which Luther himself disavowed as they appeared.[1]

To avoid this kind of impasse I want to examine certain groups of ideas through significant texts. The unfolding of Luther's doctrine in these writings does not give a complete picture of his thought, but leads us towards an accurate perception of its essential nature. By tracing a thread through this reading, a perspective emerges which is felt to be authentically Luther's and which can be recognized from one text to the others.

Everything suggests that we should begin by investigating how Luther speaks of the Gospel, particularly in the period following the confrontation at Worms.

1. Luther's Stand at Worms

On 18 April 1521, alone in the midst of the imperial diet and in

the presence of the young emperor, Charles V, Luther declared
that he neither could nor would retract the ideas for which he stood
accused, and he declared himself ready to suffer the consequences.
Only a little earlier Pope Leo X had signed the bull of excommunication, which in theory sentenced him to the stake. Soon
Luther would be placed under imperial ban. His obstinacy was
tantamount to accepting a death sentence, and he knew it.

The tortuous games of politics, however, provided a respite.
He was sheltered in the Wartburg castle by the elector of Saxony.
That seclusion gave him the leisure to write other works. He was
preoccupied in particular with a new version of the "postille"
sermons, from which the priests drew inspiration for their
preaching on the Epistles and Gospels for Sundays and festivals.
To that end he drafted a complete collection of sermons for the
period from the First Sunday in Advent to the Sunday After
Epiphany. This work was printed at Wittenberg in the spring of
1522, complete with the introduction which we shall be reading.

The subject matter of this text is the Gospel. What Luther says
here has a very special flavor. It was to witness to his conception of
the Gospel that he let himself be shut out from church and society.
Freed from the necessity of defending himself or going on the
attack, because he was already condemned and for the moment
away from the struggle, he explains very simply what is close to his
heart. In spite of several obscure points, the text has a real clarity. It
avoids the extraneous issues which are often a problem when
dipping directly into Luther's writings to illustrate his thought. It
shows that the "Gospel" for Luther arises out of the whole Bible
and concerns the promise of Christ announced by the prophets.

This discourse about the Gospel is one of the best expressions
of what Luther stood for. He wagered everything on this conception, and many followed him precisely because of it.

2. A Brief Instruction on What to Look for and Expect
in the Gospels[2]

*It is a common practice to number the gospels and to name
them by books and say that there are four gospels. From this
practice stems the fact that no one knows what St. Paul and St.
Peter are saying in their epistles, and their teaching is regarded as
an addition to the teaching of the gospels, in a vein similar to that
of Jerome's introduction.[3] There is, besides, the still worse practice
of regarding the gospels and epistles as law books in which is*

supposed to be taught what we are to do and in which the works of Christ are pictured to us as nothing but examples.[4] Now where these two erroneous notions remain in the heart, there neither the gospels nor the epistles may be read in a profitable or Christian manner, and [people] remain as pagan as ever.

One should thus realize that there is only one gospel, but that it is described by many apostles. Every single epistle of Paul and of Peter, as well as the Acts of the Apostles by Luke, is a gospel, even though they do not record all the works and words of Christ, but one is shorter and includes less than another. There is not one of the four major gospels anyway that includes all the words and works of Christ; nor is this necessary.

The Gospel, a Sure Message About Christ, Encountered Throughout the Bible

Gospel is and should be nothing else than a discourse or story about Christ, just as happens among men when one writes a book about a king or a prince, telling what he did, said, and suffered in his day. Such a story can be told in various ways; one spins it out, and the other is brief. Thus the gospel is and should be nothing else than a chronicle, a story, a narrative about Christ, telling who he is, what he did, said, and suffered—a subject which one describes briefly, another more fully, one this way, another that way.

For at its briefest, the gospel is a discourse about Christ, that he is the Son of God and became man for us, that he died and was raised, that he has been established as a Lord over all things. This much St. Paul takes in hand and spins out in his epistles. He bypasses all the miracles and incidents [in Christ's ministry] which are set forth in the four gospels, yet he includes the whole gospel adequately and abundantly. This may be seen clearly and well in his greeting to the Romans [1:1-4], where he says what the gospel is, and declares, "Paul, a servant of Jesus Christ, called to be an apostle, set apart for the gospel of God which he promised beforehand through his prophets in the holy scriptures, the gospel concerning his Son, who was descended from David according to the flesh and designated Son of God in power according to the Spirit of holiness by his resurrection from the dead, Jesus Christ our Lord," etc.

There you have it. The gospel is a story about Christ, God's and David's Son, who died and was raised and is established as Lord.

This is the gospel in a nutshell. Just as there is no more than one Christ, so there is and may be no more than one gospel. Since Paul and Peter too teach nothing but Christ, in the way we have just described, so their epistles can be nothing but the gospel.

Yes even the teaching of the prophets, in those places where they speak of Christ, is nothing but the true, pure, and proper gospel—just as if Luke or Matthew had described it. For the prophets have proclaimed the gospel and spoken of Christ, as St. Paul here [Rom. 1:2] reports and as everyone indeed knows. Thus when Isaiah in chapter fifty-three says how Christ should die for us and bear our sins, he has written the pure gospel. And I assure you, if a person fails to grasp this understanding of the gospel, he will never be able to be illuminated in the Scripture nor will he receive the right foundation.

The Good News·

Be sure, moreover, that you do not make Christ into a Moses, as if Christ did nothing more than teach and provide examples as the other saints do, as if the gospel were simply a textbook of teachings or laws. Therefore you should grasp Christ, his words, works, and sufferings, in a twofold manner. First as an example that is presented to you, which you should follow and imitate. As St. Peter says in I Peter 4, "Christ suffered for us, thereby leaving us an example." Thus when you see how he prays, fasts, helps people, and shows them love, so also you should do, both for yourself and for your neighbor. However this is the smallest part of the gospel, on the basis of which it cannot yet even be called gospel. For on this level Christ is of no more help to you than some other saint. His life remains his own and does not as yet contribute anything to you. In short this mode [of understanding Christ as simply an example] does not make Christians but only hypocrites.[5] You must grasp Christ at a much higher level. Even though this higher level has for a long time been the very best, the preaching of it has been something rare. The chief article and foundation of the gospel is that before you take Christ as an example, you accept and recognize him as a gift, as a present that God has given you and that is your own. This means that when you see or hear of Christ doing or suffering something, you do not doubt that Christ himself, with his deeds and suffering, belongs to you. On this you may depend as surely as if you had done it yourself; indeed as if you were Christ himself.[6] See, this is what it means to have a proper grasp of the gospel, that is, of the overwhelming goodness of God, which neither prophet, or apostle, or angel was ever able fully to express, and which no heart could adequately fathom or marvel at. This is the great fire of the love of God for us, whereby the heart and conscience become happy, secure, and content. This is what preaching the Christian faith means. This is why such preaching is called gospel, which in German means a joyful, good, and comforting "message"; and this is why the apostles are called the "twelve messengers."[7]

Concerning this Isaiah 9[:6] says, "To us a child is born, to us a son is given." If he is given to us, then he must be ours; and so we must also receive him as belonging to us. And Romans 8[:32], "How should [God] not give us all things with his Son?" See, when you lay hold of Christ as a gift which is given you for your very own and have no doubt about it, you are a Christian. Faith redeems you from sin, death, and hell and enables you to overcome all things. O no one can speak enough about this. It is a pity that this kind of preaching has been silenced in the world, and yet boast is made daily of the gospel.

Now when you have Christ as the foundation and chief blessing of your salvation, then the other part follows: that you take him as your example, giving yourself in service to your neighbor just as you see that Christ has given himself for you. See, there faith and love move forward, God's commandment is fulfilled, and a person is happy and fearless to do and to suffer all things. Therefore make note of this, that Christ as a gift nourishes your faith and makes you a Christian. But Christ as an example exercises your works. These do not make you a Christian. Actually they come forth from you because you have already been made a Christian. As widely as a gift differs from an example, so widely does faith differ from works, for faith possesses nothing of its own, only the deeds and life of Christ. Works have something of your own in them, yet they should not belong to you but to your neighbor.[8]

So you see that the gospel is really not a book of laws and commandments which requires deeds of us, but a book of divine promises in which God promises, offers, and gives us all his possessions and benefits in Christ. The fact that Christ and the apostles provide much good teaching and explain the law is to be counted a benefit just like any other work of Christ. For to teach aright is not the least sort of benefit. We see too that unlike Moses in his book, and contrary to the nature of a commandment, Christ does not horribly force and drive us. Rather he teaches us in a loving and friendly way. He simply tells us what we are to do and what to avoid, what will happen to those who do evil and to those who do well. Christ drives and compels no one. Indeed he teaches so gently that he entices rather than commands. He begins by saying, "Blessed are the poor, Blessed are the meek," and so on [Matt. 5:3, 5]. And the apostles commonly use the expression, "I admonish, I request, I beseech," and so on. But Moses says, "I command, I forbid," threatening and frightening everyone with horrible punishments and penalties. With this sort of instruction you can now read and hear the gospels profitably.

The Gospel and the Christian

When you open the book containing the gospels and read or hear how Christ comes here or there, or how someone is brought to him, you should therein perceive the sermon or the gospel through which he is coming to you, or you are being brought to him. For the preaching of the gospel is nothing else than Christ coming to us, or we being brought to him. When you see how he works, however, and how he helps everyone to whom he comes or who is brought to him, then rest assured that faith is accomplishing this in you and that he is offering your soul exactly the same sort of help and favor through the gospel. If you pause here and let him do you good, that is, if you believe that he benefits and helps you, then you really have it. Then Christ is yours, presented to you as a gift.

After that it is necessary that you turn this into an example and deal with your neighbor in the very same way, be given also to him as a gift and an example. Isaiah 40[:1,2] speaks of that, "Be comforted, be comforted my dear people, says your Lord God. Say to the heart of Jerusalem, and cry to her, that her sin is forgiven, that her iniquity is ended, that she has received from the hand of God a double kindness for all her sin," and so forth. This double kindness is the twofold aspect of Christ: gift and example. These two are also signified by the double portion of the inheritance which the law of Moses [Deut. 21:17] assigns to the eldest son and by many other figures.

The Dignity of the Scriptures

What a sin and shame it is that we Christians have come to be so neglectful of the gospel that we not only fail to understand it, but even have to be shown by other books and commentaries what to look for and what to expect in it. Now the gospels and epistles of the apostles were written for this very purpose. They want themselves to be our guides, to direct us to the writings of the prophets and of Moses in the Old Testament so that we might there read and see for ourselves how Christ is wrapped in swaddling cloths and laid in the manger [Luke 2:7], that is, how he is comprehended [Vorfassett] in the writings of the prophets. It is there that people like us should read and study, drill ourselves, and see what Christ is, for what purpose he has been given, how he was promised, and how all Scripture tends toward him. For he himself says in John 5 [:46], "If you believed Moses, you would also believe me, for he wrote of me." Again [John 5:39], "Search and look up the Scriptures, for it is they that bear witness to me."

This is what St. Paul means in Romans 1 [:1, 2], where in the beginning he says in his greeting, "The gospel was promised by God through the prophets in the Holy Scriptures." This is why the evangelists and apostles always direct us to the Scriptures and say, "Thus it is written," and again, "This has taken place in order that the writing of the prophets might be fulfilled," and so forth. In Acts 17 [:11], when the Thessalonians heard the gospel with all eagerness, Luke says that they studied and examined the Scriptures day and night in order to see if these things were so. Thus when St. Peter wrote his epistle, right at the beginning [I Pet. 1:10-12] he says, "The prophets who prophesied of the grace that was to be yours searched and inquired about this salvation; they inquired what person or time was indicated by the Spirit of Christ within them; and he bore witness through them to the sufferings that were to come upon Christ and the ensuing glory. It was revealed to them that they were serving not themselves but us, in the things which have now been preached among you through the Holy Spirit sent from heaven, things which also the angels long to behold." What else does St. Peter here desire than to lead us into the Scriptures? It is as if he should be saying, "We preach and open the Scriptures to you through the Holy Spirit, so that you yourselves may read and see what is in them and know of the time about which the prophets were writing." For he says as much in Acts 4 [3:24], "All the prophets who ever prophesied, from Samuel on, have spoken concerning these days."

Therefore also Luke, in his last chapter [24:45], says that Christ *opened the minds of the apostles to understand the Scriptures. And Christ, in John 10[:9, 3], declares that he is the door by which one must enter, and whoever enters by him, to him the gatekeeper (the Holy Spirit) opens in order that he might find pasture and blessedness. Thus it is ultimately true that the gospel itself is our guide and instructor in the Scriptures, just as with this foreword I would gladly give instruction and point you to the gospel.*

But what a fine lot of tender and pious children we are! In order that we might not have to study in the Scriptures and learn Christ there, we simply regard the entire Old Testament as of no account, as done for and no longer valid. Yet it alone bears the name of Holy Scripture. And the gospel should really not be something written, but a spoken word which brought forth the Scriptures, as Christ and the apostles have done. This is why Christ himself did not write anything but only spoke. He called his teaching not Scripture but gospel, meaning good news or a proclamation that is spread not by pen but by word of mouth. So we go on and make the gospel into a law book, a teaching of commandments, changing Christ into a Moses, the One who would help us into simply an instructor.

What punishment ought God to inflict upon such stupid and perverse people! Since we abandoned his Scriptures, it is not surprising that he has abandoned us to the teaching of the pope and to the lies of men. Instead of Holy Scripture we have had to learn the Decretales *of a deceitful fool and evil rogue.[9] O would to God that among Christians the pure gospel were known and that most speedily there would be neither use nor need for this work of mine. Then there would surely be hope that the Holy Scriptures too would come forth again in their worthiness. Let this suffice as a very brief foreword and instruction. In the exposition we will say more about this matter. Amen.''*

3. The Gift of the Word

Writings of this kind are common in Luther's works. Even when he undertook to prove one of his points or refute an opponent, he allowed himself—and his reader with him—to be caught up by his extraordinary awareness of the mystery of Christ and the need he felt to speak of it, to make its various aspects shine forever undimmed, to draw out its lessons.

The basis of his thought is that the Gospel is good news and preaching the text first of all elucidates the good news of the gift of

Christ against the false and inadequate ideas of the Gospel which were widespread at this time. But good news is good news only if it is announced. Luther's discourse is indeed more than an "explanation." It signifies the Gospel itself: Christ is truly imparted to the reader who welcomes in faith the promise which Luther draws from Scripture.

In Luther's conception of the Gospel no distinction is made between the message and the teaching on which it is based. The proclamation of the Gospel is born of the teaching about Christ which runs through Scripture and which Paul formulates at the beginning of the Epistle to the Romans. Christ comes to man through the preached Word. Luther expounds this theme in one of his Wartburg sermons:[10]

> Christ came to everyone through public preaching after his resurrection from the dead. It was with a view to such a coming that he came bodily in human form. The incarnation would have been of value to no one if it had not resulted in a Gospel, so that the whole world would know him and that the reason for his coming would be revealed; namely, that the promised blessing would be dispensed to those who believe in Christ by the Gospel—as St. Paul says: The Gospel was promised by God . . . (Rom. 1:2). It is as if he wanted to say that God was more concerned for the Gospel and his public advent through the Word than for his birth and bodily advent among men. For him it is a matter of the Gospel and of our faith. He willed that his Son should become man, so that the Gospel could be preached by him and that thus his salvation could draw near to the whole world through the public preaching of the Word.[11]

By being the first to preach the Gospel, of which he himself is the substance, Christ has given the Church an inexhaustible treasure. He has unveiled the meaning of Scripture which, the Gospel makes clear, speaks only of him. He has established the norm for preaching, and become communicable to every conscience through the Word, which will be preached until the end of time.

This conception was developed in response to the situation which prevailed then in the Church. There was scarcely any preaching and especially not of the Gospel—or very little. In its place the Church was noising abroad the doctrines of men. In the gospels people were looking for good stories, miracles, edifying examples, moral precepts. There was no longer any understanding of the originality of Scripture, this book unlike all others. The imagery of the Old Testament was eclipsing what nevertheless remained "Scripture" above all else. No one any longer knew how to see in the Gospel the discourse which brings to life the inspired texts. For want of such discourse there was no longer any check to the inventions of speculative theology and popular religiosity.

Luther diagnosed centuries ahead of time the de-Christian-ization of the Middle Ages which the historian today perceives. Where the message of the Gospel is abandoned, Christianity fails even to preserve its appearance, and the people return to paganism. It was to try to reverse this tendency that the Wartburg outlaw sought to liberate for his contemporaries a genuine ardor for the Gospel. In this purpose he made himself the instrument, centuries later, of the prophetic song: "To us a child is born, to us a son is given" (Is. 9:6). Since he is *given*, is he not wholly for us, and must we search for another doorway to the fullness of salvation? In the Word we have the key to all revelation, the means of making present for all time the coming of the Risen One.

The welcoming God whose boundless goodness the Gospel makes plain was a great novelty for a time which sought in the Law and its rigors the standard of authentic religion. It was wholly a discovery to rely on God through his promise, to grasp the truth that Scripture is nothing but a book of promises. Moses was not God's last word for the Christian, but the Church of Christ was much better at proposing laws to be observed, examples of sanctity to be copied, and relics to be venerated. . . . It is Jesus in person, received as a "gift," who creates the believer. With him God conceded all the rest (Rom. 8:32), "double for all her sins" (Is. 40:1 ff.).

The Gospel appeals to faith, and it is the task of the sermon to nourish and train faith daily by disclosing the promises of Scripture. In the history of the Church Luther inaugurates the age of the rediscovered Bible. The man of faith can draw from the Bible all that his faith needs. At the Wartburg Luther undertook his German translation which would give to his people a language, no less than a new understanding of Christian existence. The Reformation would open schools where all would learn to read. The clergy would no longer be able to impose its law or its ideas on an ignorant body of the faithful.

There, in a sense, we have the complete definition, if not explicit in all points, of the evangelical Christianity which we call

"Protestantism." Under its diverse forms it continues the task of evangelical preaching conceived by Luther at the Wartburg: to bring Christ near by the Word and to lead men to him so that they can believe in him and become in turn a "gift" for others.

Beyond this fundamental thrust the *Brief Instruction* initiates the themes which we will see raised again in different contexts, themes whose meaning will then appear more clearly. We should note that Luther was aware that he stood alone in his way of thinking; for example, when he says that the preaching of the first article of the Gospel has become rare. And so what matters now is to show that though his teaching has a very personal character, there is nothing improvised about it.

3

The Problem of Salvation

How Luther Became Luther

Luther never brought into question his conception of the Gospel. It became part of him and cost him dearly through the long psychological, intellectual, and religious crisis of his youth. This, as all the books recognize, was the crucible in which "Lutheranism" forged itself.

This crisis was a crisis of faith. Unbelief had certainly never been one of Luther's problems. But his faith had "changed," at least in the sense that Catholicism no longer recognized its truth. We have just seen an illustration of this. The Luther of 1521—22 taught, in effect, that Christ is received in a quasi-sacramental manner by the one who receives the Word in faith. This communion is the equivalent of that of the Catholic who receives the consecrated host. Luther was himself a priest and had never doubted the real presence of Christ in the Eucharist.[1] However, it is with respect to the Word and not the holy Sacrament that we can talk, as far as Luther is concerned, of "eucharistic" piety. The power of the Word in every human life is not imaginary but real. Was Luther expressing, in this specific case, anything other than the faith of the Church, in a different mode?

To understand this modification in his thinking, it is necessary to go back to the time when Luther, the young Catholic, discovered that the religion which he had been taught led to an impasse. His personal problems were there for a reason. but everything was also contributing to make of the young monk and theologian the man through whom the Catholicism of this time would undergo the crucial test which would reveal its weaknesses. It was in confronting problems which were neither his alone, nor invented by him, that this contemporary of Christopher Columbus reached a new spiritual world.

The path taken by his reflections passed through the problem of salvation, and we know the terms in which he posed it: It is faith that delivers man from sin, death, and hell; it makes Christians of us for good and all, giving us in Christ the foundation of salvation.

Such teaching produced the Reformation. In the Church today it is scarcely credible that opinion would be so shaken by launching a debate on the individual's eternal salvation. This is the age of collective salvation, liberation within this world rather than the next. The question of personal salvation is swept away in the decline of "bourgeois" culture which distorted religion into a private affair with each looking after his own self-interest.

Luther was not, however, the first to confer an exclusive importance on the problem of sin, death, and hell. Are these realities anything more than the expression of our own individual solitude? The declaration of personal salvation is as old as Christianity itself. It flows from the words of the Christ of the Gospels to the unknown believer: "Go, your faith has saved you."

It was his perception of salvation which made Luther the witness of the Gospel. The amazing thing is that the search by this young Christian for the basis of his own salvation could have unleashed such an upheaval in the Church and the Western world. We should try to understand why this was so.

This subject cannot be treated without raising the question of Luther's psychological difficulties bordering, some would say, on the pathological. This monk, anxious for his salvation, centered on himself and depicted by certain writers as consumed by a morbid obsession with hell and the devil—was he really "balanced"? Luther was certainly a man caught up in anxiety. What he said of the religious anguish of his youth alerts us to certain problems. His superiors, beginning with Staupitz, had to reassure him. But Staupitz had also seen that it was through this experience that Luther would have a role to play within the Church.[2]

The evidence scarcely allows us to reduce Luther's life to the "case studies" of the psychiatric books. The fragmentary materials on which they rest their pessimistic diagnoses of his anxiety and his mental and emotional balance take up very few of the 70,000 pages of the Weimar Edition. Everything we are told of his psychology explains only imperfectly how his anxiety as a young Catholic led him to his reforming certainty. We must therefore begin by showing what the facts were, without doing away with the psychological problem, but without any longer attributing to it an inordinate importance. I will pause at that point in the following chapter only when I have given Luther a lengthy opportunity to speak for himself.

1. The Impasse of Justification by Works

Luther became Luther under the impetus of his religious education. Of that, there is no doubt. It only remained for the Church to make of the young Martin Luther a Christian other than he had been. She should not have condemned him so precipitately in 1518—21, for what he was teaching was the consequence of what the Church herself was like at this moment.

As far as one can judge,[3] Luther received a Christian education typical of the young men of his time. Everything indicates that he was an amenable pupil. His ecclesiastical masters made of him a Christian for life. The young Luther believed very deeply in God. He feared offending Him by doing evil, and dreaded His judgment and the dangers of hell. These convictions would remain with him throughout his life.

He knew the Bible very little. The figure of Christ frightened him, for he saw in him the judge of the *Dies irae*. His name evoked the Last Judgment: that scene which still transfixes tourists in ancient Churches, corresponding to a tragic apprehension of the final balance sheet of human history.[4] For a long time Luther was unaware of the consoling side of faith in Christ. The religion which had been his from the beginning was not distinguishable from that of many of his contemporaries. No one would have picked up any hint of a disturbing future.

Of all that he was taught, what concerned him most was his personal salvation. This young man did not want to go to hell. From some centuries distance, the feeling about hell inculcated in Luther seems much the same as the one I remember from my first Communion retreat. But the young Luther experienced the fear of hell more dramatically than Catholic children of the first half of the 20th century. Death came easily in those times. Terrible epidemics decimated the population, and the survivors experienced the visitations of bands of mercenaries, killing and pillaging everything in their way. The assurance that death could strike at any moment gave an urgency to the preoccupation with salvation; anything was preferable to risking sudden death in a state of mortal sin.

To begin with, Luther relied on the Church to lead him to salvation. He became a monk.[5] Now the monastic life limits occasions for sin and provides a favorable climate for works of holiness. An inexperienced and overrigorous disposition must have seen in it the ideal framework for making sure of salvation.

Nothing really provided for the young postulant of the Erfurt Augustinians an adequate guide to the life which he took up on 17 July 1505. His father held monks to be worthless. Luther himself loved life, as has been said, and he does not seem to have been attracted by any specific values of the consecrated life. He would say one day that one can be a good enough Christian by serving God in the life of the world.

Many of his writings, on the other hand, attest his concern about hell. He sometimes described its torments "as if he were there," a sign of a reflectiveness pushed to the point of the anguish of the damned, who are helpless in their predicament. The word hell became part of his vocabulary, along with law, sin, death, devil, divine anger. Luther's vocation can be explained by his awareness of God and his piety. But faith in God and the conviction that nothing escapes his judgment are quite as much the basis of his anxiety about hell.

Luther was a good monk. He had entered the monastery for that purpose. He had, thus, in principle found what he was seeking: the greatest guarantee that is humanly possible for an individual to obtain assurance of his soul's salvation. Yet he did not find peace.[6] As a monk he experienced the impossibility of purity,[7] the futility of all attempts to dry up the inner source of evil, and terror in the presence of an angry and threatening God. He wanted to feel that God accepted his ardor and his works. Instead of that, he felt himself always at fault, not primarily in outward shortcomings, but at the level of his deeper dispositions.

The subjective element in this feeling of failure in his monastic life is clearly of prime importance. Some of his writings indicate a genuine welling-up of anguish.[8] The only thing that was able to bring tranquillity to Luther was the ability to convince himself that the divine punishment had not been visited on him. For a whole period of his life he could do no more than try to cling to prayer, mortification, and absolution. But it really seemed that he had done nothing but proceed down this path of deception and disillusionment.

His studies provided him with the means of clarifying his

problems. But, while giving him the extensive doctrinal knowledge on which he would draw throughout his life, they also
nourished his uneasiness. All that he knew of God's mercy was
powerless to reassure him. He was one of those who cannot be
distracted from a source of anxiety as long as they believe it to be
well-founded.

The question of salvation had, indeed, always had its solution,
which is that Christ died for all men. But the point under
discussion was the conditions under which each one obtained
redemption for himself. To be saved, it was necessary to be
baptized and to live (or at least die) "in a state of grace." A single
serious sin put a question mark over salvation. To sin is to violate
the commandments of God and the church, and even evil desires
and thoughts are sins. The moral theologians distinguished
between serious or "mortal" sins and "venial" sins—slight faults.
The young Luther had nothing for which to reproach himself.[9]
But he discovered that the external purity of the monk was unable
to suppress the sinful tendencies of the heart. He believed that he
could not cease to be a sinner, and in his eyes every sin was
"serious."[10]

The remedy for sin is to confess it and to receive absolution in
the right frame of mind. The priest judges the sincerity of the
penitent, and can put him to the test by delaying absolution until
later. But the penitent absolved in the name of Christians of the
Church can be certain of God's pardon.

This was the accepted teaching from the earliest years of the
Church, and Luther had submitted to it for a long time. The study
of the Bible and of St. Augustine nevertheless assured him that the
best of Christians remained sinners, no matter what they did.
Augustine, for example, in opposition to the Briton Pelagius,
raised a question about the deep sincerity of our actions.[11] Do we
not often do what is good because it suits us? And isn't it the fear of
punishment which restrains us from committing serious offenses?
But in that case, surely we are not fulfilling the Law whole-
heartedly and by a pure love of the good. Perhaps we even hate the
good because we are constrained to do it. Christians, and even
monks, free themselves only with difficulty from this duplicity
which really hides an unacknowledged hatred of God's will.

Assurance was given that all faults, whether hidden or openly
acknowledged, can be atoned for by meritorious works. If the evil
which lies within the heart and in the inescapably ambiguous

arena of human action cannot be stamped out, at least compensation can be made for the inevitable shortcomings of a virtuous life by an abundance of good works. But the young monk found that merit brought no change in the difficulty of being justified in the eyes of God, for the value of an act depended on the uprightness of its author.[12] This rectitude was for him a problem, as we have seen, inasmuch as evil lies at the heart of the meritorious work and undermines its merit. And if meritorious acts are infected by sin, what is the good of adding to them? Men make mistakes, and how can they escape from Him "who tries the minds and hearts" (Ps. 7:9).

On the level of analysis of the secret motivations of the human heart, the view which Luther followed had no solution. If righteousness is the complete disappearance of every suspicion of sin in man, it is not of this world. Catholicism, indeed, had for a long time tempered Augustinian rigor by regulating morality according to concrete actions, rather than the appreciation of subjective intentions.[13] But the young Luther's education had committed him to the narrow pathway of an impossibly super-human perfection.

Deprived of every solution from human nature on the one side, he was bound to seek a way out from God on the other, which corresponded to the depth of his religious feelings. Haunted as he was by the evidence of God's reality, it was out of the question that he would be content with his own imperfection by cherishing the hope of "progressing" little by little.[14]

The theology which had been taught to him made of God a sovereign, arbitrary being. Not only could nothing bind him, especially not the doubtful merits of man, but his decisions were unpredictable. God gave grace to whom he wished, when he wished, for motives known only to him. That doctrine arose out of a very high notion of God's freedom.[15] It could drive to despair: No one can be sure, in the absolute sense, of the divine verdict. On the contrary, it was clearly a wrong move to try to impose on God by merits what he was not obliged to take into account.

The nominalist theologians thought God took it on himself to accept our merits. But the Scriptures said nothing of such a doctrine, and its consequences appeared contrary to the Augustinian conception of the gratuitous nature of salvation and the persistence of sin in man. The element of truth lay here—that a "voluntarist" God depended only on himself. Luther had been so

imbued with this idea, characteristic of a whole stream of
scholastic thought, that his solution, as we shall see, would be only
an application of it. The way out of his crisis was, in effect, the
discovery that God in his sovereignty *commands* that faith in Jesus
Christ is necessary to salvation.[16]

This outline representation of the impasse within which
Luther's final destiny was played out allows us to understand why
some would have it that his drama applied only to him, to his
psychology, to his bad theology as well as his dishonesty, and not,
in any event, to the Church.

What followed shows, however, that the problem he ran up
against was one of the genuine problems of the Catholicism of his
day. Some authors, who pass over too quickly the state of the
Church in which Luther grew up, judge that the young monk
should have relied on the goodness of God, "who does not desire
the death of the sinner." R. Dalbiez makes the judgment that
Luther was the victim of a pessimistic, despairing theology which
considered the impulses of concupiscence as intrinsically blame-
worthy.[17] That would explain why he had seen sin everywhere.
But Luther's ordeal did not rest, in the final analysis, on his
insistence on sin, for the Bible, from this point of view, goes just as
far as he does, and as far as the authors cited by Dalbiez. Man's sin
is the central thread of the Biblical teaching, and Luther, generally
speaking, said hardly any more in this regard than the old
Augustinian tradition, notably St. Bernard. The conception of sin
here is only the backdrop of a debate which was already present in
another form and was generally associated with a rigid sense of
righteousness. So much is attested by Luther's writings and by all
that we know in general about him.

In this respect Luther was a son of his people, that powerful
Germanic "nation" to which all the peoples of Western Christendom were related. Since the barbarian invasions, which had put an
end to the Roman Empire, the Roman Church had been Ger-
manized—imbued with the point of view and the customs of the
new people who had come over to it and who provided it with its
thinkers and leaders. The social system of the Germanic tribes gave
evidence of a special concern to make compensation for infrac-
tions. There existed a whole set of sanctions geared to restoring the
stability of the central network of relationships, if threatened,
and to effect restitution where necessary. This sense of a logical
and unavoidable sanction had been preserved in a Christian

context, and it dominated the question of relationships with heaven. The Western Church had been induced to endow itself with a penitential system which, in Luther's time, entailed the obligation of confessing at least once a year, the distinction between mortal and venial sins, the rigors of excommunication no less than the facilities for "indulgences." At the summit of the edifice was God, avenger of evil, dreaded master of hell and purgatory, author of the Law—the concept with which Luther struggled all his life.[18] No one remained untouched by the theory which permanently supported this religious framework and which many found to be a heavy yoke. No account was ever taken of the fact that it perpetuated more and more within itself a culture which was on the way to being abandoned, for modern times had already begun.

Luther found himself placed by the particular nature of his intellectual and religious evolution at the very junction of these two epochs. Pious German that he was, he could expect to find in the Bible the confirmation of the religious regime in force. But in his eyes the letter of Scripture made the demands of the system worse, to the point of absurdity, in contradiction with the compromises of churchmen, canonists, and theologians. Furthermore, it opened up perspectives which seemed to have totally disappeared from Church teaching and practice. Everything happened as though the Germanization of the Church, justified as it had been in the past and in principle, had reached the limit of its possibilities and was henceforth bent on operating in opposition to the new necessity of preaching the Gospel. At the initial stage of the new phase which began with Luther the striking thing was that the Wittenberg monk could not avoid being trapped by the logic which demanded that every sin be detected so that it could be more surely blotted out and expiated.

The spectacular evidence that the Church had become bogged down in its pursuit of justification by works was the progress at that time of the traffic in indulgences. This traffic illustrated the defects in the doctrine of salvation which struck Luther in the course of his desperate search: the simplistic popular idea of a righteous God fussing over trifles and the abuse of easy solutions which no longer deceived any but the ignorant. This traffic in indulgences was to bring the conflict of a whole society to a head even though in itself, for the Luther of the 95 Theses, it had only a secondary importance. Nothing in his psychology or his conception of things led him to envisage a far-reaching action in relation to a subject so trivial. He would dissociate himself quickly enough from what remained. But it is true that in attacking a reality familiar to all he provoked the issue of conscience which echoed his own.

It is essential that we take account of the way Luther was imbued with the mentality of the Germany and the Catholicism of his day. If his problems and his ideas related only to his subjectivity, how could his massive following be explained? Denifle took the trouble to publish the documents of the tradition which taught, well before Luther, the evangelical conception of the righteousness of God. But that academic demonstration was beside the point. We must rather consider the logic in which a serious and candid intellect could find itself imprisoned, while the present life of the Church revolved around threats of the hereafter and the multiplication of frauds and loopholes. The theologians taught that in theory man could love God above all things, by his own powers. But the pope exploited what was patently obvious, that man could do nothing of the sort, in order to extract from the faithful, by indulgences, the money necessary for the reconstruction of the Basilica of St. Peter in Rome.

Pious souls saw the evil especially in the abuses of the system, and already, in consequence, sought to correct them, as did the Council of Trent, to some extent. But Luther knew enough to show that the anxiety and uncertainty of salvation proceeded from a real deviation from the truth. His success owed much to the fact that his doctrine took to the extreme point the conviction of the powerlessness of man before evil, the demands of God's holiness, and the experience of the marvel of forgiveness which is given to us in Jesus Christ. It seemed as if no theologian, since Augustine, knew how to hold all these positions at once as did Luther, and the other Reformers after him.

When he was still unknown, Luther discovered these problems for himself. Others, formed in the same mold and subject to the same regime, did not know that dread of impossible righteousness. Some, doubtless, did not even think of hell. Most were satisfied with the official religion. The difference with Luther was the young monk's fervor and his consciousness of God.[19] Some authors find it abnormal that Luther remained insensitive to the reassuring words of his friends.[20] Such colleagues pointed out from time to time the solution which would be his one day, as he would come to see in due course. But they sought in reality only to lessen the rigors of the system against which Luther was struggling, without questioning the principles leading to the conclusion with which he felt constrained to deal. They did nothing but skate around the real question: where to find, in God or in man, the unquestionable reasons for acknowledging that God gives his grace to the sinner despite the imperfections of human life. The difficulty presented itself in concrete form in a multitude of specific problems. The unique character of Luther's experience was that he found himself the first Catholic theologian who could no longer hold himself back from doing everything possible to bring these problems out into the open.

His stubbornness in pursuing a certainty which evaded him at almost every point was one expression of Renaissance man's yearning to end once and for all what we have come to know as the "Middle Ages." Until then, the obligation to submit to the priest was accepted without question, in the certain knowledge that in doing as he prescribed, one would be saved. For a long time this self-abandonment to the direction of the Church had been the general attitude. But man in the 16th century seemed to have lost that unquestioning trust in the clergy. The ecclesiastical institution rarely obtained from him more than grudging assent, often even less. Many in their spiritual life were in pursuit of a solid basis of support within themselves, independent of the representatives of established religion. Luther would increasingly become the incarnation of that tendency of his generation. He would carry it to its conclusion, first of all for himself, and in doing this he would define that Christian perspective which was gradually growing everywhere in diverse forms and with which a good many people identified themselves.

The demand for personal certainty related him in advance to Descartes. Like the French philosopher, Luther would not rest until he had clarified his thinking concerning the theology of salvation. However, he never entertained the idea of a "methodological doubt" which began by wiping the slate clean of every conviction in order to start afresh. Doubt with Luther was instructive, arising out of a living, existential difficulty. It called for an affirmation: "I believe, therefore I am." But elements of certainty remained which Luther would seek to amplify with the aid of Scripture, directing himself towards a growing feeling of trust in God, a disposition to seek from God alone the solution to the problem of salvation. What finally mattered to him was salvation before God.

Would the disquiet which had come upon him lead him thus to uncover his true problem, the great problem of his life and of his age: how the individual can be assured of finding favor before God?

Such analyses can be found in many authors, such as Febvre, Lortz, and Chaunu. More caution is shown about the timing of the stages of Luther's progress. In this regard we are often reduced to conjecture. Strohl has, nevertheless, given a suggestive documented account of Luther's religious and doctrinal evolution to 1520. I will content myself with a few observations, drawn from the young Luther's writings.

The actual duration of the crisis is uncertain. Only the result can be clearly discerned in the expansion of Luther's public activity in every direction, beginning from 1517—18. At this stage Luther appears sure of himself; and nothing is going to stop him. The monk's crisis gives way to the open crisis of the Church.

For the earlier period the intense intellectual and pastoral activity of the young religious, his efforts within the Augustinian order, and the favorable impression he made on those around him make it difficult to recognize that he had experienced a continued state of depression for several years. The documents say nothing of it, except for some of the old Luther's *Table Talk*, which has to be carefully interpreted.[21] His life was not that of a man tormented by anxiety all along the way. And where would a sick man have found such energy? Moments of tension in his day-to-day existence are misleading. The stress was a matter of the spirit rather than the emotional life. As throughout the rest of his life, even after the discovery of the Gospel, Luther had attacks of depression, but at other times he was sustained by a consoling certainty. His writings show that his convictions fell into place progressively. He was reconciled, for example, to the thought of hell by discovering the *resignatio ad infernum:* the "resignation to hell" which came to him from medieval spirituality; instead of dreading hell, the Christian surrendered himself to God's will. Even if damned, he would still have the supreme joy of doing as God willed. The Gospel of mercy was outlined in many ways through the pen of the young professor of Holy Scripture, and it is therefore fair to assume that he had had long periods during which he felt only moderately the sharp edge of the debate which he pursued with himself. But it is true that at certain moments anxiety over-whelmed him.

His youthful writings show the power and richness of his theological research, which contrasts with the platitudes of so many of his contemporaries. The young Luther was the great beneficiary of the campaign led by Erasmus and Lefèvre d'Etaples for the return to the Bible. He at least understood. The Bible was the sole source of his teaching, and the great novelty was that he knew how to read it.

His research did not unfold in a methodological void. Luther followed step by step the path which was his own, from certainty to certainty.[22] The passage already cited from the *Lectures on Romans*—from faith to faith—shows that from 1515—16 he conceived of faith as a continually deepening reality. His progress does not bear the marks of a sharp break: no conversion, no abandonment. What stands out rather is a progressive displace-ment of the center of his spirituality and his doctrine.

His anxiety, which he called *Anfechtung*,[23] became the very substance of his theological development. That set him apart from others, who were inclined to minimize the problems. In the end he found a way of hoping against all hope. He learned to unravel the meaning of the inward despairing into which God plunges especially those whom he loves best. God was for him at this moment the "hidden" God[24] who saves man *a contrario*, in doing the opposite of what man expects. He forgave his servants nothing: "No man living is righteous before thee" (Ps. 143:2). But the strange work of God (*opus alienum*) is only the other side of his proper work, the salvation of man. So the worse he became, the more sure he was, for the more God put man to the test, the more he demonstrated that he was dealing with him. God is the one who acts, and salvation is his work. Man is "acted upon."[25]

That bold interpretation acceded to the demands outlined above. Was it already the Reformation doctrine of Luther, or still simply another pre-Reformation conception? No doubt the truth is that in the young Luther's situation the understanding of the main point was hindered by the abundance of unresolved prob-lems. We can begin to grasp what will finally appear as the solution, yet not establish the connection with the central concern and not see that *that* is the solution. Nothing is gained unless all the ideas fall into place. The difficulty of reconstructing the history of Luther's evolution from his first writings is that the present-day interpreter establishes that some primitive text already contains a formulation of Luther's solution to the problem of salvation, without knowing whether Luther himself took account of the significance of what we understand better than he. His retrospective observations attest that the formula which he sought was given him several times. But he also said that, until the decisive turning point, there was within his thought a resistance molded by his education, which led him at first to acknowledge only provisionally the facts which emerged from his research. He could not see how the content of his lectures formed the unified whole that we now discern after the event. However, we should retain the coherence of his development, even in this period, and the emphasis on faith in God. Luther saw every step as based on the Bible, even if to us the young man appears to be dependent for a long time on contemporary patterns of spirituality.[26]

At a later stage he no longer hesitated to confront the fact of sin and to eliminate easy solutions. Instead of fearing sin, he declared, it must be accorded its full significance. The *Lectures on Romans* (1515—16) open on this theme: The purpose of the epistle, Luther explains, is to magnify sin, in order to understand how necessary Christ is.[27] Later—ch. 4 of the epistle—he reproaches the scholastics for having oversimplified the problem of sin, for having robbed it of its significance.[28] He himself abandoned this theology, encouraged by the reading of St. Augustine and, to his great surprise, by some works from the end of the Middle Ages: Tauler and the German Theology. He was amazed to discover in German—not in Latin, the language of theology—a teaching so much at one with his view of man, Adam, sin, Christ, and grace.[29] It was then that he began to criticize openly the doctrine of works, of free will, of "doing what is within oneself."[30]

The growth within him of a new certainty can be measured by the increasing virulence of his critique of current theology. For his part, Luther was already sure of himself. In 1517 he undertook the reform of theological studies at the University of Wittenberg and in a short time turned his students away from the study of Aristotle.[31]

All this, indeed, in a closed atmosphere within the restricted framework of a young university which still hovered on the periphery of the great centers of culture. For Luther to arrive at the stage he reached in the writings following Worms there had to be a genuine discovery, an illumination, with a definite character of

finality about it. The Reformation arose out of this. It amounted
to a breakthrough on the doctrinal front, and Luther would spend
the rest of his life drawing out its full significance.

2. The Discovery of Mercy

The question of Luther's Reformation discovery is a curiosity
of Luther studies. The ceaseless debates springing up on this point
remain always unresolved, but every time something is learned
from them. The fact of an "illumination" of the young Luther, at
the beginning of the Reformation, has always been acknowledged
on the testimony of explicit texts. Denifle could nevertheless write
without fear of refutation that the Protestants themselves were
unable to indicate the date or the content of Luther's discovery.[32]
That sparked off a profusion of new researches which have been
pursued down to our own time, without definitive conclusion.[33]
Today we know Luther's discovery much better than in Denifle's
time, but we are still reduced to a choice between the opinions of
various authors or forming our own hypotheses.

The Third International Congress of Luther Research
(Helsinki, 1966) was the occasion of a colloquium on this
question, and there was some hope of a solution, but on the third
day the matter had to be abandoned. No one was up to solving the
points under dispute.[34]

I hold to the view that the best approach to the problem is the
Preface composed by Luther in 1545 for the first volume of the
complete edition of his Latin works. This text is the only one in
which Luther gives a detailed account of his discovery to a wide
public. It seems, in fact, to pose more problems than it solves, but
its indications provide support for various theories—none altogether convincing—built up over so many years.

In these pages, written a year before his death, Luther
introduced the collection of his writings for the years 1517—19[35] by
an account of the events that marked the beginning of the
Reformation crisis, beginning with the indulgence affair. This
version of the origins of the Reformation by the principal
character involved includes, on the one hand, the rapid sequence
of events to 1519, in conformity with the contents of the volume,
and, on the other hand, the detailed account of a single event, not
exactly dated and in some ways standing outside the text. It
concerns Luther personally and furnishes, so to speak, the

supreme explanation, the key, of the whole story, namely the discovery of the "Gospel."

Research has not given enough attention to the fact that the Luther of 1545 placed the discovery of the Gospel among the foundation events of the Reformation. It is an integral part of the authentic story of the beginnings of the Lutheran movement. For the Luther of 1545 this story cannot be understood without his discovery. Nothing, therefore, can take the place of the careful examination of what he intended to say about this decisive moment in his career, placing it as he did in so explicit a context. The passage appears as follows:

Meanwhile, I had already during that year returned to interpret the Psalter anew. I had confidence in the fact that I was more skillful, after I had lectured in the university on St. Paul's epistles to the Romans, to the Galatians, and the one to the Hebrews. I had indeed been captivated with an extraordinary ardor for understanding Paul in the Epistle to the Romans. But up till then it was not the cold blood about the heart, but a single word in Chapter 1 [:17], "In it the righteousness of God is revealed," that had stood in my way. For I hated that word "righteousness of God," which, according to the use and custom of all the teachers, I had been taught to understand philosophically regarding the formal or active righteousness, as they called it, with which God is righteous and punishes the unrighteous sinner.[36]

Though I lived as a monk without reproach, I felt that I was a sinner before God with an extremely disturbed conscience. I could not believe that he was placated by my satisfaction. I did not love, yes, I hated the righteous God who punishes sinners, and secretly, if not blasphemously, certainly murmuring greatly, I was angry with God, and said, "As if, indeed, it is not enough, that miserable sinners, eternally lost through original sin, are crushed by every kind of calamity by the law of the decalogue, without having God add pain to pain by the gospel and also by the gospel threatening us with his righteousness and wrath!" Thus I raged with a fierce and troubled conscience. Nevertheless, I beat importunately upon Paul at that place, most ardently desiring to know what St. Paul wanted.

At last, by the mercy of God, meditating day and night, I gave heed to the context of the words, namely, "In it the righteousness of God is revealed, as it is written, 'He who through faith is righteous shall live.'" There I began to understand that the righteousness of God is that by which the righteous lives by a gift of God, namely by faith. And this is the meaning: the righteousness of God is revealed by the gospel, namely, the passive righteousness with which merciful God justifies us by faith, as it is written, "He who through faith is righteous shall live." Here I felt that I was altogether born again and had entered paradise itself through open gates. There a totally other face of the entire Scripture showed itself to me. Thereupon I ran through the Scriptures from memory. I also found in other terms an analogy, as, the work of God, that is, what God does in us, the power of God, with which he makes us strong, the wisdom of God, with which he makes us wise, the strength of God, the salvation of God, the glory of God.

And I extolled my sweetest word with a love as great as the hatred with which I had before hated the word "righteousness of God." Thus that place in Paul was for me truly the gate to paradise. Later I read Augustine's The Spirit and the Letter, *where contrary to hope I found that he, too, interpreted God's righteousness in a similar way, as the righteousness with which God clothes us when he justifies us. Although this was heretofore said imperfectly and he did not explain all things concerning imputation clearly, it nevertheless was pleasing that God's righteousness with which we are justified was taught. Armed more fully with these thoughts, I began a second time to interpret the Psalter. And the work would have grown into a large commentary, if I had not again been compelled to leave the work begun, because Emperor Charles V in the following year convened the diet at Worms.* (LW 34, 336—38)

The account clearly turns on an exegetical difficulty, on the meaning of the first half of Rom. 1:17: "In it [the Gospel] the righteousness of God is revealed." The problem was that the righteousness of God means first of all that God is righteous, with an inflexible righteousness that makes no compromise with evil. Luther did not maintain that this was the meaning of Rom. 1:17 or even that he had been taught to read the verse in this sense. He said only that for a whole period St. Paul's formulation had made him believe that the Gospel, even if it is the proclamation of mercy, does not lessen in any way the demands of the retributive justice of God. The proclamation of mercy, therefore, could not relieve the disturbed conscience of the reckoning to be given to the righteousness of God. Luther's evocation of his experience as a monk gave a practical demonstration of how Paul's words faced the Christian with the persistence of God's threatening righteousness and at the same time the consoling aspects of the Gospel.

Understood in this way the formula of Rom. 1:17, which for Luther had the authority of Scripture[37] itself, held him back from relying on God's mercy. The rest of the Preface explains how he succeeded in grasping that the righteousness of God (of Rom. 1:17) is that of the righteous man who lives by faith. It is "of God" because it comes from God, but the text does not allude to the divine attribute of righteousness. The Bible contains other expressions constructed with the genitive "of God" for which Hebrew grammar allows the sense claimed by Luther.

Luther had, besides, sought the support of an authority recognized within the Church. He knew enough of Augustine's *De spiritu et littera* to know that this treatise on the spirit and the letter includes a consistent, sustained exegesis of the Epistle to the Romans. He had had to read many times the passage relating to Rom. 1:17 without seeing if Augustine interpreted St. Paul on this point in a significant way. This time he scrutinized it word by word and verified joyfully that Augustine explained the words *iustitia Dei* exactly as "the righteousness with which God endows us when he justifies the unrighteous,"[38] and that without reference to the other righteousness of God, of which, moreover, St. Paul no longer speaks in the verse in question.

The initial exegetical difficulty is thus overcome by the fact that the words "righteousness of God" in Rom. 1:17 should be explained by what follows, in the sense of the "righteous man who lives by faith," without appealing to a scholastic doctrine. There is, indeed, a plane on which the only reality is mercy, and that is the plane of faith.

This is what Luther identified in 1545 as the decisive discovery of the Reformation. What is clear is the essential place of the conception of the Gospel in this presentation, and the importance of the Scripture which had been at the basis of both the problem and its solution.

It is certainly possible to find other interpretations of the 1545 Preface. I should say a word about these, in such a way as to give some idea of the discussion about Luther's Reformation discovery without summarizing it all.

The major reason for the differences between the authors is that

many of them analyze the 1545 text on the basis of their own
conception of the discovery. It is, as a matter of fact, possible to
begin with other texts. But as it is unavoidable to say something
about the testimony of the Preface, which is unique in its kind, it is
not uncommon to find scholars applying to its theories inspired
by other statements of Luther's. It is affirmed, for example, that the
text which we have just read reports Luther's discovery of the
doctrine of justifying faith, an idea already present in the *Lectures
on Romans*. Or again, it is suggested that the Luther of 1545
speaks of the distinctions between the "two righteousnesses of
God": that by which God is righteous in himself (active righteousness) and that which we freely receive from him (passive
righteousness). In this case the discovery described in 1545 would
be the discovery of mercy. But the text can also suggest that Luther
simply recounts his discovery of the meaning of Rom. 1:17, and
this leads to a search in his early writings for the moment when the
exegesis defined in the Preface appears.

Explanations of this kind often bypass the main point, which
is what the text of the Preface itself says. Taken in itself, it seems to
me difficult to give it a meaning other than the one I have
indicated. It pinpoints a problem which is precise and clearly
defined, in itself by no means based on the epistle itself, namely,
that Luther was at first convinced that St. Paul gave an important
role to the active righteousness of God in his conception of the
Gospel.

Such a conception implies that Luther knew—like every
Christian—that the Gospel is nothing but mercy. He did not have
to "discover" the Gospel, which he found clearly articulated in the
Epistle to the Romans, not to mention in the liturgy and the
theological tradition, as Denifle has pointed out. But the importance accorded to the retributive righteousness of God in his
Romano-Germanic Catholicism prevented him from believing
that the Scriptures invite us to take the Gospel in its absolute
meaning, since we read from Paul's own pen that "in the Gospel
the righteousness of God is revealed." We must verify the meaning
of such a formulation. Did Paul wish to place the Gospel outside
the constricting framework of righteousness and of the Law, or
not? This was the young Luther's precise question according to
the 1545 Preface.

Denifle asserts that Luther on this occasion distorted the truth
in terms of his "Lutheran" evolution, and also of his public. One

can actually think that the Preface was intended to make Lutherans understand the origin of the doctrine of justification by faith alone, without works, by which doctrine they distinguished themselves from Catholics faithful to Rome. The reproach made against Augustine, of not having explained "imputation" well— that is to say, that God asks nothing of us except to believe—is a strong indication of this meaning.

But if this was the Reformer's view of things at the end of his life, how can we know what the discovery can really have been for the young, Catholic Luther, who was its beneficiary and who was for a long time unable to speak in the terms of the Preface's account? None of the young Luther's writings indicates a discovery, before a letter of 31 May 1518 to Staupitz, which accompanied the *Explanations of the Ninety-five Theses* to Rome.

The difficulty is to indicate at what date we should look for the event described in 1545—the Preface is not precise about it.[39] One's Latin is simply unequal to the task of investigating the pluperfect tenses—*redieram, captus fueram*, etc.—by which Luther marks out the stages leading to his solution. Moreover, certain interpreters stick to the indication that the discovery took place at the time of the second commentary on the Psalms, that is to say, in 1518. But H. Bornkamm, followed by the majority of recent authors, asserts that the situation evoked by the Preface is that of the beginning of the lectures on the Epistle to the Romans (1515—16).

Earlier commentators go back before the first commentary on Psalms (1513—15) and take the view that the Luther of the Preface has confused his two works on the Psalter.

The context of the account (the story of the origins of the Reformation from 1517 to 1519) suggests despite everything that Luther intended to speak of his second commentary on the Psalms. What is less sure, in the light of the text, is whether he was careful to date his discovery correctly. Was the date important for him? Did he even have a date to indicate?

The other texts in this collection are no more explicit in this regard. They concern declarations in which Luther, from the beginning of 1518—19, defends his new interpretation of the righteousness of God or even indicates that he has discovered it after a long personal ordeal.[40] To this we may add various texts of the period 1513—18 in which, it is believed, ideas that are already reformatory can be discerned. Analysis of these texts, whose dates we often know, allows us perhaps to reveal this reversal of thought from one day to the next of which the Preface speaks.

There are some factors which seem to me to favor the date 1518 among all those possibilities which the 1545 text suggests.[41] The main one is that the account is placed explicitly in the context of the years 1517—19. That given fact can be connected to the indication, in the last lines of the Preface, that Luther did not find the truth all at once, but gradually. This suggests a continued process, of which the Preface describes the final stage under the form of an exegetical discussion adapted to the evidence of the time. Whatever could have been the reality 30 years earlier, it could only with difficulty be seen as a matter of a sudden revelation of truth unsuspected in every respect. Retrospectively, the event appeared to Luther as the moment when his last hesitation had ceased. It was only in finding the answer to the objection arising out of Rom. 1:17 that his conception of the Gospel became operative, and the Reformation emerged from there, no less than from the external events of the years 1517—19.[42]

The memorandum Luther addressed to Cajetan at Augsburg in October 1518 spelled out a long list of Scriptural proofs for the doctrine of justifying faith, citing first of all Rom. 1:17 (LW 31, p. 270). That development expressed a recent and deepening reflection of Luther on this point. Would he have perceived at this moment how much Rom. 1:17 allowed him to lay the foundation of his doctrine?[43] The evidence suggests that from 1518 he was completely liberated. At that date, at least, something had changed, in the sense of a transition from the common faith of the Church to Luther's faith.

Research into the date of the Reformation discovery also depends on the question of its content. It is less easy to take these questions one after the other than to treat them together. As for the content, it would be necessary to know how the events took place, and therefore at what moment. The old Luther said that he had been for a long time in anguish at the thought of the righteousness of God, to the point of being unable to pray Psalms like Ps. 31:1: "In thy righteousness deliver me!" He specified that it was Rom. 1:17 that lifted him out of his difficulties. But the fundamental reversal is explained in a variable way from one text to the next. The opposition "active/passive righteousness" is explicitly found only in some texts. The Preface follows the line of the *Table Talk*, which confirms that at the end of his life Luther restricted the episode to a tension about the meaning of the righteousness of God in Rom. 1:17. But the letter of 31 May 1518 says that Luther had been put on the path by understanding that true penitence (*metanoia*) comes not at the end but at the beginning of our efforts. At that time the theme of the righteousness of God was no longer pressing on his thoughts.

Should we conclude that Luther was the first to lose interest in precision about the facts, beyond the affirmation that the principle of justification by faith appeared plainly to him at one moment after long questioning? The "discovery," in any case, whatever it could have been,[44] depended on the intuition of a principle of extreme simplicity: The basis of Christian reality is that sinful man communicates with the merciful will of God, who demands of each one nothing else than to welcome Christ in faith—and to live in him.

Through that perception the young Luther's anguish was finally overcome.[45] He knew the decisive reason for no longer dreading God's anger. He stopped pursuing his efforts along the lines of his early education. From now on he had his doctrine, which appears to constitute, with due deference to Denifle, an incredible novelty at this moment in the Church's life. Luther's crisis in the monastery was a crisis mediated by the spiritual searching of his time. He did not even have to ask himself if his solution could satisfy others. In fact, scarcely had he begun preaching publicly in the Church in the name of the Gospel than he saw opinion divide into opponents and partisans, all equally under the spell of his preaching.

3. The Clash with the Church

The Luther "armed more fully with these thoughts" who returned to the interpretation of the Psalms in 1518—19 was burdened with a message, the key to which still remained hidden. If it depended only on him, he would perhaps be content to deepen his new intuition with the help of Scripture for the benefit of his students. But since 31 Oct. 1517 the story of his life was intertwined with that of the beginnings of the Reformation. He himself indicated in 1545 that his summoning to Worms by Charles V ended what appears to us the most favorable possibility of a Luther who would have peacefully helped the Church to recognize that she was the creature of the Gospel.

"Luther's theology is not a way of thinking intrinsically at odds with the Church, in so far as it is not centered on the Church but on salvation. The conflict broke out about indulgences and was, therefore, a problem of pastoral practice concerning salvation in a situation of tension peculiar to the Empire."[46] Pierre Chaunu, from whom I have borrowed these lines, analyzes, better than I can do, the circumstances which made Luther's personal discovery of mercy the rapidly ripening seed of a new growth of Christianity. The indulgences theses reveal only imperfectly what Luther represented,[47] in terms of redressing the shallowness of religious life. The reaction was an unleashing of anti-Roman passion, as if Germany was only waiting for the opportunity. The papacy was soon on the defensive and could think of nothing better to do than to drag Luther before its courts. Rome had no doubt that the choice between the pope and the monk would be easily made. What could not be foreseen was that public opinion took the part of the monk, in whom it discovered what it had ceased to hope for in the Bishop of Rome: the Word of God.

The Brief Instruction of 1522 allows us to grasp the message which had made so much more of an impression on Luther's sympathizers than the outward clamor.

The need of a renewal in church and religious life, and also in social and cultural affairs, was not part of the call for Reformation such as had taken place. The latter had been defined little by little, very much at the mercy of events. But it had acquired stability only on the basis of the principles brought to light by Luther: Scripture, the Word of God, the Gospel, Christ, faith. Luther's advent gave to the movement the force of his remarkable originality, in a Church imprisoned in its habits. Luther, wrote Söderblom, created "a new ideal of life, a new assurance and a new liberty, through an inward experience and the Gospel. Considered from the point of view of the history of religions, he is, after St. Paul, the greatest prodigy, the creative genius of Christianity."[48] His discovery was "that of the absolutely universal and creative dimension of faith. It is here that is found the creative center of all Christian existence, the righteousness of God in Jesus Christ, by which we live before God from beginning to end and are renewed progressively in the Spirit."[49]

Similar judgments were expressed by those contemporary with the indulgences affair. Among those who took on the role of rejecting and combating Luther, a host of earnest souls, many still faithful to Rome perceived that the Wittenberg monk bore within him the potential for a rebirth unprecedented within the old religion. The saintly bishop of Würzburg, who received Luther one evening in April 1518, on his way to Heidelberg, wrote to his prince, the elector of Saxony, to recommend protection. Such a man of God should not be allowed to fall into the hands of those who already wanted to see him dead.[50] Erasmus himself threw his weight behind attempts to check the pursuit of Luther in 1519—20.[51]

Christians in this period, we should always remember, did not have the conception of Catholicism which has become ours since the Council of Trent. It would need nearly 20 years at Trent to overcome what Lortz called "theological confusion." Since Avignon and the Great Schism the papacy was no longer un-challenged, and the election of an Alexander VI, a Julius II, and a Leo X was perceived as the end of a line, even in Rome. Something new was expected; the situation, it was felt, could not last.

Luther answered these expectations: He presented Christ reestablished in His role of unique Savior; a doctrinal authority which could not be deceived, the Scriptures; a religion of faith instead of a practice degraded by "works." (Concerning the latter, the point had been reached where relics were passed around and handled before the reception of the Eucharist.) Nor should we forget Luther's return to the Augustinian sources of Western thought, dried up by Aristotelianism. This strong return to Augustine's influence would make Catholicism a prey to Jan-senism, which was proclaimed at Louvain from the time of St. Pius V. Luther also declared an end to fear, the liberty of a conscience set free from priestly tyranny. In him there was realized a Christianity which would not have been thought possible. The startling changes he triggered off in the Church resembled what we knew for a brief moment with John XXIII. There could be no doubt that Luther appeared to many Catholics, despite everything pointing in an opposite direction, as the apostle of an *aggiornamento* within the Church.

But it is true that Luther's faith was, from the beginning, in conflict with the Church. The antipapal theses which Luther publicly upheld at the Leipzig debate in July 1519 aggravated the tension with Rome. The pope, Luther affirmed, could be deceived because he had already been deceived. His is a human power, and he does not in any way rule the Church by "divine right." Already the basis of the Reformer's thought, bearing the marks of the

German context and inheriting the antipapal polemics of the preceding century, is clear; the pope was the Antichrist, that is, the one who sees himself or is seen to be Christ, but whose actions bring about results in opposition to the Gospel. In the name of such principles Luther would plunge more and more into the morass of a struggle against "papism," sweeping away pilgrimages, religious orders, the cult of saints and relics, the rosary, and the doctrine of the seven sacraments.

Undoubtedly, our analysis should not pass over these difficulties. But to concentrate only on Luther's errors is to miss altogether, from a Catholic point of view, a true consideration of the deep themes of the drama. Luther's errors have been exploited to the point of absurdity. There was another side of things, a "passion" for the Church itself, inflamed by this leap of faith which cast a piercing light on his life and his theology. After its long, internal triumph over Protestant "heresy," Rome is not always up to acknowledging that the Reformation is its Damascus Road: "I am he whom you are persecuting." Luther, indeed, was not a heretic like the others. He was among those who put themselves in the wrong without leaving their judges the least opportunity of being wholly right. What mattered, and matters still above everything, is to ponder the message he brings: the Pauline claim of the rights of Christ in the Church that bears his name.

4
Being Justified, By Faith

The Lesson of the Epistle to the Romans

In Luther's life and writings St. Paul's Epistle to the Romans looms large. His lectures at Wittenberg on this epistle (1515—16) confirm that he had studied it with extraordinary ardor, as he declared in 1545. Volumes 56 and 57 of the Weimar Edition, which are devoted to the young Luther's lectures on St. Paul, are among the best sources we have at our command for understanding his quest.[1]

Moreover, there is a long introduction by Luther to this epistle, which is contemporary with the *Brief Instruction on the Gospel* and was published with the German translation of the New Testament (1522). It lays open in all its power Luther's conception of faith and "righteousness." He used the Epistle to the Romans to set out the complete framework within which his perception developed. This mature expression of his thought merits our attention, for here we see, among other things, sound answers to theories based on his psychology which tend to attribute to his subjectivity the ultimate explanation of his doctrinal originality.

Faith, he says, is "a living, daring confidence in God's grace, so sure and certain that the believer would stake his life on it a thousand times."[2] For the Catholic writer Roland Dalbiez that notion of faith was the means contrived by Luther in the end to resist the temptation to suicide. This thinking rests on a closed argument, and the only viable alternative to it is to understand Luther's own comments about his situation. Accordingly, this is the way I intend to approach the problem of Luther's anxiety.

The *Preface to the Epistle of St. Paul to the Romans*, the entire text of which we are going to read, includes a study of St. Paul's terminology and an analysis of the epistle. It is not exegesis in the modern sense of the word, but at least every Christian can profit directly from it. Luther, as we have seen, was concerned about democratizing the knowledge of Scripture. The Bible is not a book for clerics and specialists. If it had been up to Luther alone, Catholics would have known the Bible better than has actually been the case over the last 400 years. The Epistle to the Romans is still for many priests and many of the faithful just one text among others. Apart from some passages, which the liturgy or seminary lectures have made more familiar, the prevailing impression is that here, as elsewhere in St. Paul, anything can be found. But Luther discerns in the development of the apostle's subject a discussion quite fundamental for the understanding of the faith.

It is easy to understand this debate in terms of an ideal still abroad today, of the "good" Christian, who seeks to live a holy and honest life observing the commandments of God and the Church. St. Paul was speaking to believers converted from Judaism who had such an ideal. To use his language, which we meet again in Luther, his Roman correspondents were trying to fulfil the Law by performing the "works" which it laid down and avoiding what was forbidden. In their view, as in Christian opinion right down to our time, a life conformed to the Law and rich in good works is worthy of being called righteous. It is outwardly irreproachable, and no one could doubt its inherent sincerity.

But it appears that Christianity demands more. This is Paul's thought, and Luther changes nothing. His achievement was to bring to light everything in this epistle which enables us to understand the righteousness of faith and to recognize the insufficiency of the righteousness of works, that is, of all perfection outside Christ.

To begin with, Luther asks each person to question himself with deep honesty before God: Even when we do as he wishes, can we be sure that we truly love his will? That question had thrust itself on the young monk, and the text which follows shows the point to which he had taken it.

1. Preface to the Epistle of St. Paul to the Romans (1522)[3]

This epistle is really the chief part of the New Testament, and is truly the purest gospel. It is worthy not only that every Christian should know it word for word, by heart, but also that he should occupy himself with it every day, as the daily bread of the soul. We can never read it or ponder over it too much; for the more we deal with it, the more precious it becomes and the better it tastes.

Therefore I too will do my best, so far as God has given me power, to open the way into it through this preface, so that it may be the better understood by everyone. Heretofore it has been badly obscured by glosses and all kinds of idle talk,[4] though in itself it is a bright light, almost sufficient to illuminate the entire holy Scriptures.

To begin with we must have knowledge of its language and know what St. Paul means by the words: "law," "sin," "grace,' "faith," "righteousness," "flesh," "spirit," and the like. Otherwise no reading of the book has any value.

PAUL'S VOCABULARY

LAW—The Law of God Should be Fulfilled Wholeheartedly

The little word "law" you must here not take in human fashion as a teaching about what works are to be done. That is the way with human laws; a law is fulfilled by works, even though there is no heart in the doing of them. But God judges according to what is in the depths of the heart. For this reason, his law too makes its demands on the inmost heart; it cannot be satisfied with works, but rather punishes as hypocrisy and lies the works not done from the bottom of the heart. Hence all men are called liars in Psalm 116[:11], because no one keeps or can keep God's law from the bottom of the heart. For everyone finds in himself displeasure in what is good and pleasure in what is bad. If, now, there is no willing pleasure in the good, then the inmost heart is not set on the law of God. Then, too, there is surely sin, and God's wrath is deserved, even though outwardly there seem to be many good deeds and an honorable life.

No-one Fulfills the Law by Doing Good Works

Hence St. Paul concludes, in chapter 2[:13], that the Jews are all sinners, saying that only the doers of the law are righteous before God. He means by this that no one, in terms of his works, is a doer of the law. Rather, he speaks to them thus, "You teach one must not commit adultery, but you yourself commit adultery" [2:22]; and again, "In passing judgment upon another you condemn yourself, because you, the judge, are doing the very same things" [2:1]. This is as if to say, "You live a fine outward life in the

*works of the law, and you pass judgment on those who do not so
live. You know how to teach everyone; you see the speck that is in
the eye of another, but do not notice the log that is in your own
eye" [Matt. 7:3].*

*For even though you keep the law outwardly, with works, from
fear of punishment or love of reward, nevertheless you do all this
unwillingly, without pleasure in and love for the law, but with
reluctance and under compulsion. For if the law were not there,
you would prefer to act otherwise. The conclusion is that from the
bottom of your heart you hate the law. What point is there then in
your teaching others not to steal, if you yourself are a thief at heart,
and would gladly be one outwardly if you dared? Though, to be
sure, the outward work does not lag far behind among such
hypocrites! So you teach others, but not yourself; nor do you
yourself know what you are teaching—you have never yet understood the law correctly. Moreover the law increases sin, as St. Paul
says in chapter 5[:20], because the more the law demands of men
what they cannot do, the more they hate the law.*

The Law Is Spiritual

*For this reason he says, in chapter 7[:14], "The law is
spiritual." What does that mean? If the law were for the body, it
could be satisfied with works; but since it is spiritual, no one can
satisfy it—unless all that you do is done from the bottom of your
heart. But such a heart is given only by God's Spirit, who fashions
a man after the law, so that he acquires a desire for the law in his
heart, doing nothing henceforth out of fear and compulsion but
out of a willing heart. The law is thus spiritual in that it will be
loved and fulfilled with such a spiritual heart, and requires such a
spirit. Where that spirit is not in the heart, there sin remains, also
displeasure with the law and hostility toward it even though the
law itself is good and just and holy.*

Fulfilling the Law by Faith and Doing the Works of the Law

*Accustom yourself, then, to this language, that doing the
works of the law and fulfilling the law are two very different
things. The work of the law is everything that one does, or can do,
toward keeping the law of his own free will or by his own powers.
But since in the midst of all these works and along with them there
remains in the heart a dislike of the law and compulsion with
respect to it, these works are all wasted and have no value. That is*

what St. Paul means in chapter 3[:20], when he says, "By works of the law will no man be justified in God's sight." Hence you see that the wranglers and sophists practice deception when they teach men to prepare themselves for grace by means of works. How can a man prepare himself for good by means of works, if he does good works only with aversion and unwillingness in his heart? How shall a work please God if it proceeds from a reluctant and resisting heart?

To fulfil the law, however, is to do its works with pleasure and love, to live a godly and good life of one's own accord, without the compulsion of the law. This pleasure and love for the law is put into the heart by the Holy Spirit, as St. Paul says in chapter 5[:5]. But the Holy Spirit is not given except in, with, and by faith in Jesus Christ, as St. Paul says in the introduction. Faith, moreover, comes only through God's Word or gospel, which preaches Christ, saying that he is God's Son and a man, and has died and risen again for our sakes, as he says in chapters 3[:25], 4[:25], and 10[:9].

So it happens that faith alone makes a person righteous and fulfills the law. For out of the merit of Christ it brings forth the Spirit. And the Spirit makes the heart glad and free, as the law requires that it shall be. Thus good works emerge from faith itself. That is what St. Paul means in chapter 3[:31]; after he has rejected the works of the law, it sounds as if he would overthrow the law by this faith. "No," he says, "we uphold the law by faith"; that is, we fulfill it by faith.

SIN—The Root of Sin is Unbelief[5]

Sin, in the Scripture, means not only the outward works of the body but also all the activities that move men to do these works, namely, the inmost heart, with all its powers. Thus the little word "do" ought to mean that a man falls all the way and lives in sin. Even outward works of sin do not take place, unless a man plunges into it completely with body and soul. And the Scriptures look especially into the heart and single out the root and source of all sin, which is unbelief in the inmost heart. As, therefore, faith alone makes a person righteous, and brings the Spirit and pleasure in good outward works, so unbelief alone commits sin, and brings forth the flesh and pleasure in bad outward works, as happened to Adam and Eve in paradise, Genesis 3.[6]

Hence Christ calls unbelief the only sin, when he says in John 16[:8-9], "The Spirit will convince the world of sin . . . because they do not believe in me." For this reason too, before good or bad works take place, as the good or bad fruits, there must first be in the heart faith or unbelief. Unbelief is the root, the sap, and the chief power of all sin. For this reason, in the Scriptures it is called the serpent's head and the head of the old dragon, which the seed of the woman, Christ, must tread under foot, as was promised to Adam, Genesis 3[:15].

GRACE, GIFT—God Is Gracious to the Believer

Between grace and gift there is this difference. Grace actually means God's favor, or the good will which in himself he bears toward us, by which he is disposed to give us Christ and to pour into us the Holy Spirit with his gifts. This is clear from chapter 5[:15], where St. Paul speaks of "the grace and gift in Christ," etc. The gifts and the Spirit increase in us every day, but they are not yet perfect since there remain in us the evil desires and sins that war against the Spirit, as he says in Romans 7[:5ff.] and Galatians 5[:17], and the conflict between the seed of the woman and the seed of the serpent, as foretold in Genesis 3[:15]. Nevertheless grace does so much that we are accounted completely righteous before God. For his grace is not divided or parceled out, as are the gifts, but takes us completely into favor for the sake of Christ our Intercessor and Mediator. And because of this, the gifts are begun in us.

In this sense, then, you can understand chapter 7.[7] There St. Paul still calls himself a sinner; and yet he can say, in chapter 8[:1], that there is no condemnation for those who are in Christ, simply because of the incompleteness of the gifts and of the Spirit. Because the flesh is not yet slain, we are still sinners. But because we believe in Christ and have a beginning of the Spirit, God is so favorable and gracious to us that he will not count the sin against us or judge us because of it. Rather he deals with us according to our faith in Christ, until sin is slain.

FAITH

Faith is not the human notion and dream that some people call faith. When they see that no improvement of life and no good works follow—although they can hear and say much about faith—they fall into the error of saying, "Faith is not enough; one must do works in order to be righteous and be saved." This is due to the fact that when they hear the gospel, they get busy and by their own powers create an idea in their heart which says, "I believe"; they take this then to be a true faith. But, as it is a human figment and idea that never reaches the depths of the heart, nothing comes of it either, and no improvement follows.

Faith Is a Work of God in Us

Faith, however, is a divine work in us which changes us and makes us to be born anew of God, John 1[:12-13]. It kills the old Adam and makes us altogether different men, in heart and spirit and mind and powers; and it brings with it the Holy Spirit.[8] O it is a living, busy, active, mighty thing, this faith. It is impossible for it not to be doing good works incessantly. It does not ask whether good works are to be done, but before the question is asked, it has already done them, and is constantly doing them. Whoever does not do such works, however, is an unbeliever. He gropes and looks around for faith and good works, but knows neither what faith is nor what good works are. Yet he talks and talks, with many words, about faith and good works.

Faith is a living, daring confidence in God's grace, so sure and certain that the believer would stake his life on it a thousand times.[9] This knowledge of and confidence in God's grace makes men glad and bold and happy in dealing with God and with all creatures. And this is the work which the Holy Spirit performs in faith. Because of it, without compulsion, a person is ready and glad to do good to everyone, to serve everyone, to suffer everything, out of love and praise to God who has shown him this grace. Thus it is impossible to separate works from faith, quite as impossible as to separate heat and light from fire. Beware, therefore, of your own false notions and of the idle talkers who imagine themselves wise enough to make decisions about faith and good works, and yet are the greatest fools. Pray God that he may work faith in you. Otherwise you will surely remain forever without faith, regardless of what you may think or do.

RIGHTEOUSNESS

Righteousness, then, is such a faith. It is called "the righteousness of God" because God gives it, and counts it as righteousness[10] for the sake of Christ our Mediator, and makes a man to fulfil his obligation to everybody. For through faith a man becomes free from sin and comes to take pleasure in God's commandments, thereby he gives God the honor due him, and pays him what he owes him. Likewise he serves his fellow-men willingly, by whatever means he can, and thus pays his debt to everyone. Nature,

*free will, and our own powers cannot bring this righteousness into
being. For as no one can give himself faith, neither can he take
away his own unbelief. How, then, will he take away a single sin,
even the very smallest? Therefore all that is done apart from faith,
or in unbelief, is false; it is hypocrisy and sin, Romans 14[:23], no
matter how good a showing it makes.*[11]

FLESH AND SPIRIT

*Flesh and spirit you must not understand as though flesh is
only that which has to do with unchastity and spirit is only that
which has to do with what is inwardly in the heart. Rather, like
Christ in John 3[:6], Paul calls everything "flesh" that is born of
the flesh—the whole man, with body and soul, mind and senses—
because everything about him longs for the flesh. Thus you should
learn to call him "fleshly" too who thinks, teaches, and talks a
great deal about lofty spiritual matters, yet does so without grace.
From the "works of the flesh" in Galatians 5[:19-21], you can learn
that Paul calls heresy and hatred "works of the flesh."*[12] *And in
Romans 8[:3] he says that "the law is weakened by the flesh"; yet
this is said not of unchastity, but of all sins, and above all of
unbelief, which is the most spiritual of all vices.*

*On the contrary, you should call him "spiritual" who is
occupied with the most external kind of works, as Christ was when
he washed the disciple's feet [John 13:1-14], and Peter when he
steered his boat and fished. Thus "the flesh" is a man who lives
and works, inwardly and outwardly, in the service of the flesh's
gain and of this temporal life. "The spirit" is the man who lives
and works, inwardly and outwardly, in the service of the Spirit and
of the future life.*

*Without such a grasp of these words, you will never understand
this letter of St. Paul, nor any other book of Holy Scripture.
Therefore beware of all teachers who use these words in a different
sense, no matter who they are, even Origen, Ambrose, Augustine,
Jerome, and others like them or even above them.*[13] *And now we
will take up the epistle.*

THE CONTENT OF THE EPISTLE

The Revelation of Sin

*It is right for a preacher of the gospel in the first place by
revelation of the law and of sin to rebuke and to constitute as sin*

everything that is not the living fruit of the Spirit and of faith in Christ, in order that men should be led to know themselves and their own wretchedness, and to become humble and ask for help. This is therefore what St. Paul does. He begins in chapter 1 to rebuke the gross sins and unbelief that are plainly evident. These were, and still are, the sins of the heathen who live without God's grace. He says: Through the gospel there shall be revealed the wrath of God from heaven against all men because of their godless lives and their unrighteousness. For even though they know and daily recognize that there is a God, nevertheless nature itself, without grace, is so bad[14] that it neither thanks nor honors God. Instead it blinds itself, and goes steadily from bad to worse until, after idolatry, it blatantly commits the most shameful sins, along with all the vices, and also allows others to commit them unreprimanded.

In chapter 2 he extends his rebuke to include those who seem outwardly to be righteous and who commit their sins in secret. Such were the Jews and such are all the hypocrites who without desire or love for the law of God lead decent lives, but at heart hate God's law, and yet are quick to judge other people. This is the nature of all hypocrites, to think of themselves as pure, and yet to be full of covetousness, hatred, pride, and all uncleanness, Matthew 23[:25-28]. These are they who despise God's goodness, and in their hardheartedness heap wrath upon themselves. Thus St. Paul, as a true interpreter of the law, leaves no one without sin, but proclaims the wrath of God upon all who live well simply by nature or of their own volition. He makes them to be no better than the obvious sinners; indeed, he says they are stubborn and unrepentant.

In chapter 3 he throws them all together in a heap, and says that one is like the other: they are all sinners before God. Only, the Jews have had the word of God. Though not many have believed that word, this does not mean that the faith and truth of God are exhausted. He quotes incidentally a verse from Psalm 51[:4], that God remains justified in his words. Afterward he comes back to this again and proves also by Scripture that all men are sinners, and that by the works of the law nobody is justified, but that the law was given only that sin might be known.[15]

Revealing the Righteousness of God

Then he begins to teach the right way by which men must be justified and saved. He says: They are all sinners making no boast of God; but they must be justified without merit [of their own][16] *through faith in Christ, who has merited this for us by his blood, and has become for us a mercy-seat by God. God forgives all former sins to demonstrate that we are helped only by his righteousness, which he grants in faith, and which was revealed at that time through the gospel and was witnessed to beforehand by the law and the prophets. Thus the law is upheld by faith,*[17] *though the works of the law are thereby put down, together with the boasting of them.*

Faith Alone, Without Works

After the first three chapters, in which sin is revealed and faith's way to righteousness is taught, St. Paul begins in chapter 4 to meet certain remonstrances and objections. First he takes up the one that all men commonly make when they hear that faith justifies without works. They say, "Are we, then, to do no good works?" Therefore he himself takes up the case of Abraham, and asks, "What did Abraham accomplish, then, with his good works? Were they all in vain? Were his works of no use?" He concludes that Abraham was justified by faith alone, without any works, so much so that the Scriptures in Genesis 15[:6] declare that he was justified by faith alone even before the work of circumcision. But if the work of circumcision contributed nothing to his righteousness, though God had commanded it and it was a good work of obedience, then surely no other good work will contribute anything to righteousness. Rather, as Abraham's circumcision was an external sign by which he showed the righteousness that was already his in faith, so all good works are only external signs which follow out of faith; like good fruit, they demonstrate that a person is already inwardly righteous before God.

With this powerful illustration from the Scriptures, St. Paul confirms the doctrine of faith which he had set forth in chapter 3. He cites also another witness, David, who says in Psalm 32[:1-2] that a man is justified without works—although he does not remain without works when he has been justified. Then he gives the illustration a broader application, setting it over against all other works of the law. He concludes that the Jews cannot be Abraham's heirs merely because of their blood, still less because of the works of the law; they must inherit Abraham's faith, if they would be true heirs. For before the law—before the law of Moses and the law of circumcision—Abraham was justified by faith and called the father of all believers. Moreover the law brings about wrath rather than grace, because no one keeps the law out of love for it and pleasure in it. What comes by the works of the law is thus disfavor rather than grace. Therefore faith alone must obtain the grace promised to Abraham, for these examples too were written for our sakes [Rom. 15:4], that we too should believe.

The Works of Grace

In chapter 5 he comes to the fruits and works of faith, such as peace, joy, love to God and to every man, as well as confidence, assurance, boldness, courage, and hope amid tribulation and suffering. For all this follows, if faith be true, because of the superabundant goodness that God shows us in Christ, causing Christ to die for us before we could ask it of him, indeed, while we were still enemies. Thus we have it that faith justifies without any works; and yet it does not follow that men are therefore to do no good works, but rather that the genuine works will not be lacking. Of these the work-righteous saints know nothing. They dream up works of their own in which there is no peace, joy, confidence, love, hope, boldness, or any of the qualities of true Christian work and faith.

Christ, the New Adam

After this he digresses and makes a pleasant excursion, telling whence come sin and righteousness, death and life, and comparing Adam and Christ. He means to say that Christ had to come as a second Adam bequeathing his righteousness to us through a new spiritual birth in faith, just as the first Adam bequeathed sin to us through the old fleshly birth. Thus he declares and proves that no one by his own works can raise himself out of sin into righteousness, any more than he can prevent the birth of his own body. This is proved also by the fact that the divine law—which ought to assist toward righteousness, if anything can—has not only not helped, but has even increased sin. For the more the law forbids, the more our evil nature hates the law, and the more it wants to give reign to its own lust. Thus the law makes Christ all the more necessary, and more grace is needed to help our nature.

The Work of Faith

In chapter 6 he takes up the special work of faith, the conflict of the spirit with the flesh for the complete slaying of the sin and lust that remain after we are justified. He teaches us that we are not by faith so freed from sin that we can be idle, slack, and careless, as though there were no longer any sin in us. Sin is present; but it is no longer reckoned for our condemnation, because of the faith that is struggling against it.[18] *Therefore we have enough to do all our life long in taming the body, slaying its lusts, and compelling its members to obey the spirit and not the lusts. Thus we become like the death and resurrection of Christ, and complete our baptism— which signifies the death of sin and the new life of grace—until we are entirely purified of sin, and even our bodies rise again with Christ and live forever.*

All this we can do, he says, because we are under grace and not under law. He himself explains what this means. To be without the law is not the same thing as to have no laws and to be able to do what one pleases. Rather we are under the law when, without grace, we occupy ourselves with the works of the law. Then sin certainly rules [us] through the law, for no one loves the law by nature; and that is great sin. Grace, however, makes the law dear to us; then sin is no longer present, and the law is no longer against us but one with us.

This is the true freedom from sin and from the law. He writes about this down to the end of the chapter, saying that it is a freedom only to do good with pleasure and to live well without the compulsion of the law. Therefore this freedom is a spiritual freedom, which does not overthrow the law but presents what the law demands, namely, pleasure [in the law] and love [for it] whereby the law is quieted and no longer drives men or makes demands of them. It is just as if you owed a debt to your overlord and could not pay it. There are two ways in which you could rid yourself of the debt: either he would take nothing from you and would tear up the account, or some good man would pay it for you and give you the means to satisfy the account. It is in this latter way that Christ has made us free from the law. Our freedom is, therefore, no carefree fleshly freedom which is not obligated to do anything, but a freedom that does many good works of all kinds, and is free of the demands and obligations of the law.

In chapter 7 he supports this with an analogy from married life. When a man dies, his wife is also alone, and thus the one is released entirely from the other. Not that the wife cannot or ought not take another husband, but rather that she is now for the first time really free to take another—something which she could not do previously, before she was free from her husband. So our conscience is bound to the law, under the old man of sin; when he is slain by the Spirit, then the conscience is free, and the one is released from the other. Not that the conscience is to do nothing, but rather that it is now for the first time really free to hold fast to Christ, the second husband, and bring forth the fruit of life.

Then he depicts more fully the nature of sin and of the law, how by means of the law sin now stirs and becomes mighty. The old man comes to hate the law all the more because he cannot pay what the law demands. Sin is his nature[19] and of himself he can do nothing but sin; therefore the law to him is death and torment. Not that the law is bad, but the old man's evil nature cannot endure the good, and the law demands good of him; just as a sick man cannot stand it when he is required to run and jump and do the works of a well man.

Therefore St. Paul here concludes that the law, correctly understood and thoroughly grasped, does nothing more than to remind us of our sin, and to slay us by it, making us liable to eternal wrath. All this is fully learned and experienced by our conscience, when it is really struck by the law. Therefore a person must have something other than the law, something more than the law, to make him righteous and save him. But they who do not correctly understand the law are blind. They go ahead in their presumption, thinking to satisfy the law by means of their deeds, not knowing how much the law demands, namely, a willing and happy heart. Therefore they do not see Moses clearly; the veil is put between them and him,[20] and covers him [Exod. 34:29-35; II Cor. 3:12-16].

Then he shows how spirit and flesh struggle with one another in a man. He uses himself as an example, in order that we may learn how properly to understand the work of slaying sin within us. He calls both the spirit and the flesh "laws"; for just as it is in the nature of the divine law to drive men and make demands of them, so the flesh drives men and makes demands. It rages against the spirit, and will have its own way. The spirit, in turn, drives men and makes demands contrary to the flesh, and will have its own way. This tension lasts in us as long as we live; though in one person it is greater, in another less, according as the spirit or the flesh is stronger. Nevertheless the whole man is himself both spirit and flesh, and he fights with himself until he becomes wholly spiritual.

In chapter 8 he comforts these fighters, telling them that this flesh does not condemn them. He shows further what the nature of flesh and spirit is, and how the Spirit comes from Christ. Christ has given us his Holy Spirit; he makes us spiritual and subdues the flesh, and assures us that we are still God's children, however hard sin may be raging within us, so long as we follow the spirit and resist sin to slay it. Since, however, nothing else is so good for the mortifying of the flesh as the cross and suffering, he comforts us in suffering with the support of the Spirit of love, and of the whole creation, namely, that the Spirit sighs within us and the creation longs with us that we may be rid of the flesh and of sin. So we see that these three chapters (6—8) drive home the one task of faith, which is to slay the old Adam and subdue the flesh.

Predestination

In chapters 9, 10, and 11 he teaches of God's eternal predestination—out of which originally proceeds who shall believe or not, who can or cannot get rid of sin—in order that our salvation may be taken entirely out of our hands and put in the hand of God alone. And this too is utterly necessary. For we are so weak and uncertain that if it depended on us, not even a single person would be saved; the devil would surely overpower us all. But since God is dependable—his predestination cannot fail, and no one can withstand him—we still have hope in the face of sin.

Here, now, for once we must put a stop to those wicked and high flying spirits who first apply their own reason to this matter. They begin at the top to search the abyss of divine predestination, and worry in vain about whether they are predestinated. They are bound to plunge to their own destruction, either through despair, or through throwing caution to the winds.

But you had better follow the order of this epistle. Worry first about Christ and the gospel, that you may recognize your sin and his grace. Then fight your sin, as the first eight chapters here have taught. Then, when you have reached the eighth chapter, and are under the cross and suffering, this will teach you correctly of predestination in chapters 9, 10, and 11, and how comforting it is. For in the absence of suffering and the cross and the perils of death, one cannot deal with predestination without harm and without secret anger against God. The old Adam must first die before he can tolerate this thing and drink the strong wine. Therefore beware that you do not drink wine while you are still a suckling. There is a limit, a time, and an age for every doctrine.

True Worship

In chapter 12 he teaches what true worship is, and makes all Christians priests. They are to offer not money or cattle, as under the law, but their own bodies, with slaying of the lusts. Then he describes the outward conduct of Christians, under the spiritual government, telling how they are to teach, preach, rule, serve, give, suffer, love, live, and act toward friend, foe, and all men. These are the works that a Christian does; for, as has been said, faith takes no holidays.

In chapter 13 he teaches honor and obedience to worldly government. Although worldly government does not make people righteous before God, nevertheless it is instituted in order to accomplish at least this much, that the good may have outward peace and protection and the bad may not be free to do evil in peace and quietness, and without fear. Therefore the good too are to honor it even though they themselves do not need it. Finally, he comprehends it all in love, and sums it up in the example of Christ: as he has done for us, we are also to do, following in his footsteps.

In chapter 14 he teaches that consciences weak in faith are to be led gently, spared, so that we do not use our Christian freedom for doing harm, but for the assistance of the weak. For where that is not done, the result is discord and contempt for the gospel; and the gospel is the all-important thing. Thus it is better to yield a little to the weak in faith, until they grow stronger, than to have the teaching of the gospel come to nothing. And this work is a peculiar work of love, for which there is great need even now, when with the eating of meat and other liberties, men are rudely and roughly— and needlessly—shaking weak consciences, before they know the truth.

In chapter 15 he sets up Christ as an example: we are to tolerate also those other weak ones who fail in other ways, in open sins or in unpleasing habits. We are not to cast them off, but to bear with them until they too grow better. For so Christ has done with us, and still does every day; he bears with our many faults and bad habits, and with all our imperfections, and helps us constantly.

Then, at the end, he prays for them, praises them, and

commends them to God. He speaks of his own office and of his preaching, and asks them kindly for a contribution to the poor at Jerusalem. All that he speaks of or deals with is pure love.

The last chapter is a chapter of greetings. But he mingles with them a noble warning against the doctrines of men, which break in alongside the teaching of the gospel and cause offense. It is as if he had certainly foreseen that out of Rome and through the Romans would come the seductive and offensive canons and decretals and the whole squirming mass of human laws and commandments,[21] which have now drowned the whole world and wiped out this epistle and all the Holy Scriptures, along with the Spirit and faith itself; so that nothing remains anymore except the idol, Belly, whose servants St. Paul here rebukes. God save us from them. Amen.

In this epistle we thus find most abundantly the things that a Christian ought to know, namely, what is law, gospel, sin, punishment, grace, faith, righteousness, Christ, God, good works, love, hope, and the cross; and also how we are to conduct ourselves toward everyone, be he righteous or sinner, strong or weak, friend or foe—and even toward our own selves. Moreover this is all ably supported with Scripture and proved by St. Paul's own example and that of the prophets, so that one could not wish for anything more. Therefore it appears that he wanted in this one epistle to sum up briefly the whole Christian and evangelical doctrine, and to prepare an introduction to the entire Old Testament. For, without doubt, whoever has this epistle well in his heart, has with him the light and power of the Old Testament. Therefore let every Christian be familiar with it and exercise himself in it continually. To this end may God give his grace. Amen.

2. Saving Faith

These pages show in what terms Luther sought to bring back to the Church the forgotten doctrine of justification by faith. Those who followed him became "Protestants"; the others continued to hold the view which Luther denounced as a return to the righteousness of works condemned by St. Paul.

This text was conceived as an introduction. It has to be read and reread along with the epistle. The explanation of Paul's vocabulary provides a key to the reading. It defines a "hermeneutic," that is, a method for making clear the meaning Luther discerns in the text. He himself excels in extracting from the apostle's thought everything that can contribute to a more effective appropriation of justification by faith. He assimilates Paul's teaching to the point of giving it out again as his own; one feels that the apostle himself is speaking. But doubtless more than one reader would fail to recognize here what he has been taught to read in the Epistle to the Romans.

Luther is clearly convinced that the reader who approaches the epistle as he does will get the most out of it and apprehend its true meaning. We must therefore pay close attention to his procedure. The idea of beginning with a study of vocabulary allows him to open up the discussion with the question of the Law. We know that the Law was the specter which had haunted the young Luther and forced him to revise everything he had been taught. In the epistle the theme of the Law appears at chapter 2, in reference to the Jews, but it is within the context of Paul's argument directed to Christians still imbued with Judaism.

Luther emphasized the fact that the fulfillment of the Law is impossible for man because he does not love the Law. His analysis of the problem came to him from St. Augustine and St. Jerome, but it was inspired by his own past experience. The impossibility of fulfilling the Law with one's whole heart meant that the works of the Law could not make anyone "righteous" before God. St. Paul made this point in all his letters. Now, for Luther's first readers perfection consisted precisely in the accumulation of good works. Instead, Luther teaches us to be concerned for the true love of the Law which is the gift of God's Spirit, and to do good works freely. And he raises a burning issue: How can it be said that by doing his best, by free will and personal effort, by his own works, man can put himself in the position of receiving God's grace? To imagine that we can please God is an illusion. What can we hope to obtain from God for the price of works which can only displease him? The purpose of these objections is to clear the ground for what is later said about grace: It is "a disposition which God has within himself towards us"—a spontaneous divine disposition, for God's grace cannot be bought.

Having thus unraveled the theme of the Law from the perspective of works, Luther introduces the reality of faith in Jesus Christ, as Paul had done before. Once again we find the now familiar language: "Faith comes only through God's Word or gospel, which preaches Christ, saying that he is God's Son and a man, and has died and risen again for our sakes. . . . So it happens

that faith alone makes a person righteous and fulfills the law."
The Law is fulfilled not by works, as theology and Church
teaching would have it, but by faith.

This masterly opening introduces the definition of sin: Sin is
unbelief, that is, the opposite of faith (or rather, unbelief is the
absence of faith). Luther's originality here is to bring to light that
"sins" are only the fruits of a tree rooted in the being of man
himself. Evil works do not in themselves constitute the decisive
point of the question of righteousness, any more than good works
do. Compared with prevailing views of that time, this represents
an immense shift in thought: Instead of looking at guilty actions,
all attention is concentrated on the guilty person, the one who does
evil.

It is a matter for discussion whether Luther here is really
following St. Paul, whom he does not cite. But his course is against
the stream of medieval theology's multiplication of categories of
sin, and the practices instituted by the Church as a remedy for
them. The problem does not lie there. It is the guilty man who is
the object *as such* of divine grace; how could God bring grace to a
righteous man? Luther explains that when God bestows grace it is
without conditions and without half measures. He gives grace,
nothing else. That is possible, of course, only through the Holy
Spirit, who gives us faith through the gift of Jesus Christ. But "as
long as the flesh is not dead, we remain sinners." God accepts us as
righteous on account of Christ, our mediator "while waiting for
sin to die." This provides the explanation of one of Luther's
famous sayings: *simul peccator et iustus*, "at the same time a
sinner and a righteous man." Such a teaching went against the
conviction that the Christian, purified by absolution, is without
sin. He challenged Catholicism to be faithful to St. Paul. The idea
that the justified man is protected against all sin, as long as he does
not deliberately do evil again, or that the sinner cannot be called
"righteous," is easily explained by the principles of Aristotle. But
Aristotle knew neither original sin nor Christ. In taking its
inspiration from him, the Church not only opened the door to a
deficient morality but also ignored the direction which Paul
indicated for Christians who were seeking the righteousness of
works and of the Law.

Luther focused on faith. It was the "divine work in us which
changes us and makes us to be born anew of God." It is less clear
than Aristotle's morality. But it frees the Christian life from the

round of confessions, undertaken once a year in order to go to
Communion—then dropped until Easter comes around again.
Between the two, God alone could see what new birth there was!
Luther attributes to faith, in addition to its bringing us the
forgiveness of sins, the capacity for motivating us to do good.
There is the sign of authentic faith; the tree is recognized by its
fruits. In itself faith is confidence, surrender, certainty. Scholasticism had made of it a "supernatural, intellectual faculty," which
helped no one. Church people were corrupted by the caricatures of
faith which produced a superstition flourishing on the emptiness
of theology. "Revealed truths" are not enough to define faith. In
dogmatic terminology, Luther substituted for the scholastic view a
Pauline style of discourse which had already captured the imagination of the young Dominican Martin Bucer at the time of the
Heidelberg Disputation in 1518.

As for righteousness, it is nothing but faith. Luther does not
return here to the beginning of the epistle, to the fateful verse Rom.
1:17. The explanation to follow begins with verse 18. Thus the
pages on the apostle's vocabulary play the role of a commentary on
Luther's prolog to Paul's epistle. They are a full explanation of
justification by faith, and an examination of the epistle shows that
this constitutes a complete formula for the Christian life.

Luther thus appears to have found in the Epistle to the
Romans the guide for a new line of Christians. The faith which
saves gives rise to a style of Christian life which cannot be reduced
to any discipline of works. Faith is freedom.

It is worth asking whether Luther understood St. Paul
properly. Catholics have usually claimed that he did not.[22]
Modern exegesis certainly takes the view that Pauline doctrine
does not amount purely and simply to justification by faith, and
Protestants freely recognize this.[23]

But this discussion bypasses the real debate. In taking up the
battle against the righteousness of works, Luther was in fact
tackling a permanent problem in Christianity. The problem is
that every time Christians consider themselves "righteous" for one
reason or another, they slip away from Christ and the Gospel.
Perfection becomes an idol. Luther often remarks that he who
judges himself irreproachable is merciless when it comes to the
faults of others. Only faith in Christ bestows on the heart the
wisdom to see oneself as one is and the humility to accept others as

they are. In the Epistle to the Romans Paul attacks the pharisaism of the first Christians in Rome. His letters present other formulations of the righteousness of the Christian, but when dealing with the righteousness of works the only remedy was the doctrine of justification by faith. Augustine, who encountered the problem with the Pelagians, refuted Pelagius in *The Spirit and the Letter* by a commentary on the Epistle to the Romans. Luther could not but borrow from his two predecessors in arguing against late medieval Catholicism's notion of the righteousness of works. The Reformation had its origins in this difficulty, and there was only one way Luther could answer it, only one interpretation he could give of Paul.

However, it was not for exegetical reasons that Rome condemned Luther. His attacks against works were objected to because of their practical consequences. Even today, the Catholic is not ready to renounce the meritorious value of good deeds. When Paul was discussing this point, it was not a question of man's merit at all; only after him did the Church become wedded to a theology of merit. For Catholics in Luther's time to deny any saving value to works was to encourage a lack of zeal and indolence; if the good that one does serves for nothing and has no importance, what is the point of it, and why put oneself out? Some have even found in this an explanation of the instances of immorality in early Protestantism.[24]

Justification by faith appeared to be nothing so much as an easy way out. If all that was required was "belief," what then? Theologically, it was difficult to see how such a role could be attributed to faith when simple believers are often incapable of grasping what theologians know. The persistence of sin in the righteous seemed inherently absurd. The theory of forensic justification, stemming from Melanchthon, appeared to be the most plausible interpretation of Luther's conception: God would "impute" righteousness just as a tribunal can acquit an accused man, even though he is guilty.[25] The *simul peccator et iustus*, which results in the negation of all merit even after justification, seemed to exclude the possibility of grace transforming man. Luther has an explanation of this, as we have seen. But it is true that he does not take up the theology of grace after justification.[26] All his energy was directed towards centering on Christ once more the essential doctrine of salvation, which had deviated into justification by works. The second generation of the Reformation, under Calvin, sensed what was lacking and emphasized sanctification.

Luther was so much at odds with the theology of his time that it has been claimed that he invented the doctrine of justification entirely for his own needs. This was Grisar's view, [27] and his ideas have recently surfaced once more in Roland Dalbiez's study of Luther's anxiety. This reassertion of an old view by a specialist in scholasticism doubling as an informed psychologist is typical of Catholic attempts to reduce Luther's faith to nothing. Further discussion is needed here, for what can be said of this product of Catholic polemic against Luther goes for all the others: Whatever way the evidence is taken, the result is to show that, despite all his personal problems, what mattered most for Luther was nothing else than the historic faith.

3. Luther's Anxiety and Special Faith

In his book,[28] published in 1974, Dalbiez analyzes the psychological origins of the "process of decatholicization" in Luther's soul. Ever since the writings of Dr. Paul Reiter it has been possible to argue that Luther suffered from a "manic-depressive psychosis."[29] Dalbiez reaches an analagous diagnosis which, as I am no doctor, I will not discuss, except to say that in my opinion the patient usually bore up rather well.[30] But the essential point is the other assertion of Dalbiez, who saw Luther's mind as obscured by a theology which exacerbated his morbid qualms of guilt. Dalbiez saw Luther as managing to overcome this anxiety only by inventing his theory of "special faith."[31] A "heretic in order to survive," Luther chose religious suicide as a means of escaping suicide pure and simple.

Some effort is needed to unravel the threads of this theory; was it a question of Luther's psychology and his medico-mental dossier, of his faith, or of his theology of justification by faith? Dalbiez refrains from going beyond the point of the ideological break between Luther's faith and the Catholic faith. His question is: "How did Luther reach a conviction ineradicably opposed to Catholic dogma?" (p. 11). But "every dogmatic edifice of Luther collapsed" (p. 14) from the time when "the cornerstone of his structure . . . that is, the doctrine of necessary guilt," had to be rejected.

It is doubtful whether the importance given by the young Luther to the problem of sin is the real question. Whether the guilt was necessary or unnecessary, Luther's problem was to explain how God pardoned the guilty. The text of Rom. 1:17 disturbed him because it seemed to limit the scope of the Gospel as a declaration of mercy. His rigid sense of God's righteousness, his awareness of God and His law, turned him from the way which Dalbiez seems to interpret specifically as Catholic orthodoxy: that is, the way of those theologians who exhort seekers after holiness to abound in guiltless acts. Does the saint ever boast of the goodness of his actions before the One who tests the mind and the heart? Whatever could have been the young Luther's conception of guilt, his "Biblical, Pauline, Augustinian" development[32] prevented him in advance from making of it the "cornerstone of his structure." How could the author of *L'angoisse de Luther* have reached the point of according such a role to necessary guilt in the origins of the Reformation and of Protestantism?

The die is cast from the beginning of the book. While Protestants warn against taking a superficial conception of the importance of the doctrine of justification by faith as the first principle of Luther's theology,[33] Dalbiez begins by defining on this sole basis "the essence of Luther's system," and he borrows the formulation of it from Bossuet, content to put the finishing touches on the observations of the author of the *Variations*.[34]

Luther's structure would rest on the three ideas of extrinsic justification, special faith, and necessary guilt,[35] which "put him in opposition to Catholic dogma" (p. 15). What is non-Catholic about such a system, according to Dalbiez, is that Luther excludes the disappearance of sin in the righteous man, and the possibility of being guiltless, and grants to autosuggestion the efficacy of grace under the pretext of "special faith": "I am justified because I believe I am justified"—the Coué method raised to the dignity of a sacrament![36]

The first two problems are serious ones. We have seen that in maintaining that the righteous man is at the same time a sinner, Luther throws down a challenge to Catholic theology. Necessary guilt amounts to the negation of free will.[37] But the definition of special faith borrowed from Bossuet is ridiculous. To say that a man is righteous because he believes that he has righteousness is not out of Luther but Molière! Luther speaks specifically of believing in God's promise, as we saw in the *Brief Instruction*. One can raise the question as to whether he still held to the faith in God's promise which Catholic theologians hold. But it is certain

that there is a promise of God addressed to every Christian who
believes in Jesus Christ. The young Luther's anxiety was that he
did not believe that he was justified. If we must follow Bossuet, it
amounts to saying that Luther found the remedy for his anxiety in
freedom from anxiety!

In any case, Dalbiez leaves Bossuet, from whom he borrows
only the "Lutheran" concepts, to argue directly about Luther's
anxiety itself. "For me Luther is nothing but anxiety" (p. 24). The
demonstration of this assertion, which is very serious, and is meant
to be so, consists of documenting the "Luther" case with ex-
pressive passages drawn from the Reformer's works[38] and showing, with the aid of psychology books, that the mental picture
which emerges from this study justifies a despairing prognosis;
such a patient was a candidate for suicide.

From that point there unfolds the explanation of Luther's
transition to convictions irreconcilable with the Catholic faith.
The theological current of necessary guilt fed the morbid anxiety
of the young Luther. Judging himself to be always guilty, he
concluded that justification cannot make sin disappear. But if one
believes that one is justified, then it is so in spite of sin. To find a
basis for this conviction Luther, according to Dalbiez, always
interpreted Scripture in his own way.

Thus everything rested on an aberrant theology and, in the last
analysis, on Luther's anxiety, by which his allegiance to this
current of scholastic thought was sealed. "To be justified it is
necessary and sufficient to believe that one is justified. This belief
arose out of his unconscious and imposed itself on him in a
deterministic way" (p. 352). This anxiety takes away all authority
from his doctrine, which is the doctrine of a sick man. But it also
removes his responsibility: "Luther was not free to adhere or not to
adhere to his heresy" (p. 349).

Does this shallow conclusion of seeing Luther taken away
from the Protestants as irresponsible, and plucked from the
personal hell to which some have assigned him, merit more than
these few pages? Roland Dalbiez is afraid of offending Luther's
friends. I am no less afraid of taking my critique too far, but there is
more to be said.

There is, in fact, something altogether different to say about
Luther's faith, special faith, than to reduce it to a product of his
anxiety and his unconscious. First of all we should realize how
little Luther's anxiety matters. My own view is simply the one

which I indicated in the previous chapter. But I have no special competence in psychology, and everyone is free to accept or reject my views. On the other hand, I have studied for some years to form my judgment of what Luther set down in his writings. Even supposing that the Luther of history justified the worst psychological diagnosis possible, there still remain his written explanations of his doctrine of special faith, and what everyone can read from his own pen is not the caricature born of Bossuet's imagination.

Without taking up the analyses put forward by Congar, which go to the heart of the question,[39] we must underline the necessity for enlarging Bossuet's apparent conception of faith. He sees in it only something to be reduced to the formula: "I am justified." Faith has a divine guarantee, and if I *believe* that, I am justified. Now Luther did not take refuge in this "subscholasticism." He believed, first of all, in God and in the Word of God. If his faith was certain, it was so in the sense that no one should doubt God. In that, Luther was "Catholic." His theological creation was to make clear, according to Scripture, that God asks us to welcome his Son by faith in order to be saved, and that this is the justification others seek through works. It is a matter of *my* justification, because faith is always the faith of *someone*. It does not exist in itself. And it is not general but special, because the important thing finally is that every human being should personally welcome Jesus Christ. One cannot rest content with the general truth that Christ died for all men.

If the "decatholicization" of Luther in this aspect of doctrine can be shown, then this is what ought to be discussed. In fact, Catholic theologians are less and less likely to contend this. But let us rather hear what Luther has to say, in an extract from his writings for which Dalbiez offers a trenchant critique.

In October 1518 Luther appeared at Augsburg before Cardinal Cajetan, the papal legate. He was asked to retract, and we know that he refused to do so. Among the points taken up by Cajetan was special faith. The "prince of theologians" judged that in the sacrament of penance Luther minimized sacramental absolution in favor of the efficacy of special faith.

Luther replied in these terms:

The other objection is that in Thesis 7 I stated that no one can be justified except by faith. Thus it is clearly necessary that a man believe with firm faith that he is justified and in no way doubt that he will obtain grace. For if he doubts and is uncertain, he is not justified but rejects grace. My opponents wish to consider this theology new and erroneous.

This I answer by saying:

1. It is an infallible truth that no person is righteous unless he believes in God, as stated in Rom. 1[:17]: "He who through faith is righteous shall live." Likewise, "He who does not believe is condemned already" [John 3:18] and dead. Therefore the justification and life of the righteous person are dependent upon his faith. For this reason all the works of the believer are alive and all the works of the unbeliever are dead, evil, and damnable, according to this passage: "A bad tree cannot bear good fruit. Every tree that does not bear good fruit is cut down and thrown into the fire" [Matt. 7:18-19].

2. Faith, however, is nothing else than believing what God promises and reveals, as in Rom. 4[:3], "Abraham believed God, and he reckoned it to him as righteousness" [Cf. Gen. 15:6]. Therefore the Word and faith are both necessary, and without the Word there can be no faith, as in Isa. 55[:11]: "So shall my word be that goes forth from my mouth; it shall not return to me empty."

3. I must now prove that a person going to the sacrament must believe that he will receive grace, and not doubt it, but have absolute confidence, otherwise he will do so to his condemnation.

I prove this first through the word of the Apostle in Heb. 11[:6] "For whoever would draw near to God must believe that he exists and that he rewards those who seek him." According to this it is clear that we dare not doubt but must firmly believe that God rewards those who seek him. If we must believe that God is one who rewards, then we must above all believe that he justifies man and gives his grace to those still living. Without grace he gives no reward.

Second, in the face of the peril of eternal damnation and the sin of unbelief, we must believe these words of Christ: "Whatever you loose on earth shall be loosed in heaven" [Matt. 16:19]. Therefore if you come to the sacrament of penance and do not firmly believe that you will be absolved in heaven, you come to your judgment and damnation because you do not believe that Christ speaks the truth when he says, "Whatever you loose," etc. [Matt. 16:19]. And with your doubt you make of Christ a liar, which is a horrible sin. If, however, you say, "What if I am

unworthy and unfit for the sacrament?" I answer as I did above.
Through no attitude on your part will you become worthy,
through no works will you be prepared for the sacrament, but
through faith alone, for only faith in the word of Christ justifies,
makes a person alive, worthy, and well prepared. Without faith all
other things are acts of presumption and desperation. The just
person lives not by his attitude but by faith. For this reason you
should not harbor any doubt on account of your unworthiness.
You go to the sacrament because you are unworthy and so that you
may be made worthy and be justified by him who seeks to save
sinners and not the righteous [Cf. Luke 5:32]. When, however, you
believe Christ's word, you honor it and thereby are righteous.[40]

Here, in his own words, is Luther's complete version of his
position. He follows it up with nine Scriptural proofs and the
witness of St. Augustine and St. Bernard.

Dalbiez rightly accords a major importance to these explanations, for Luther is here defending his doctrine against the
greatest theologian of his time (p. 294). Dalbiez announces that he
is going to discuss each point and gives the reader the Latin text
and his translation side by side. But to begin, instead of letting
Luther speak, he himself states the argument which he proposes to
criticize: "Understand well Luther's position," he writes. "Luther
maintains that no one can be justified, where the sacrament of
penance is concerned, if he does not believe *with absolute certainty*
that he himself is justified" (italics by Dalbiez). Second, he cites
and translates the passage: "I stated that no one can be justified
except by faith. Thus it is clearly necessary that a man must believe
with firm faith that he is justified and in no way doubt that he will
obtain grace. For if he doubts and is uncertain, he is not justified
but rejects grace." Third, he explains Luther's position in this
way: "Here is a poor, scrupulous man who questions whether he
has preserved an attachment to sin, and lacked contrition, and
who, *in consequence* (italics by Dalbiez) fears that the absolution
which he receives will not be valid. According to Brother Martin
this unfortunate neuropath rejects grace. For the Reformer contrition signifies absolutely nothing; only faith is necessary, not
general but special faith, faith in personal justification. The
necessary and sufficient condition for being justified is to believe
absolutely that one *is* justified." That precisely is the point on
which Luther opposed Cajetan (pp. 294—95).

It is easy for anyone to notice the switch from Luther's problem
to his interpreter's. The symptom of this is the leap, without any
connecting steps, from Luther's initial treatment of the idea of
unworthiness to its final development. Furthermore, Dalbiez
portrays a "scrupulous neuropath" while Luther's exposition
states a general principle which is valid for those in perfect health.
Dalbiez neglects everything Luther draws out of Rom. 1:17 and
concludes: "To sum up, Luther in his doctrine of justification
eliminates free will, contrition, charity, sacramental efficacy *ex
opere operato* and replaces them with special faith: the individual's absolute belief in his own justification" (p. 295).

What follows only makes explicit the misunderstanding
between Luther's Scriptural perspective and the reductionist
psychological interpretation of Dalbiez. He goes on to scrutinize
Luther's proofs, an examination "indispensable if we are to
penetrate Luther's psychology. It is quite obvious from this that
only a soul absolutely submerged by the anxiety of guilt could take
seriously six of the interpretations which Luther gives to the nine
Scriptural texts, for only three of them are worthy of being
discussed. The worthlessness of the others is self-evident to a
beginner" (p. 296). Indeed!

The first "absurd" development of the matter is Luther's
interpretation of the faith of the Canaanite woman (Matt. 15:21-
28). For Dalbiez the woman comes to Christ "absolutely certain of
the power" which Christ has to heal her daughter; but would he
use it? There is no mistaking "the certain, absolute faith of this
pagan woman in the power of Christ, and his wish, his desire to
use this power to heal her daughter." According to Dalbiez, we
must always distinguish "two stages in the Canaanite woman's
faith: general faith in the power of Christ joined to the very
humble desire that he should accede to her prayer; and following
this, and only after Christ said to her·*Fiat tibi:* 'Let it be done to
you,' the special faith that her daughter would be healed. Special
faith presupposes special revelation, Christ's intimation to the
Canaanite woman that he freely willed to use his power in her
favor" (pp. 297—98). In short, "the woman believed first in the
power of Christ, and it was by that general faith that she procured
his granting of her request; she had special faith in the deliverance
of her daughter only *after* Christ's acknowledgment that he
accepted her prayer" (p. 298).

According to this exposition by Dalbiez, the progressive steps of the Canaanite woman represented 1. general faith in Christ's power to heal her daughter, 2. her desire that Christ use this power, and 3. the special faith that her daughter would be healed according to the promise Christ made to her.

Luther, declares Dalbiez, on the one hand confused the faith of the Canaanite woman in Christ's power and her desire that he exercise this power, and that confusion was the very basis of his argument. On the other hand, he compressed into one the two stages of her faith.

Before letting Luther speak, let us note that the evangelist says: "And her daughter was healed instantly" (Matt. 15:28). It is thus not a question of special faith after Christ's reply that the child was going to be healed. The evangelist concludes the episode directly by the *fait accompli* of the healing. All he wanted to show of the Canaanite woman's faith is summed up in Christ's word: "Great is your faith!" The account is a crescendo of rebuffs which show how great indeed was the woman's faith. That is something else than the general faith and the humble desire of which Dalbiez speaks! It is the faith which nothing can rebut, certain faith, faith in healing by Christ—before the healing—faith which obtains healing immediately, from the moment when she proves unshakable.

But let us listen to Luther:

> He had commended this faith to us in many ways in the gospel. First, when he said to the woman of Canaan: "O woman, great is your faith! Be it done for you as you have believed" [Matt. 15:28]. This shows that not faith in general is meant here, but the special faith which was concerned with the daughter who was to be healed in answer to her mother's prayer. For she boldly believed that this would be done, that Christ could and would do it, and so her prayer was fulfilled. She never would have obtained this, however, if she had not believed. Therefore she was made worthy of this answer to her prayer, not by her attitude, but by faith alone."[41]

Luther reads in Matthew's text that he who relies on Christ in unshakable fashion obtains what he wants by virtue of his singleminded disposition of faith. Does Matthew say anything radically different? Does not the theological principle Luther draws from the apostle have an explanation other than a pathological one?

The following analyses by Dalbiez pose the same problems and call for the same kind of observation. His feeling about the emptiness of Luther's explanations comes from the fact that

Luther has no idea of the notion that was attributed to him and simply proceeded with the proof of his statements to Cajetan.

For example, Luther's second Scriptural argument, which for Dalbiez is likewise one of those "whose patent absurdity would be apparent even to a beginner," concerns the blind men to whom Christ said, "Do you believe that I am able to do this?" (Matt. 9:27-31). Dalbiez notes that Luther's confusion is even more flagrant here. He interprets it thus: "Jesus asks the two blind men not if they believe that he is going to heal them, but if they believe that he has the power to heal them" (p. 298).

What should we say of that "restriction of thought" attributed to Jesus in the framework of a dialog which begins, "Have mercy on us, Son of David" and ends with, "According to your faith be it done to you." When Jesus asks, "Do you believe that I am able to do this?" and those involved reply, "Yes, Lord," there is no need to be a psychologist to understand that everyone thinks of the *effect*, the healing of the blindness. As usual, Jesus wanted to know if the person believed sufficiently in him to be sure in advance of the result from the time he was appealed to. His evangelistic mission did not consist in convincing the people of his supernatural power. What would he have made of a naively magical faith in his gifts of thaumaturgy?

Luther wrote more correctly: "They were certain that it would come to pass as they petitioned. Therefore it came to pass without any preparation on their part. If, however, they had doubted the outcome, they would not have prayed well or received what they had prayed for."[42]

If, from the beginning, Luther set special faith as a unique inclination of man towards justification in opposition to every other "meritorious" disposition, he did not make of it the exclusive cause of salvation. Bossuet rendered a disservice to Dalbiez in furnishing him with a distorted simplification throughout his book, which annuls the result in advance.

Such therefore is this misleading judgment of Luther's faith in the name of psychology. So many others·who were not Luther believed the same as he! Luther had his psychology, and one will always be grateful to competent persons to explain it to us.[43] He had his *bêtes noires:* his father, the angry God, the pope, the devil,[44] while the Bible was his mother (he also called it "my Katherine von Bora"). But what of all that?

Except for the worst cases, the problem of psychology is not to know what one has but what can be made of it. What Dalbiez finds pathological will without doubt appear to the reader of this book as a healthy reaction: the belief that being a good Christian is relying on God, not knocking one's head against the wall of justification by works. As Luther put it himself: "This is the reason why our theology is certain: it snatches us away from ourselves and places us outside ourselves, so that we do not depend on our own strength, conscience, experience, person, or works but depend on that which is outside ourselves, that is, on the promise and truth of God, which cannot deceive" (LW 26, 387).

5

Believing in Jesus Christ

The Practice of Faith

Luther's struggle for special faith was the consequence of his discovery of the Gospel. That discovery had put him on the path of a new way of expressing faith in practice, based on the certainty of laying on Christ everything necessary for a life of righteousness before God.

For 2,000 years without interruption, faith in Christ has raised up generations of Christians. Over the years it has been able to assume very diverse forms. With Luther it reappeared as in the beginning, for Luther's special faith mirrors the attitude of those whom the gospels show coming to Christ expecting everything from him.

This reawakening occurred at a time when the "priestly and imperial" Church had had its day, though it still remained apparently intact. Churchmen took the view that eternal Rome, the repository of truth, had nothing more to learn, and especially not from Luther. But the new man who slowly broke free from the convulsions of the closing Middle Ages aspired to emancipate himself from the tutelage of king and priest. He had not yet lost faith, and he looked for a religious "New Deal," not primarily in the sense of a Church better adapted to the world but in the sense of a different style of Christian existence. Luther's response to this quest went beyond everything imaginable to that point: He showed, in fact, that people no longer knew what purpose Christ served and how he could become real to each person's faith.

Today we are more interested in "Luther's Christ" than in the past. None of the Reformation controversies focused on Christological dogma, and the theological manuals have, for a long time, found nothing to draw from Luther on this subject, at least outside

Protestantism. Many authors speak of Luther without giving any attention to his faith in Jesus Christ.[1]

Generally speaking, the Reformer had a thoroughly traditional doctrine of Christ. Admittedly, it was not by this means that he influenced his contemporaries. But some recent works show that, over and above his concern for the articles of the Creed and the truths essential to the faith, his constant objective was to restore Christ to each believer and to reveal in him the unique Lord of the Church. Ian D. Kingston Siggins opens his study of Luther's doctrine of Christ with these words of the Reformer: "This should be the Christian's only skill, to learn Christ aright."[2] The Lutheran Marc Lienhard, of the University of Strasbourg, approaches the subject through the *fides Christi*, the faith which is a living relationship to Christ.[3] Siggins also shows in conclusion that the Church is defined, according to Luther, by its way of preaching Christ,[4] yet it habitually fails to do this in a convincing—or convinced—way.

There is abundant evidence of the intense appeal such ideas exercised in all settings. Hans Sachs' poem "The Wittenberg Nightingale" showed all the animals, even the wild beasts, drawn to the Lamb by the bewitching bird. Many Catholics followed Luther in this way for a long time, for his teaching about Christ, hoping that time would quieten the conflicts; they abandoned him only when his audacity terrified them or when they were driven into a corner by the anathemas of the Council of Trent.

Luther's writings provide us with a faithful echo of this discourse about faith. They speak to us of Christ for us (Gal. 3:13), of the Emmanuel (God with Us: John 1:14), and of the cross. These themes, rather than the dogmatic theses, represent Luther's original contribution to a living understanding of Jesus Christ.

1. Christ for Us

In the Wittenberg Sermons Luther followed up the idea that Christ is the gift from God promised by the prophets, what he calls "the first article of the Gospel." In relation to Heb. 1:3, "he . . . made purification for our sins," he remarks that the author "here characterizes the Gospel exactly." This affirmation leads him to a kind of synthesis of what we have learned from the previous texts.

Whatever we may be taught about Christ is of no help to us until we grasp that it is all said for our good and profit. Why would it be necessary to preach to us if it were done only for him? But in fact, it has to do entirely with us and our salvation.

Let us therefore listen with joy to these immeasurably pleasing words. Christ, who is so great, the heir of all things, the brightness of God's glory, the image of the divine nature, who upholds all things not with outside power and help but through his own actions and his own power—who is, in short, all in all—this Christ has served us, has poured out his love for us, and has made purification for our sins. The text says: "our sins," not his own sins, and not the sins of unbelievers. For purification is not for the unbeliever, and cannot profit him.[5]

Christ has not achieved this purification through our free will, our reason, or our power, nor through our works, our contrition, or repentance—for all this is nothing before God—but through himself. How? By taking upon himself our sins, on the holy cross, as Is. 53:6 says. But that is still not enough to explain how he purifies us "by himself." For it also signifies that if we believe in him, and believe that he has done this for us, then he dwells within us by our faith, and because of it, and daily by his own work continues to purify us; and nothing apart from Christ can contribute in any way to the cleansing of our sin. Now he cannot dwell in us and work this purification except in and through faith.

Listen, then, you deceivers of the world and leaders of the blind—pope, bishops, priests, monks, learned men and idle prattlers, who teach the purification of sin through the works of men and satisfaction for sins, who give indulgence letters and sell imaginary purifications for sin. Hear that there is no purification for sin in works but only in Christ and through Christ himself.

Now Christ cannot be communicated to us through any work of ours, but only through faith, as St. Paul says in Eph. 3:17: "that Christ may dwell in your hearts through faith." It must certainly be true, then, that the purification of sins is faith, and whoever believes that Christ has cleansed him of his sins is certainly purified by that faith, and in no other way. St. Peter therefore speaks truly when he says that our hearts have been cleansed by faith (Acts 15:9).

When this faith is already present, and purification has been accomplished by Christ himself, then let us do good works, hate our sins, and repent of them. These works are good—but before faith they are of no value, and encourage false confidence and trust. For sin is such a powerful thing, and its purification is so costly, that a person as exalted as we read Christ was had to intervene himself and cleanse sinners. What could the poor, vain attempts of us who are creatures—indeed sinful, weak, corrupt creatures—achieve where so much was required? We might just as well presume to burn heaven and earth with an extinguished brand. The payment for sin must be as great as God himself, who is wronged by sin.[6]

This text has numerous parallels in the Wartburg sermons and in the Weimar Edition. It expresses the outlaw's reflection on the Gospel for which both church and state were persecuting him. The position he adopted is the same one as arises out of this study: Every person finds in his faith in Christ the free remission of his sins. On this point Luther never deviated.

His Gospel is nothing other than this conjunction of traditional, Biblical, or peculiarly Lutheran elements forming the thread of this passage. The first lines define Luther's Christ: Everything that is said of Christ has to do entirely with us and our salvation. Now, at this time in the Church, "everything that was said of Christ" had to do instead with Him: the birth of the uncreated Word in the soul, for the mystics, or the stories of the Passion, with stress on realism to sway the crowds.[7] Christ was the Example to follow or the Judge to be feared. As for salvation, it was a matter for the Church. It asserted its indispensability on all sides, through the sacraments, the discipline of works, or in borrowing from the "treasury" of the merits of Christ, the Virgin, and the saints for distributing indulgences at will. Luther linked salvation to Christ and elucidated the rich principle that the mystery of the Son of God made man is only revealed to us because it is a matter *for us.*

The art of being a Christian, therefore, lies first of all in apprehending that the preaching of Christ is for our benefit—our gain. It is not enough to "understand" better. Preaching is a school addressing itself to apprentices who should try to practice Christ, and they are the ones who have joy in hearing what the greatness of Christ means.

Christ is all things by his own power, not by the power of another, and he has been our servant. In the figure of the Lord's Servant in Isaiah 53 Luther sees the Servant of men. He has come to us as the One who serves (cf. Matt. 20:28), and it is to Christ in this role that Luther looks for his understanding. He means to show the Church the One whom it really serves, and Christians their need to avail themselves of him.

The idea that Christ has by love accomplished the purification of sin is the traditional dogma of the Redemption. But we must be attentive here to Luther's particular accents: He asserts that Christ has taken our sins on the cross for a purification which owed nothing to our free choice, our will, our power, our contrition or penitence. This fact, evident in the very act of the Passion, becomes a theological principle: Nothing we can do is any more useful for the remission of sins in our life than it was in the death of Christ. Purification remains the exclusive action of Christ, in whom we have faith. That faith is all that is required of us; because of it, Christ can dwell in us and accomplish in each believer the redemption of Calvary.

Faith is thus raised to a function at variance with the intellectual properties which theology saw in it (namely, knowledge of the mysteries). The change has to do first with the object of faith. What is believed is the "Gospel" of the remission of sins and not simply belief in Christ. For the one who believes in him, it is remission of sins on a special individual level, and not only on the general level of the redemption of mankind. "If we believe . . . that he has done this for us, then he dwells within us by our faith, and because of it, and daily by his own work continues to purify us." The basis of such a conviction is God's gift of Christ: "To us a child is born, to us a son is given" (Is. 9:6). Luther finds in this gift a meaning which can only make the Christian long to have within him, and for his own benefit, the very deed of Calvary, by faith anchored in God's promise.

The idea of Christ dwelling within us is traditional. But Luther made that presence of Christ depend on faith in the purification accomplished by Christ alone for the present as well as for the past. He thus gives unexpected significance to a form of piety advanced within the sphere of the New Devotion. That presence of Christ, which was being made a privilege for pure souls, is remission of sins and is for everyone.

The consequence of this is the appearance of the "certain" principle that the purification of sin is faith, not works. The latter cannot be a remedy for sin, nor can they put Christ within us, just as one cannot enter into the good graces of someone who has been offended by showering that person with gifts. At this stage of the argument (quite distinct from the abuse leveled at the clergy, which figures very largely) the important point is the affirmation that there is no purification of sin in works.

We have seen the reason for Luther's position in the *Preface to the Epistle of St. Paul to the Romans*. Here Luther contents himself with specifying the role of faith. The text of Eph. 3:17, "that Christ may dwell in your hearts through faith," serves his thought admirably. But Paul had certainly never subscribed to the theology taught just prior to Luther. The latter's logic, which can appear very sketchy, was a response to the inconsistencies of a theology of which the apostle could not have conceived.

Chief among these inconsistencies was the development of the theory and system of works and of practices indispensable to salvation, in such a way that a phrase like "that Christ may dwell in your hearts through faith" appears at best a pious formula for preachers to introduce for effect at an opportune moment. A better way had been found since St. Paul; things had become more "precise." However, the New Testament makes it very clear, as Luther emphasizes, that there is no other way to salvation than faith. The Acts of the Apostles report the discussion of the Council of Jerusalem on the necessity to practice the Law for purification. And it is Peter himself who declares that it is by faith (not by the Law) that the Spirit has cleansed their hearts (Acts 15:9). He even specifies that Christian Jews who practice the Law were, just like the pagans, saved by the grace of the Lord Jesus (v. 11). Both the letter of the text and its context make clear the idea that faith is a principle of inward purification in Luther's sense. Luther himself elsewhere unfailingly refers to Acts 15:9 in this kind of debate.

His error is undoubtedly that he does not attribute any inherent value to the Church's experience. The doctrine of works had been admitted over the centuries by serious and truly Christian souls. Luther was content with recognizing that, once purification is gained, from the atonement procured by Christ himself, Christian behavior is what the Church teaches: the practice of good works, the struggle against sin, and penitence. But, contrary to what was said to the faithful, that was useless for the purification of sin, which remained exclusively the work of faith. Moreover, the zealous Christian runs the risk of putting confidence and assurance in his own goodness, which is an illusion and a failure to recognize the grace of Christ. To cast off this peril, one must remember that sin yields only before the power of Christ glorified in the resurrection. We are only creatures, "sinful, weak, corrupt," thoroughly incapable of having taken on such a problem "as great as God himself."[8]

This completes our outline of Luther's thought, the whole force of which is the conviction that individual sin is taken over by Christ himself, who makes the understanding of the Gospel operative in the soul by faith. The edifice holds together by its logic. It is not without mystical overtones, but the point of view is strictly theological, indeed abstract, like a theorem. The introduction of the psychic or sentient factor would risk bringing back into the debate problems which Luther precisely intended to exclude. His explanation implies the rejection of all other action against sin but that of Christ, that action being dependent on him and his grace.

Such a position should exercise an irresistible fascination for those who have no specific reasons for holding back. Luther announces to the Christian the complete and certain purification of his sin before God. He makes Christ everything for the individual Christian's life and gives an unexpected luster to the most familiar texts about Christ in Scripture, tradition, and the liturgy. Faith becomes the master word, whose explicit doctrine is often not perceived except latently, or more often not at all. Now faith is in itself a personal initiative of the individual (under the impulse of the Holy Spirit), independent of the functioning of the ecclesiastical institution. Luther's teaching makes of it the principle of a greater personal autonomy in the religious domain. Faith finds what it needs in a certain reading of Holy Scripture, whose affirmations suddenly become very eloquent under Luther's pen. "Luther's Bible" is characterized by key passages which we begin to know well: Heb. 1:3; Eph. 3:17; Acts 15:9; Is. 9:6; Rom. 1:1-4, 17; 8:32. Or again, in this context, 1 Cor. 1:30: "He is the source of your life in Christ Jesus, whom God made our wisdom, our righteousness and sanctification and redemption."

Luther's influence was due to the wide-ranging character of his evangelical preaching. Each aspect touches a category of individuals. What seems to have remained his secret was the discourse itself. His followers drew from it "Lutheran" doctrines in which he would not recognize himself. Very quickly these Lutherans lost the background of their master's rich experience, which had been nourished by his monastic education no less than by the Scriptures. So his principles tended to lose their strength and even to wither like dried flowers.

BELIEVING IN JESUS CHRIST

The interpretation of Heb. 1:3 presents the heart of Luther's Christology, from the point of view of the purification of sins. Most often, Luther brings together the remission of sin and the acquisition of righteousness. Theology made a distinction between the two questions, and Luther had as much to say on one as on the other.

The treatise on *The Freedom of a Christian* unites them in the theme of the "wonderful exchange"—the *admirabile commercium* of the Christmas liturgy, inspired by the sermon of St. Leo and here transformed by Luther. The basic idea is that Christ has taken our human nature and in return communicates to us participation in his divinity. The human desire to have access to the divine, one way or another, explains the success of this theme, from which the influence of Platonism cannot be excluded—in the New Testament the idea of a divinization of the believer remains within the limits of Jewish thought, which Christian Hellenism was to ignore. Luther transposes this schema on the plan of his conception of the Gospel, substituting for the terms "humanity" and "divinity" those of the "righteousness of God" and the "sinful human condition." For him Christ takes upon himself our sin (not merely removing it, but becoming it himself), and in exchange he communicates his righteousness to us. This teaching can rest on the "tropological" interpretation of the allegory of Eph. 5:23 ff., concerning the marriage of Christ and the church.[9] What the text says of the Church is in this case applied to the believer's soul—an exegesis by no means illegitimate, especially in that epoch.[10] It reflects the juridical character of marriage under the rule of the community: spouses married under this rule have everything in common; what belongs to each belongs to the other. Thus Christ has his righteousness in common with the soul and shares with it the sinful condition.

Faith not only gives the soul so much that she becomes, like the divine Word, full of all graces, free and blessed, but also unites the soul with Christ, like a bride with her bridegroom; and out of this marriage, as St. Paul says, Christ and the soul become one body, and share good and bad fortune, and all things in common. What Christ has belongs also to the believing soul, and what the soul has becomes Christ's. If Christ has all good things and all blessedness, these will also belong to the soul; and if the soul has only vices and sins, these will become Christ's own. So there arises that joyful exchange and struggle. Because Christ is God and man and has never sinned, and because his godliness is unconquerable, eternal, and all-powerful, so he makes the sins of the believing soul his own through the bridal ring, namely, faith. He acts just as if he had committed those sins himself, and thus they are swallowed up and drowned in him, because his invincible righteousness is stronger than any sin. So the soul is freed of her sins solely through her dowry, that is, on account of her faith. She becomes free and untrammeled, endowed with the eternal righteousness of her bridegroom Christ. . . . Her sins cannot possibly condemn her, for they now rest on Christ and are swallowed up in him. Thus she enjoys such abundant righteousness in her bridegroom that she can always stand firm against sins, though they remain in her. Paul speaks about this in 1 Cor. 15:57: "Thanks be to God, who gives us the victory through our Lord Jesus Christ" in which death is swallowed up together with sin.[11]

The citation of 1 Cor. 15:57 is another example of the amazing work of restoration carried out by Luther on the whole facade of Scripture. Texts which had been ignored find their luster and color again, revealing the true dignity of the Scriptures. Others of Luther's writings carry full theological justification for his conception of Christ for us: the *Preface to the Epistle of St. Paul to the Romans*, the *Sermon on Two Kinds of Righteousness* (1518), or a passage from the second commentary on the Psalms.[12] But we know enough, for the present, about the way he intends to establish a new Christian experience, centered on the living presence of Christ within us by faith. It is powerful teaching, in the same thought world as St. Paul, and Protestantism has lived nearly five centuries out of this theological creation, this new step in the understanding of Christianity.

That has not been the view of the Church authorities. The text cited at the beginning of this chapter allows us to see the tension between them and Luther's thought. Had the Middle Ages evolved so far in another direction that the authenticity of such a discourse about faith could not be recognized? Was Luther atoning for the error of the break with Byzantium in 1054? This schism had deprived the Western Church of the brotherly correction of the Eastern tradition and had handed it over to its people's gods: legalism, moralism, magic, fear, the tyranny of power. All that, no less than book knowledge, made her deaf to the *Tolle lege* of the new Augustine.

2. One of Us

The best answer to the notion of the "fallen monk" (Maritain) is that Luther's years in the monastery brought him to the discovery of Christ. In the gospels those who come to Christ are not locked up in the misery of their fallen state. Luther had the gift of rediscovering the enthusiasm of evangelical and apostolic times for the person of the Lord himself. He speaks of it habitually, as does St. Paul himself, who had not known Christ in the flesh. But Siggins (pp. 9—10) also draws attention to how Luther was soaked in the thought of St. John, to whom he devoted hundreds of sermons.

That stance indicates an exceptional feeling for the realism of the Incarnation, the mystery of the Son of God made man. Luther had no affinity with Arianism, though he was taken for a new Arius. Not only had he never doubted the divinity of Christ, but that aspect of Christology was really not a question for him. On the contrary, it mattered to him more than anything to show what the humanity of the Son of God means for us and to defend it against those whose doctrine would open up a chasm between the Christian and his Redeemer.

That aspect of his work once became apparent to me in Germany in Catholic churches at Christmastime—before the Council. The Catholic repertoire of this liturgical season includes some of Luther's songs, for he was also a composer. This Luther for Christmastime is at least as sound as the Luther of Good Friday, to whom I shall return later. He speaks no less highly of the Mother of God than St. Bernard, one of his favorite authors. In accordance with the most ancient tradition, which expresses itself in the Apostles' Creed, Mary was for him the guarantee that Christ is truly man—because he was born of a woman.[13]

Luther had to react, at the time, against the inclination of clergy and people for the miraculous. The balance of the mystery of Christ, God and man, is difficult to preserve when the contrivances of theology and piety on the one hand and of culture and the politico-social system on the other are no longer measured by the wonderful synthesis of the gospels. The Christ of Luther's contemporaries is the one described by works of art and studies in the history of literature. What is lacking is what is shown most clearly in the New Testament—that He is for everyone—one of us. In the tendency to draw back from this realism Luther sees man's eternal need to fashion the divine in his image, the better to guarantee his autonomy against God. The first condition for discourse about Christ was, in his eyes, to give all possible emphasis to the intent behind the first lines of the gospel: "The Word became flesh and dwelt among us" (John 1:14).

Siggins (pp. 199—200) brings together in two pages typical statements of Luther on Jesus as true man. One can say, he writes, in the same terms as Luther, that Jesus Christ is true man because one can hear and see with one's own eyes that he speaks as a human being. He let himself be seen and touched. He ate, drank, slept, worked, suffered, and died, like every human being. He had eyes, ears, a mouth, a nose, a chest, a stomach, hands and feet as you and I do. He sucked the breast of his mother, who cared for him like any other child. For 30 years his life was absolutely ordinary. His behavior in his childhood was that of any other little boy. He slept, woke up, and was tired. He was sad and happy, he cried and laughed. He was hungry and thirsty, was cold and perspired; he prattled, worked, and prayed. He knew anxiety, failure, and fear. He became poor, weak, and lowly. Her suffered the pangs of sadness, anger, and hatred. He was deeply disturbed at the approach of his death and felt miserable, alone, and abandoned when his own friends and God himself left him in this extremity. In his adult life he submitted to physical needs, was a citizen like others, led an earthly career as a preacher, was the best of friends to his disciples, and conducted himself in general like every human being—with one exception: he remained free from all sin.

Such references allow us to understand Luther's "intractable" attitude. Christ must not be taken away from him! At Augsburg, before the papal legate, as at Worms before the emperor, he always saw this concrete Christ whose presence he was able to recognize through special faith. How could he possibly retract? And just to receive a cardinal's hat? In any case, he was German, and something more than massive artillery would be necessary to make him desert his post, despite his fears.

After the break with Rome he lived to open up a new front— within his own camp. The "sacramentarians" or "enthusiasts" (*Schwärmer*) attacked the real presence of Christ in the Eucharist. Are the bread and the wine consecrated in the Mass the body and blood of the Lord, or are they not? This was a difficult question with infinite complications,[14] but the controversies surrounding it never caused Luther to forget what was at stake. "The enthusiasts strangle Christ my Lord. . . . As soon as Christ said: This is my body, his body was there, by the Word and power of the Holy Spirit" (Lienhard, ch. 4). He held to his principle that "the Word of God is true." Christianity, bound to the letter of Scripture, includes the "sacrament" in which man encounters Christ in bodily fashion, as did Mary, Simeon, and the shepherds. The living Christ of faith is the risen Christ, who ministers to us so that we know him like those who heard him speak. "Spiritualizing" is out of the question. The spirit, in Luther's teaching, is opposed to the "flesh," that is to say, to sin. It is not the quintessence of what is really human, purified of every bodily element (ibid., p. 216).

It was indeed the same struggle that Luther was fighting here, despite some apparent but easily resolved contradictions in what he says. It was a struggle to have the Word understood as another living bread, conveyed through preaching; and during Advent 1518 he had already explained it in these terms to the children and the common people, in reference to the Lord's Prayer:

> Now you see what is meant by this daily bread and that Christ is truly this bread. However, he will be of no benefit to you and you will not be able to avail yourself of him unless God translates him into words whereby you can hear and know him. What does it profit you if Christ sits in heaven or is hidden in the form of bread? He must be brought to you, prepared for you, and translated into words for you by means of the inner and external word. See, that is truly the Word of God. Christ is the bread, God's Word is the bread, and yet there is but one object, one bread. He is in the Word, and the Word is in him. To believe in this same Word is the same as eating the bread. He to whom God imparts this will live eternally.[15]

At the same time he spoke out against the practice of private Masses without a sermon, which neglect "the very thing for which masses were instituted, namely, preaching." He put forward the view that the Word makes people recognize what they never would have grasped through the Sacrament. Without the Word, the Mass becomes a pointless and sterile rite worthy only of contempt. People return from the Mass "deprived, knowing neither Christ nor themselves." So it was necessary to pray to God that he send good preachers. Now we know that this doctrine was translated within Protestantism into a cult of the Word to the detriment of the Eucharist, but such was surely not Luther's thought on the matter.[16]

This sense of Christ's presence in the Word led him to search again for the language without which there is no discourse of faith. His writings are an unending restatement of the traditional language of Catholicism, which has not taken any account of this, resulting in the situation we know today. But if Luther made little use of the language of grace or transubstantiation, which he believed was too much marked by Aristotelianism, he had a knack for putting things unforgettably.

With regard to Nestorius, for example, he wondered if the heresy of this patriarch of Constantinople condemned at the Council of Ephesus in 431 had been clearly understood. He pointed out that Nestorius did not doubt the divinity of Christ and that he did not really divide him into God and man. His difficulty was that he did not want it to be said of Mary that she was the Mother of God. Now this language is indispensable for the declaration of the Christian mystery, and the Church, in proclaiming Mary's divine mother-hood, was only defending its right to declare the faith as it perceived it and as the well-being of the faithful demanded.[17]

Joined intimately to Christ by the Word and by faith, the Christian is, like him, "priest and king." It was in this sense that Luther in *The Freedom of a Christian* developed the theme of the "wonderful exchange." The priesthood, in particular, appeared to him as a primary gift of each Christian life. He took the view that in stripping the faithful of the priesthood in order to reserve it to priests, there had disappeared with it all understanding of grace, freedom, Christian faith with everything we owe to Christ, and of Christ himself. The priests have been regarded as "other Christs," which in Luther's judgment is the definition of the Christian. For the practice of faith amounts to living "as a Christ for others,"[18] carrying to its conclusion the epiphany of the Word of God.

The question of the "ministerial" priesthood (that of the priests) remains a thorny point between Rome and Luther's heirs. It is bound to the question, which is decisive for Catholicism, of whether Luther understood the saving efficacy which the hu-manity of Christ had in itself: Is salvation the work of the man Jesus Christ or the work of God alone acting "through him"?[19]

3. Christ Made Sin for Us: The Theology of the Cross

The texts show that for Luther the classical question of the merits of Christ (the fact that Jesus earned our salvation by the obedience of his human will) comes after the fundamental concern of searching out in what way Christ is for us, one of us. That the Son of God was made man, and that he was true man no less than true God, Luther did not doubt for a moment. Where his Christology appeared to deviate from the traditional faith, it is clear that his intention was to hold to the Nicene Creed.[20] On the merit of Christ he had essentially neither more nor less to say than any other theologian,[21] but as far as he was concerned the scholastic speculation about Christ's humanity "in itself" was bad theology. The work of Christ must be understood from the complete reality of the Christ of faith and of history, the Son of God and of Mary. Moreover, concern for the moral perfection of Jesus is, for Luther, a way of sidestepping the question which is at the basis of the problem of salvation. Nothing is more readily understandable than that the Son of God made man was a perfect man. But man is in fact a sinner. The redemptive incarnation cannot therefore be explained solely in terms of humanity. Christ must come to *sinful* man.

Lutheran (and Augustinian) realism which sees man from the perspective of his sinful condition would not surprise a modern man, for the newspapers show the existence of evil far better than the works of theology do. Every person is sufficiently aware of the "less good" aspects of his nature so that he feels himself responsible, or puts the blame on others, or on circumstances. So it should not be difficult to grasp Luther's question: Has the Son of God, in making himself man, met us in the very depths of human misery? Has he known the times when we despair of ourselves, of God, and of everything?

This was an unusual question for Christianity through the ages. Experience persuades the Christian spontaneously to attribute to Christ the measure of purity which he does not count on attaining himself. Christ at least is pure, and the beginning of purity is recognizing him as Master and Lord. Theology sees in him the Son of God and the boundless merit of his sacrifice. Thus sin has no part in him. But then, is he truly one with us and with the darkness in which we are formed? Isn't he only the benefactor who visits the shantytown one afternoon, hands out small change and promises, then leaves for that other life forever unknown to the desolate in this corner of the world?

Luther took the view that everything said of Christ is pointless if it is forgotten that he is *for us.* But Christ is for us only if he is one of us, that is to say, in one way or another a sinner like us. That may seem unthinkable, since Christ is innocence itself. Everything, however, points to the fact that Luther saw the Crucified One more and more as the victim of sins which he has taken to his own account. He was encouraged in this by Scripture no less than by his confidence in the Gospel. "For our sake he made him to be sin who knew no sin, so that in him we might become the righteousness of God" (2 Cor. 5:21). That was Paul's declaration, not Luther's invention. It signified for him that Christ redeems us not merely by creating the possibility of infinite human merit by his incarnation and death, his obedience and suffering, but by identifying in such a way with sin that his death becomes the death of sin itself.

At stake was a theology other than the current one, a new way of speaking about faith, which Luther called the theology of the cross: "of the cross" because it was on the very fact of the cross, of the Crucified, that his thought was fastened. This was improper theology from the point of view of those who would imagine that it has Jesus succumbing to temptation. But without wishing to justify all the audacity of a theologian as little worried about what people would say as Luther is said to have been, it is important not to forget that it was St.Paul who spoke first of all of the scandal and stupidity of the cross (cf. 1 Cor. 1:18-29).

The notion of Christ being one with sinners at least prevents us from thinking that a good God made his innocent Son perish for the guilty. It was as a guilty one that Jesus died. He was not substituted (as the one who pays for others) but was the same as we. He was like Père de Montcheuil, who secured the chaplaincy of the Vercors underground during his holidays as professor at the Catholic Institute, and wanted to be executed with the others, though the German authorities recognized that he was not a freedom fighter. In an analagous way Jesus wanted to be with us and for us, a sinner like us all. And because he was himself innocent, the sin and death which came to strike sin down—for death is the wages of sin—were destroyed by his purity, and we have been delivered.

Luther explained all this in a very long commentary on Gal. 3:13: "Christ redeemed us from the curse of the Law, having become a curse for us—for it is written: 'Cursed be everyone who hangs on a tree'" (LW 26, 276 ff.). This was a work of his maturity. At that time (1531—35) he was sure of what he asserted: "In my heart there rules this one doctrine, namely, faith in Christ. From it, through it, and to it all my theological thought flows and returns, day and night; yet I am aware that all I have grasped of this wisdom in its height, width, and depth are a few poor and insignificant firstfruits and fragments" (LW 27, 145). The decisive aspect lay in his daring to imagine that Christ's true humanity was to be directed towards those whom everyone, including the religious, condemned. Luther's Christ was not the "beautiful God" of the Cathedrals.[22]

That interpretation was inspired within him by his own *Anfechtungen.* His sense of the mystery of Christ progressed, in fact, parallel to the clarification of his debate within himself. He only began to find an opening from God's side through understanding that for the sinner God cannot be found because he is hidden. Sin is something so serious that it cannot be erased as a blackboard is erased. God saves us, while accentuating our sense of being evil and prey to his anger.[23] It is in this sense that the Epistle to the Romans (ch. 1) says that everything begins with the preaching of sin. Luther came very early to the view that it is not in seeing our faults disappear that we progress, but by better understanding the seriousness of the evil we continue to commit.

This knowledge is accompanied by the feeling that God is more and more angry and that we have less and less chance of being reunited with him. At the end of the route is hell, eternal separation from God and his heaven. The solution is to believe in the righteousness which God gives to the one who believes in Christ, for Christ comes precisely to bring to birth that new attitude of faith through a personal relationship with God.

Christ himself, in the midst of his Passion, had cried out in his turn: "My God, my God, why hast thou forsaken me?" (Mark 15:34). For Luther, here was the cry of the man oppressed by the consciousness of sin. In the case of Christ, the knowledge was that of the sins of men, not just the sin which he took on himself, but the sins which he had made his own, as if he were himself guilty. Luther did not hesitate to write, in commenting on Psalm 21, that Christ knew hell in this way to test a God who was deeply angry with him as a sinner, experiencing in himself feelings towards God which would be outright blasphemy for us.[24]

Such reflections, besides being strong wine which those who are not yet weaned should refrain from taking,[25] are against all logic—except the logic of the Gospel.

The clear meaning of the Gospel is that Christ is the One who is ready to do all things for us. The Gospel, moreover, is truth. If, in order to be true and believable, Christ had to go the whole way in his meeting with man, to give himself up completely with us to sin's dominion, one can be sure that he has done it. This, in any event, is the invariable line of Luther's teaching.

His theology of the cross was really discovered only in the 20th century. Earlier Protestantism drew out of it the adventurous notion of the *kenosis*,[26] without digesting to the same degree its soundly evangelical teaching. The studies that have poured out for some decades often make much of the paradoxes that arise at each step of that essentially dialectical teaching. But with Jürgen Moltmann's book *The Crucified God*,[27] a significant effort was made to show in the cross of Christ, following Luther, the basis and the critique of all Christian theology. The theology of the cross appears particularly as the response to the scandal of evil which causes doubt about God (in the sense that one says: If there were a good God, none of this would have happened). Without being the whole of theology, it provides the criteria for all truth and the criticism of all pretense. The Crucified One is for Christian faith and for the church "the one who liberates them most radically from lying and vanity, from the struggle for power and from fear" (p. 2). In this way the theology of the cross can become the standard of a practical response in which man is truly liberated.

This was indeed how things happened with Luther, at least in relation to the Church and the Catholicism of his time. In attacking, in the name of the Gospel, the glorification of the man who is strong in good works, and the pursuit of power by the clergy, he wanted to bring the Christian community back to the nakedness of the cross, which leaves room only for the act of faith by the thief or the centurion. And all this for man and his personal freedom.

Moltmann (pp. 72—73), however, notes that Luther scarcely saw beyond inner salvation or liberation within the framework of ecclesial society. He remained notoriously insensitive to the peasants' movement for politico-social liberation.[28] He allowed the princes that power over the Church which he refused to the pope. His thought gave little place to the critical function of the cross with respect to civil society. His behavior at the time of the Peásants' War is denounced even today as a repudiation of his

Gospel. Did he not preach total submission to the rebels, and in his prayers call for their repression? Did the bishop who traveled through his diocese, reconquered from the rebels, with an executioner on his heels for speedy retribution do anything more than the Reformer had demanded in his 1525 pamphlets?

In view of these facts, there is certainly material here for an investigation which would find the Reformer guilty before the court of history. But his inability to surmount his *petit bourgeois* conservatism, devoted to order and defiant of the common people, is not the only explanation of his prejudice. At a deeper level, it is necessary to look for the reason in his passion for defending the Gospel against all compromises, or even against all-too-human viewpoints. Two extracts from his *Admonition to Peace: A Reply to the Twelve Articles of the Peasants in Swabia*, which defined his initial stance in the conflict, can help us to understand this observation. The first recalls Luther's ideal at the beginning of the Reformation, namely, the advancement of matters solely by the preaching of the Word of God. The second exhorts the peasants to practice the theology of the cross.

Now what have I done that the more pope and emperor raged, the more my gospel spread? I have never drawn a sword or desired revenge. I began neither conspiracy nor rebellion, but so far as I was able, I have helped the worldly rulers—even those who persecuted the gospel and me—to preserve their power and honor. I stopped with committing the matter to God and relying confidently at all times upon his hand. This is why God has not only preserved my life in spite of the pope and all the tyrants—and this many consider a really great miracle, as I myself must also confess—but he has made my gospel grow and spread. Now you interfere with what I am doing. You want to help the gospel and yet you do not see that what you are doing hinders and suppresses it most effectively (LW 46, 31).

In saying this it is not my intention to justify or defend the rulers in the intolerable injustices which you suffer from them. They are unjust, and commit heinous wrongs against you . . . however . . . Christians do not fight for themselves with sword and musket, but with cross and with suffering, just as Christ, our leader, does not bear a sword, but hangs on the cross. Your victory, therefore, does not consist in conquering and reigning, or in the use of force, but in defeat and weakness, as St. Paul says in II Corinthians 1 [10:4], "The weapons of our warfare are not material, but are the strength which comes from God," and "Power is made perfect in weakness" [II Cor. 12:9]. (LW 46, 32).

For Luther, in this issue as in many others, everything comes back to the paradox of the weakness of God, victorious over evil in the Crucified One. All his life he taught that only Christ makes possible the knowledge of God in this, the only beneficial way. The exaltation of divine perfection by theology and official religion responds to man's desire, smitten as he is with glory, wealth, and power. God, the God of Jesus Christ, is not the one who loves and seeks his own advantage in everything. Rather, he seeks out what is of no account, and worthless, to re-create it; he makes perfect those whom he loves, and favors no one in particular.[29] It is along these lines that there emerges the deepest and most common aspiration of all currents of the Reformation: that God should be God.

Luther would have liked to believe that this teaching could help the peasants resolve their problems by some means other than violence. But did he himself believe and want to believe that he could love the papal Church despite the unfaithfulness he discovered in her—and to reform her without deforming her? That question, an inevitable one on the part of a Catholic brought up to believe in principle in the Church as she is, no more throws doubt on the validity of Luther's Gospel than do his pamphlets against the peasants. But it invites us look more closely at how and why such a Gospel could bring with it a break between the Church and the Reformation.

6
What Kind of Reformation?

The Church and the Gospel

We come now to the question posed to the Church by Luther's faith. The Gospel of Christ only took on such importance in his life because he was reacting to the decidedly unevangelical climate of the Church of Alexander VI, Julius II, and Leo X. His research could only have interested a handful of followers. But the question of the Gospel in the Church became the question of a whole generation, and opened up within Western Christianity a debate which is still not closed.

This is undoubtedly the most profound question in the history of the Reformation,[1] and the most far-reaching one, in view of the still insurmountable division between Catholics and Protestants. How was it that a movement to further the Gospel could lead to an impasse for which there is no resolution even centuries after the events?

The reasons for this situation are not exclusively religious.[2] But at the point where we stand after Vatican II, the problem amounts to a search for Christian unity and the changes this implies. The divided churches cannot separately manage the tasks of evangelization. From the Catholic point of view, it is a matter of whether Rome can recognize Catholicism's misunderstanding of the Gospel as it came down to us from the Middle Ages. Rome has never seen fit to admit that the situation of the Church at the beginning of the 16th century called for a Luther, that is, for an advocate of the Gospel. Now we have seen that Luther himself did not grasp the totality of the problem. Where he looked only for the "justice" of God, today everything indicates that there is good reason for preoccupation with justice in the world. He and his followers nevertheless experienced the tension between the revolutionary demands of the Gospel and traditional Catholicism to the point of breaking with the papacy. Concern with unity cannot but persuade the Catholic scholar to pay attention to the challenge posed to his faith by Protestantism's enduring preoccupation with the question raised by the Wittenberg monk.

In accordance with the pattern followed so far, I propose to examine this debate on the basis of texts and in historical context. But I would like to begin by defining the facts of the case as they appear to me.

1. The Question of the Gospel in the Church

The schema "Gospel-Church" corresponds to the two stages of the 16th-century crisis: the appearance of Luther's Gospel and the reaction of the Church at the Council of Trent. Luther summed up his doctrine as "Gospel" just as Rome spoke of "the Church." That stylization of a complex historical and doctrinal record clearly invites objection.[3] Its purpose is to emphasize the profound question which Luther raised within the Church and the importance of Rome's refusal to allow such a question.[4]

Luther took aim not at the Church in general but at the Roman or papal Church, the Church that depended on the pope, the successor of Peter, to whom Christ had committed authority over the Christian world. This dogma of papal primacy was traditional in the West, and it was this which was at stake in the conflict between Rome and the Reformation.

The Gospel of justification by faith aroused two opposing responses in the bosom of the Church; that of the Reformer's supporters, and the official view of the Council of Trent (1545—63). Many sided with the "Gospel" without regard to the condemnation pronounced since 1521 against Luther, his doctrine, and his disciples. The new power of the Gospel was such that it was bound to assert itself, with or without Rome. With Luther condemned, it exploded throughout the Church, bringing in its train "reforms" that rendered traditional religion unrecognizable. The Council of Trent put an end to the confusion by reinforcing "Catholicism," confirming the condemnation of Protestants and Protestantism, and blocking any development of an "evangelical" character within the Church. Thus Luther's faith appeared clearly incompatible with the Catholic faith.

The relevance of the questions raised by the Reformer cannot be denied. Surfacing at a critical period in the history of the Roman tradition, these questions had set events in train and necessitated the mobilization of a council. Though divided, Christianity at the close of the 16th century was entirely "reformed," a state which the Lateran Council (1512—17) had not been able to achieve. Luther was not mistaken about the importance of his struggle, which took him to the point of twice refusing to retract. He did the right thing in beginning by appealing to the bishops and then to the pope.[5] For the problem of the Gospel in the Church cannot be regulated without the hierarchy. But Rome's first decision was to reduce the monk to silence. The second was Trent's "No" to everything Luther had hoped for.

The Council of Trent rectified a situation which was, from the Catholic point of view, thoroughly dangerous. But, in severing all links with the Reformation, it created a violent state of affairs that has been perpetuated to our own time—the division between Catholics and Protestants, who are (in their separate ways) both involved in the making of Christians. Does it make sense to declare "outside the faith" a religious current of such depth which emerged from the very life of Catholicism? For some time Rome has recognized no alternative to inviting Protestants to "return to the fold," which was for them to renounce a religious position whose great value Luther had discovered. Tridentine Catholicism justified only too well their conviction that the Reformers had truly defended the cause of the Word of God. The persistent division is only the logical outcome of irreconcilable points of view fixed in the bitterness of the crisis.

As heirs of this situation in which they are born into the faith in "separated" Churches, Christians of today can no longer hold to it. There is a certain amount of mingling everywhere between Catholics and Protestants, without any problems. It is against all principles. But the evidence that we are—both groups of us— disciples of the Gospel is stronger than dogmatic opposition. The questionable situation prevailing after Trent, which defined "the truth" as an abstract absolute, continues to lose ground. It is not that the demands of truth have been renounced or that divergences no longer have the same importance. But the challenge thrust at Christians by the world today is above all whether they can go beyond their quarrels for the sake of common action in the name of the Gospel.

The study of Luther constantly stumbles up against the rivalry between Catholicism and Protestantism. Catholic objections to the Reformer and his work have to do particularly with the division of the Churches. This process will have no ending as long as the break remains. Denifle, who believed he had put a stop to discussion about Luther, had only given it a new lease on life, and three quarters of a century later it is still not over. But because that discussion continues to concern us, we are in a better position to see things than the fathers of the Council of Trent, the first Protestants, or even Luther himself. What they sowed has produced a harvest, and today we can try to separate the good grain from the chaff. The passing of time allows us to discern the response that would have changed the course of events for the better, and even to catch a glimpse of a resolution in the conflict in which we are still engaged.

Properly considered, the question of the Gospel in the Church is summed up in several points:

—The debate concerns first of all the Roman tradition of Christianity, rather than the origins of Protestantism as such or Luther's errors. Luther elaborated his Gospel in response to a crisis in the Roman Church, without which doubtless we would never have heard of him. The phenomenon of the Reformation represents, in all its fullness, a great historic mutation of the Western Church. It was the distant consequence of the break with the East, which had delivered the papacy over to the allurements of feudal Europe without any counterbalancing factor.

—At stake was not just a matter of "reforms" but a fundamental issue which could no longer wait or be resolved by itself—namely, the basis of the theological interpretation of revelation current at that time, the insistence on the Law and man's own power of achieving merit before God. Today the ground of the debate still remains the position of Catholicism on the relation of Law and Gospel, though discussions often take place over concrete questions like mixed marriages, intercommunion, and the recognition of ministries. The appearance of such a difficulty opened up a new chapter in the history of the Church. Nothing could stop its development, and there could be no retreat to an earlier position. Today there is no escape from the problem of the division of Christians, for reasons going back to the controversies of the 16th century.

—The decisive fact was the papal refusal to take Luther's Gospel into consideration, a refusal confirmed by Trent and maintained to our own day.[6] It was up to the pope to grasp a problem that had become a major one for the Church. The evangelical deficiency of the papal Church could not find its remedy without the papacy. But Rome admitted the need for reforms, not the radical question of the Gospel.

—This refusal had the effect of distorting the question in all its ramifications. It prevented the possibility of seeing what would have been produced out of the association of the strong Roman tradition with the no less vigorous evangelical aspiration perpetuated in Protestantism. The evangelical Reformation asserted itself without and against the Roman Church. This provoked the Counter-Reformation, which resolved to defend the Church without any concession to Luther's Gospel, indeed to the Gospel itself. The Church and the Gospel became two absolute antagonists, the principles of two forms of Christian life. The Gospel of justification ceased to be an article of the traditional Church, and this led in turn to the formation of new churches.[7] Each party denounced in relation to the other the absence of the Church, or of the Gospel.

—The papal refusal of the question of the Gospel is the obstructive factor preventing the restoration of the visible unity of Christians. In the 16th century there was no getting beyond the religious division of the West into Catholic and Protestant. Rome's initial refusal pushed the faithful into two distinct pathways: the Gospel (outside the Church) and the Church (without the Gospel). Today's dialog about unity has to do with irreconcilable dogmas fixed in consequence of this problematical situation, which was perverted from the very beginning. But the logic of division could not be that of unity. Instead of lowering dogmatic barriers, a dialog on that basis does nothing but maintain them.

—Rome will not be able to avoid grasping the problem of the nonevangelical aspect of Catholic orthodoxy. That was the question of 1517 and the only question still valid today. There is no other way out of the impasse into which the papacy's initial strategic error led the Christian West astray from the time of Luther's condemnation. The evangelical idea defined by Luther with a view to the renewal of the Church did not produce in Protestantism all that it could have. Catholicism, for its part, did not recover from being separated from those who were expressing in the most vigorous way possible the evangelical yearning of the Western Christian soul. What was lacking from the beginning ould now take place: The pope should persuade Catholicism to the path of evangelical transformation in which the Protestants, in the name of the same tradition of faith, have led the way for some centuries.

—The ecumenical movement and Vatican II have raised in a new way the question of the Gospel in the Church: Protestantism is seeking the visible unity of the Church with a view to the proclamation of the Gospel, its mission; conciliar Catholicism is seeking the Gospel for the renewal of the Church. That is the point from which a new start should be made.

Put in these terms, the question raised in the Church by Luther's faith is that of the reality of the evangelical deficiency which Luther revealed in Catholicism, and of the grounds for Rome's obstinate refusal to enter the pathway of "Reformation." What can we say of the infidelity and resistance to the Gospel within the Roman faith?

I shall endeavor to develop the study in this way. We shall see at the start how Luther posed the question of a reform of the Church by the Gospel and the response which the Augsburg Confession (1530) represented, the first formulation of a Church renewed according to the Gospel. A final chapter will deal with the Council of Trent's verdict—*Non possumus*—and will try to indicate briefly what an evangelical reform of the Church of Rome could be like: a reform which would be neither the Counter-Reformation nor outright Protestantization.

2. A Question of Life or Death: The 1528 Confession of Faith

At the end of his great work in support of the Real Presence, Luther wanted to confess his faith. He was then (March 1528) getting over a long illness, and Wittenberg was recovering from an outbreak of the plague. Doubtless the thought of death inspired this confession of faith, yet Luther stressed that he made it in full clarity and possession of his faculties.

It is the declaration of a conscience resolved to witness to its faith, of a way of thinking which risks all in the face of the Church. The pattern of exposition is that of the Creed. It allows Luther to speak first of his faith in God, then in Jesus Christ. But to believe in Christ is to hold to the Gospel of the remission of sins by faith alone, which leads to a stern critique of free will and monastic vows, the typical expressions, according to Luther, of justification by works. From that point his reflection unfolds in a revision of

Catholicism as it was, from top to bottom, on the basis of the Gospel and in application of the principle of Scripture alone: What is against Scripture is to be rejected, what is not in Scripture is not required.

The text, which is very explicit, makes it unnecessary to consult other "reforming" writings of Luther. It has the advantage of not being distorted by polemic, which in other places sometimes obscures the dominance of the Gospel. It is easy to grasp the continuity with what has gone before without any need for an abundance of notes.

Confession Concerning Christ's Supper (1528)[8]

I see that schisms and errors are increasing proportionately with the passage of time, and that there is no end to the rage and fury of Satan. Hence lest any persons during my lifetime or after my death appeal to me or misuse my writings to confirm their error, as the sacramentarian and baptist fanatics are already beginning to do, I desire with this treatise to confess my faith before God and all the world, point by point. I am determined to abide by it until my death and (so help me God!) in this faith to depart from this world and to appear before the judgment seat of our Lord Jesus Christ. Hence if any one shall say after my death, "If Luther were living now, he would teach and hold this or that article differently, for he did not consider it sufficiently," etc., let me say once and for all that by the grace of God I have most diligently traced all these articles through the Scriptures, have examined them again and again in the light thereof, and have wanted to defend all of them as certainly as I have now defended the sacrament of the altar. I am not drunk or irresponsible. I know what I am saying, and I well realize what this will mean for me before the Last Judgment at the coming of the Lord Jesus Christ.[9] Let no one make this out to be a joke or idle talk; I am in dead earnest, since by the grace of God I have learned to know a great deal about Satan. If he can twist and pervert the Word of God and the Scriptures, what will he not be able to do with my or someone else's words?

God, Trinity, and Creator

First, I believe with my whole heart the sublime article of the majesty of God, that the Father, Son, and Holy Spirit, three distinct persons, are by nature one true and genuine God, the Maker of heaven and earth; in complete opposition to the Arians,

Macedonians, Sabellians, and similar heretics,[10] *Genesis 1 [:1]. All this has been maintained up to this time both in the Roman Church and among Christian churches throughout the whole world.*

The Son of God Made Man

Secondly, I believe and know that Scripture teaches us that the second person in the Godhead, viz. the Son, alone became true man, conceived by the Holy Spirit without the co-operation of man, and was born of the pure, holy Virgin Mary as of a real natural mother, all of which St. Luke clearly describes and the prophets foretold; so that neither the Father nor the Holy Spirit became man, as certain heretics have taught.

Also that God the Son assumed not a body without a soul, as certain heretics have taught, and was born the promised true seed or child of Abraham and of David and the son of Mary by nature, in every way and form a true man, as I am myself and every other man, except that he came without sin, by the Holy Spirit of the Virgin Mary alone.

And that this man became true God, as one eternal, indivisible person, of God and man, so that Mary the holy Virgin is a real, true mother not only of the man Christ, as the Nestorians teach, but also of the Son of God, as Luke says [1:35], the child to be born of you will be called the Son of God," i.e. my Lord and the Lord of all, Jesus Christ, the only, true Son by nature of God and of Mary, true God and true man.

The Savior and Redeemer

I believe also that this Son of God and of Mary, our Lord Jesus Christ, suffered for us poor sinners, was crucified, dead, and buried, in order that he might redeem us from sin, death, and the eternal wrath of God by his innocent blood; and that on the third day he arose from the dead, ascended into heaven, and sits at the right hand of God the Father almighty, Lord over all lords, King over all kings and over all creatures in heaven, on earth, and under the earth, over death and life, over sin and righteousness.

For I confess and am able to prove from Scripture that all men have descended from one man, Adam; and from this man, through their birth, they acquire and inherit the fall, guilt and sin, which the same Adam, through the wickedness of the devil, committed in paradise; and thus all men along with him are born, live, and die altogether in sin, and would necessarily be guilty of eternal death if Jesus Christ had not come to our aid and taken upon himself this guilt and sin as an innocent lamb, paid for us by his sufferings, and if he did not still intercede and plead for us as a faithful, merciful Mediator, Savior, and the only Priest and Bishop of our souls.

The Grace of Christ and Free Will

I herewith reject and condemn as sheer error all doctrines which glorify our free will, as diametrically contrary to the help and grace of our Savior Jesus Christ.[11] Outside of Christ death and sin are our masters and the devil is our god and lord, and there is no power or ability, no cleverness or reason, with which we can prepare ourselves for righteousness and life or seek after it. On the contrary, we must remain the dupes and captives of sin and the property of the devil to do and to think what pleases them and what is contrary to God and his commandments.

Original Sin

Thus I condemn also both the new and the old Pelagians who will not admit original sin to be sin, but make it an infirmity or defect.[12] But since death has passed to all men, original sin must be not merely an infirmity but enormous sin, as St. Paul says, "The wages of sin is death" [Rom. 6:23], and again, "Sin is the sting of death" [I Cor. 15:56]. So also David says in Psalm 51 [:5], "Behold, I was conceived in sin, and in sin did my mother bear me." He does not say, "My mother conceived me with sin," but, "I—I myself—I was conceived in sin, and in sin did my mother bear me," i.e. in my mother's womb I have grown from sinful seed, as the Hebrew text signifies.

Religious Orders, an Invention of the Devil

Next, I reject and condemn also as sheer deceptions and errors of the devil all monastic orders, rules, cloisters, religious foundations, and all such things devised and instituted by men beyond and apart from Scripture, bound by vows and obligations, although many great saints have lived in them, and as the elect of God are misled by them even at this time,[13] yet finally by faith in Jesus Christ have been redeemed and have escaped. Because these monastic orders, foundations, and sects have been maintained and perpetuated with the idea that by these ways and works men may seek and win salvation, and escape from sin and death, they are all a notorious, abominable blasphemy and denial of the unique aid and grace of our only Savior and Mediator, Jesus Christ.[14] For "there is no other name given by which we must be saved" than this, which is Jesus Christ [Acts 4:12]. And it is impossible that there should be more saviors, ways, or means to be saved[15] than through the one righteousness which our Savior Jesus Christ is and has bestowed upon us, and has offered to God for us as our one mercy seat, Romans 3 [:25].

It would be a good thing if monasteries and religious foundations were kept for the purpose of teaching young people God's Word, the Scriptures, and Christian morals, so that we might train and prepare fine, capable men to become bishops, pastors, and other servants of the church, as well as competent, learned people for civil government, and fine, respectable, learned women capable of keeping house and rearing children in a Christian way. But as a way of seeking salvation, these institutions are all the devil's doctrine and creed, I Timothy 4 [:1 ff.], etc.

The Orders Instituted by God: the Ministry, the Family, Public Office

But the holy orders and true religious institutions established by God are these three: the office of priest, the estate of marriage, the civil government. All who are engaged in the clerical office or ministry of the Word are in a holy, proper, good, and God-pleasing order and estate, such as those who preach, administer sacraments, supervise the common chest, sextons and messengers or servants who serve such persons. These are engaged in works which are altogether holy in God's sight.

Again, all fathers and mothers who regulate their household wisely and bring up their children to the service of God are engaged in pure holiness, in a holy work and a holy order. Similarly, when children and servants show obedience to their elders and masters, here too is pure holiness, and whoever is thus engaged is a living saint on earth.

Moreover, princes and lords, judges, civil officers, state officials, notaries, male and female servants and all who serve such persons, and further, all their obedient subjects—all are engaged in pure holiness and leading a holy life before God. For these three religious institutions or orders are found in God's Word and

commandment; and whatever is contained in God's
holy, for God's Word is holy and sanctifies everyt
with it and involved in it.

The Order of Love

Above these three institutions and orders is the common order
of Christian love, in which one serves not only the three orders, but
also serves every needy person in general with all kinds of
benevolent deeds, such as feeding the hungry, giving drink to the
thirsty, forgiving enemies, praying for all men on earth, suffering
all kinds of evil on earth, etc. Behold, all of these are called good
and holy works. However, none of these orders is a means of
salvation. There remains only one way above them all, viz. faith in
Jesus Christ.

For to be holy and to be saved are two entirely different things.
We are saved through Christ alone; but we become holy both
through this faith and through these divine foundations and
orders. Even the godless may have much about them that is holy
without being saved thereby. For God wishes us to perform such
works to his praise and glory. And all who are saved in the faith of
Christ surely do these works and maintain these orders.

What was said about the estate of marriage, however, should
also be applied to widows and unmarried women, for they also
belong to the domestic sphere. Now if these orders and divine
institutions do not save, what can we say about the effects of the
devil's institutions and monasteries, which have sprung up
entirely without God's Word, and further, rage and contend
against the one and only way of faith?

The Holy Spirit

Thirdly, I believe in the Holy Spirit, who with the Father and
the Son is one true God and proceeds eternally from the Father and
the Son, yet is a distinct person in the one divine essence and
nature. By this Holy Spirit, as a living, eternal, divine gift and
endowment, all believers are adorned with faith and other
spiritual gifts, raised from the dead, freed from sin, and made
joyful and confident, free and secure in their conscience. For this is
our assurance if we feel this witness of the Spirit in our hearts, that
God wishes to be our Father, forgive our sin, and bestow
everlasting life on us.

The Holy Trinity and Ourselves

These are the three persons and one God, who has given himself to us all wholly and completely, with all that he is and has. The Father gives himself to us, with heaven and earth and all the creatures, in order that they may serve us and benefit us. But this gift has become obscured and useless through Adam's fall. Therefore the Son himself subsequently gave himself and bestowed all his works, sufferings, wisdom, and righteousness, and reconciled us to the Father, in order that restored to life and righteousness, we might also know and have the Father and his gifts.

But because this grace would benefit no one if it remained so profoundly hidden and could not come to us, the Holy Spirit comes and gives himself to us also, wholly and completely. He teaches us to understand this deed of Christ which has been manifested to us, helps us receive and preserve it, use it to our advantage and impart it to others, increase and extend it. He does this both inwardly and outwardly—inwardly through the gospel, baptism, and the sacrament of the altar, through which as through three means or methods he comes to us and inculcates the sufferings of Christ for the benefit of our salvation.

Baptism and Eucharist

Therefore I maintain and know that just as there is no more than one gospel and one Christ, so also there is no more than one baptism. And that baptism in itself is a divine ordinance, as is his gospel also. And just as the gospel is not false or incorrect for the reason that some use it or teach it falsely, or disbelieve it, so also baptism is not false or incorrect even if some have received or administered it without faith, or otherwise misused it. Accordingly, I altogether reject and condemn the teaching of the Anabaptists and Donatists, and all who rebaptize.

In the same way I also say and confess that in the sacrament of the altar the true body and blood of Christ are orally eaten and drunk in the bread and wine, even if the priests who distribute them or those who receive them do not believe or otherwise misuse the sacrament. It does not rest on man's belief or unbelief but on the Word and ordinance of God—unless they first change God's Word and ordinance and misinterpret them, as the enemies of the sacrament do at the present time. They, indeed, have only bread and wine, for they do not also have the words and instituted ordinance of God but have perverted and changed it according to their own imagination.

The Church

Next, I believe that there is one holy Christian Church on earth, i.e. the community or number or assembly of all Christians in all the world, the one bride of Christ, and his spiritual body of which he is the only head.[16] *The bishops or priests are not her heads or lords or bridegrooms, but servants, friends, and—as the word "bishop" implies—superintendents, guardians, or stewards.*

This Christian Church exists not only in the realm of the Roman Church or pope, but in all the world, as the prophets foretold that the gospel of Christ would spread throughout the world, Psalm 2 [:8], Psalm 19 [:4]. Thus this Christian Church is physically dispersed among pope, Turks, Persians, Tartars, but spiritually gathered in one gospel and faith, under one head, i.e. Jesus Christ. For the papacy is assuredly the true realm of Antichrist, the real anti-Christian tyrant, who sits in the temple of God and rules with human commandments, as Christ in Matthew 24 [:24] and Paul in II Thessalonians 2 [:3 f.] declare; although the Turk and all heresies, wherever they may be, are also included in this abomination which according to prophecy will stand in the holy place, but are not to be compared to the papacy.

Remission of Sins, Confession, Indulgences

In this Christian Church, wherever it exists, is to be found the forgiveness of sins, i.e. a kingdom of grace and of true pardon. For in it are found the gospel, baptism, and the sacrament of the altar, in which the forgiveness of sins is offered, obtained, and received. Moreover, Christ and his Spirit and God are there. Outside this Christian Church there is no salvation or forgiveness of sins, but everlasting death and damnation; even though there may be a magnificent appearance of holiness and many good works, it is all in vain. But this forgiveness of sins is not to be expected only at one time, as in baptism, as the Novatians[17] *teach, but frequently, as often as one needs it, till death.*

For this reason I have a high regard for private confession, for here God's word and absolution are spoken privately and individually to each believer for the forgiveness of his sins, and as often as he desires it he may have recourse to it for this forgiveness, and also for comfort, counsel, and guidance. Thus it is a precious, useful thing for souls, as long as no one is driven to it with laws and commandments but sinners are left free to make use of it, each according to his own need, when and where he wishes; just as we are free to obtain counsel and comfort, guidance and instruction when and where our need or our inclination moves us. And as long as one is not forced to enumerate all sins but only those which oppress him most grievously, or those which a person will mention in any case, as I have discussed in my Little Book on Prayer.[18]

But the pardons or indulgences which the papal church has and dispenses are a blasphemous deception, not only because it invents and devises a special forgiveness beyond the general forgiveness which in the whole Christian Church is bestowed through the gospel and the sacrament and thus desecrates and nullifies the general forgiveness, but also because it establishes and bases satisfaction for sins upon the works of men and the merits of saints, whereas only Christ can make and has made satisfaction for us.

Prayer for the Dead, and the Invocation of the Saints

As for the dead, since Scripture gives us no information on the subject, I regard it as no sin to pray with free devotion in this or some similar fashion: "Dear God, if this soul is in a condition accessible to mercy, be thou gracious to it." And when this has been done once or twice, let it suffice. For vigils and requiem masses and yearly celebrations of requiems are useless, and are merely the devil's annual fair.[19]

Nor have we anything in Scripture concerning purgatory. It too was certainly fabricated by goblins. Therefore, I maintain it is not necessary to believe in it; although all things are possible to God, and he could very well allow souls to be tormented after their departure from the body. But he has caused nothing of this to be spoken or written, therefore he does not wish to have it believed, either. I know of a purgatory, however, in another way,[20] but it would not be proper to teach anything about it in the church, nor on the other hand, to deal with it by means of endowments or vigils.

Others before me have attacked the invocation of saints, and this pleases me. I believe, too, that Christ alone should be invoked as our Mediator, a truth which is scriptural and certain. Of the invocation of saints nothing is said in Scripture; therefore it is necessarily uncertain and not to be believed.

Anointing of the Sick, Marriage, and the Sacraments

If unction were practiced in accordance with the gospel, Mark 6 [:13] and James 5 [:14], I would let it pass. But to make a sacrament out of it is nonsense. Just as, in place of vigils and masses for the dead, one might well deliver a sermon on death and eternal life, and also pray during the obsequies and meditate upon our own end, as it seems was the practice of the ancients, so it would also be good to visit the sick, pray and admonish, and if anyone wished in addition to anoint him with oil, he should be free to do so in the name of God.

Neither is there any need to make sacraments out of marriage and the office of the priesthood. These orders are sufficiently holy in themselves.²¹ So, too, penance is nothing else than the practice and the power of baptism. Thus two sacraments remain, baptism and the Lord's Supper, along with the gospel, in which the Holy Spirit richly offers, bestows, and accomplishes the forgiveness of sins.

The Horror of the Mass and of Monastic Vows

As the greatest of all abominations I regard the mass when it is preached or sold as a sacrifice or good work,²² which is the basis on which all religious foundations and monasteries now stand, but, God willing they shall soon be overthrown. Although I have been a great, grievous, despicable sinner, and wasted my youth in a thoughtless and damnable manner,²³ yet my greatest sins were that I was so holy a monk, and so horribly angered, tortured, and plagued my dear Lord with so many masses for more than fifteen years. But praise and thanks be to his unspeakable grace in eternity, that he led me out of this abomination, and still continues to sustain and strengthen me daily in the true faith, despite my great ingratitude.

Accordingly, I have advised and still advise people to abandon religious foundations and monasteries and their vows and come forth into the true Christian orders, in order to escape these abominations of the mass and this blasphemous holiness, i.e. "chastity, poverty, and obedience," by which men imagine they are saved. Excellent as it was in the early days of the Christian Church to maintain the state of virginity, so abominable is it now when it is used to deny the aid and grace of Christ. It is entirely possible to live in a state of virginity, widowhood, and chastity without these blasphemous abominations.

Images and Cult Objects

Images, bells, eucharistic vestments, church ornaments, altar lights, and the like I regard as things indifferent. Anyone who wishes may omit them. Images or pictures taken from the Scriptures and from good histories, however, I consider very useful yet indifferent and optional. I have no sympathy with the iconoclasts.

The Resurrection

Finally, I believe in the resurrection of all the dead at the Last Day, both the godly and the wicked, that each may receive in his body his reward according to his merits. Thus the godly will live eternally with Christ and the wicked will perish eternally with the devil and his angels. I do not agree with those who teach that the devils also will finally be restored to salvation.

This is my faith, for so all true Christians believe and so the Holy Scriptures teach us. On subjects which I have treated too briefly here, my other writings will testify sufficiently, especially those which have been published during the last four or five years. I pray that all godly hearts will bear me witness of this, and pray for me that I may persevere firmly in this faith to the end of my life. For if in the assault of temptation or the pangs of death I should say something different—which God forbid—let it be disregarded; herewith I declare publicly that it would be incorrect, spoken under the devil's influence. In this may my Lord and Savior Jesus Christ assist me: blessed be he for ever, Amen.

These fervent and serious pages surely express the real Luther. They show his soul captivated by the Gospel of Christ, the only recourse for sinful man, and they show how that conviction engendered a program for Church reform.

The Catholic can be scandalized by the criticism heaped up against so many aspects of his faith still regarded as essential: free will, the religious or monastic vocation, the primacy of the pope, the Mass and the sacraments, the cult of the saints, prayers for the dead. Since the Reformation there have been opportunities enough to exploit this aspect of the "Luther case." Polemic has chosen to ignore what appears so clearly here, the fact that Luther's criticisms of Catholicism arise out of the demands of the Gospel. The most serious issue, in the last analysis, is not the scandalous character of this or that assertion but the strange ease with which Luther wipes out with a word dogmas and practices unquestioned until then. The story of the Reformation shows that the Gospel of justification by faith had the effect of opening people's eyes to those things within the Church which contradicted the absoluteness of grace—that reality beyond the reach of human efforts—and everything which tended to obscure the consciousness of Christ's mediation: intercession of the saints, the powers of the clergy, the efficacy of grace acknowledged in the rites and even in consecrated objects rather than the Word of God. All this led to the feeling that the credulity of the faithful had been abused and the affirmation that the Church of Rome was the rule of the non-Gospel, the Antichrist. On all points the Scriptural principle showed the contradictions of the papal principle or the "doctrines of men."

It was not yet 10 years since these questions had begun to be dealt with. The discovery of the Gospel was accompanied by the disappearance of the feeling that the Roman tradition was the authentic expression of the faith of the apostles. This phenomenon, which reminds us of the sudden eclipse of adherence to the monarchy at the time of the French Revolution of 1789 (in 1792 there was talk only of "tyrants"), is no more explicable than it. Such a polarization made the question of the Gospel in the Church a matter of life or death, and not only for the Roman institution but also for those who were vulnerable to the stake in their attachment to faith in Christ as revealed by Luther.

3. Towards an Evangelical Church

Through the years 1520—30 it was still possible to ask if what eventuated would not fully justify Luther. The Reformation entered into popular customs and brought lasting political changes to Germany, Switzerland, and Scandinavia.[24] It already had its martyrs.[25] But religious pluralism was then as unthinkable for statesmen as for theologians, and there was no question of anything other than one church. Since the measures taken in 1521 had had little effect, people had got used to the situation and settled into an attitude of "wait and see." How could one know which of the two parties, both unyielding, would carry the day?

After the short interlude of the reign of Adrian VI (1522—23), the papacy showed itself as incapable of putting the brakes on the truth as it was of seizing the initiative of reform. The interests of the Roman faith were taken in hand by Emperor Charles V, who supported a council to settle differences. The most difficult to convince was the pope, for Rome feared a council like the plague.[26] In 1527 the sack of Rome put the papacy at the emperor's mercy. For eight hours the Lutheran imperial footsoldiers were able to desecrate the churches with impunity and violate the seclusion of the cloisters, while the Spanish soldiers tortured the priests to relieve them of their money. From then on Charles V could carry out his ecclesiastical policy.

While waiting for a decision from Pope Clement VII, who was dragging his feet on the question, the emperor resolved to act within the framework of the Estates. He called the Diet of Augsburg and invited the representatives of the various religious points of view to give an account before him and among themselves.

The Lutherans produced a confession derived from Luther's.[27] It was read publicly at the diet on 25 June 1530 and put to the emperor. It was presented as "a confession of faith" of "certain princes and cities" (Tappert, p. 23) and was not the private writing of a single scholar, still less an attempt against Roman authority, but a political act. The competent authorities of the territories involved defined what they intended to retain of recent innovations, for a reform of the Church in conformity with the Gospel. The text was divided into 28 articles: 21 to do with doctrine, the others relating to "the abuses which have been corrected" (Tappert, p. 48). The signatories represented themselves as the voice of the ancient tradition of the Church against the developments of medieval Catholicism. While their course of action was not without its ulterior motives, their intention to list "the chief points," to introduce "nothing . . . contrary to Holy Scripture or the universal Christian church" (Tappert, p. 95) has to be taken into consideration. The Augsburg Confession is the conscientious balance sheet of 10 years of Church reform, in the name of the Gospel.

It is of interest to us here because it allows us to see how Luther's Gospel functioned as a norm for Church reform. The doctrine of justification by faith is, in effect, laid out in the first six

articles, which thenceforth serve as criteria for a series of restate-
ments involving the doctrines and practices of Catholicism.[28]

The thought is that of Luther's confession of faith, at times
taken up in the very same terms. The presentation of the
Reformer's teaching about the faith is worth examining closely,
for it is under this form that Luther's thought still governs the
faith of Lutheran churches today.

The first important point is that the article on God is followed
directly by the doctrine on original sin. The question of man thus
precedes Art. III, on the Son of God. Man, it is explained,
according to the Bible, is born full of evil desires or dispositions,
without fear of God, incapable of truly believing in Him.[29] This
innate flaw[30] is sin in the strict sense, and it destines for eternal
death those who are not born anew by Baptism, which brings the
Holy Spirit. This doctrine condemns the "Pelagians" who deny
that original sin in us is real sin, who attribute to man the power to
be good before God by his own strength—who teach, in effect, that
it is not absolutely necessary to be saved by Christ.

The inability of man without Christ to believe truly in God is
the presupposition of every Reformation doctrine. It rules out the
attainment of righteousness by the fulfillment of the Law and
leaves room only for faith. Luther's confession of faith shows that
he was implying a particular conception of man. In the nominalist
theology on which Luther relied, reality resides in the individual
in his concrete existence. The doctrine of justification should
therefore establish the basis of *individual* salvation and salvation
by Christ.

We read here, in this sense, that Christ is the expiatory victim[31]
"not only for original sin but also for all other sins." He is
"ascended into heaven, and sits at the right hand of God, that he
may eternally rule and have dominion over all creatures, that
through the Holy Spirit he may sanctify, purify, strengthen, and
comfort all who believe in him, that he may bestow on them life
and every grace and blessing, and that he may protect and defend
them against the devil and against sin" (Art. III).

Luther said much the same as this above: "All men . . . would
necessarily be guilty of eternal death if Jesus Christ had not come
to our aid and taken upon himself this guilt and sin as an innocent
lamb, paid for us by his sufferings, and if he did not still intercede
and plead for us as a faithful, merciful Mediator, Savior, and the
only Priest and Bishop of our souls." Daily Christ makes salvation

operative as "the only Priest," and the remission of sins is his exclusive action.

Theology at that time made the priests mediators between God and man, through their power to offer the sacrifice of the Mass for the daily sins of the living and the dead. The Council of Trent would not allow the Lutheran objection that such a conception of the Mass and the priest is opposed to the exclusive role of Christ. But it could not prevent Protestantism from continuing its struggle to make Christ present in the life of each believer, without having to depend on a priest.

The reason for this obstinacy was the conception of justification: "We cannot obtain forgiveness of sin and righteousness before God by our own merits, works, or satisfactions, but . . . we receive forgiveness of sin and become righteous before God by grace, for Christ's sake, through faith, when we believe that Christ suffered for us and that for his sake our sin is forgiven and righteousness and eternal life are given to us" (Art. IV). For in such faith God wants to see righteousness before him, to "impute" it to us, according to St. Paul in Romans 3 and 4. Every notion of human participation (through priest or personal merit) in the work of salvation clashes with this divine disposition. Sinful man cannot please God, who grants him grace only on account of his faith in Christ.

Preaching is the means by which man reaches such a faith. Here again, it is God who has instituted the ministry of preaching, to which is entrusted the proclamation of the Gospel and the dispensation of the sacraments, so that faith may be obtained. The Word and sacraments are like instruments by means of which the Holy Spirit is given and produces faith. Faith is response to the Gospel, which "teaches that we have a gracious God, not by our own merits but by the merit of Christ, when we believe this" (Art. V).[32]

Faith in the Gospel should produce an abundance of good works (Art. VI) in obedience to God's will and his commandments, but also out of love for him, not in order to win grace. We must not put such confidence in our works, for we are unprofitable servants (Luke 17:10). God has ordained that we should be saved by faith in Jesus Christ, that sins should be pardoned by faith alone, without merit on our part.[33]

These six articles define the Gospel, the sole message the Church has to announce to mankind. The Church is recognized by its fidelity to this message. That is the tenor of Art. VII, which begins by affirming that the Church "is to continue forever" (*perpetuo mansura sit*) but makes it, with Luther, the assembly of believers[34] "among whom the Gospel is preached in its purity and the holy sacraments are administered according to the Gospel." The mission of the Church therefore is to assure the justification of its members by the proclamation of the Word of God. After 10 years of reformation it is on this point that the claim about the Church is concentrated. But for Luther, as we have seen, the definition of the Church as the community of believers signifies that the pope is not the criterion of the true Church. For under the pope faith, the Gospel, and the true doctrine of justification can be in jeopardy. Not that there was any wish to supplant the pope at Augsburg (the editor maintained a discreet silence on that question), but his primacy was negated by the acceptance of a "functional" conception of the Church. The Church of Jesus Christ is the Church of faith in him as the source of salvation.

For the Augsburg Confession, agreement on the Gospel assures the unity of the Church without any need for universal imposition of the same cultic form.[35] Some thought was given to assuring the faithful about the validity of the sacraments administered at a time when priests were in schism with Rome and Roman doctrine was in dispute. Although the Church is, properly speaking, a community of "saints," here on earth it numbers many sinners in its ranks.[36] But the sacraments administered by unworthy ministers preserve their validity, for this comes to them from the institution of Christ. There should be no dreaming about a Church of the pure (Art. VIII).[37]

The doctrine of the sacraments rests on the teaching of Luther, who now recognized only Baptism and the Eucharist. But it was underlined, against Zwingli, that the sacraments are signs of divine favor towards us, intended to awaken and strengthen faith.[38] It is therefore necessary to use them in such a way as to call forth faith in the promises of God, which they renew in concrete form.[39]

The problems of the Christian's life in the world, his earthly vocation, are brought out in Art. XVI. The legitimate order of society is a good work of God. Christians can assume public duties, exercise justice (including the death penalty!), make war, conclude agreements, have property, give oaths before the authorities, and get married. This doctrine condemns the Anabaptists, who reject all institutions as contrary to the Gospel, but equally all those who seek evangelical perfection in the monastery, outside the common life—by works, not solely by faith or the fear of God. The Gospel commands us to see the will of God in the orders of society and to practice love there, each according to his station. Christians owe obedience to governments, except in the case where it is necessary to obey God rather than man (Acts 5:29).

The doctrine of free will (Art. XVIII) is Luther's. Article XX refutes at length the accusation that Lutheranism is against good works. It notes that the enemies of the Reformation have stopped putting works forward and speak rather more of faith.[40] It is shown that the negligence of the preachers and the troubles of the faithful have made preaching the doctrine of faith in Christ a matter of urgency. Such faith is not simply the "historic" faith (adherence to dogmas) which even the demons possess, but "such true faith as believes that we receive grace and forgiveness of sin through Christ. Whoever knows that in Christ he has a gracious God truly knows God." Faith "is a confidence in God and in the fulfillment of his promises"[41] (Heb. 11:1).

Independently of these points of doctrine, the Augsburg Confession treats "matters in dispute" and "abuses which have been corrected." The second part (Arts. XXII—XXVIII), understandably longer than the first, pleads for liberty, peace, and the consolation of consciences, while judging scandals and abuses severely. The following points which we can draw from these articles give a clear picture of the situation that brought about such a decisive change in the name of the Gospel.

—Communion in bread and wine is a command of Christ, which is the reason for holding on to it. Dividing the sign (by giving the bread without the wine) distorts the Sacrament. The Lutherans also abolished processions of the holy Sacrament which focus piety on the bread itself.[42]

—Marriage of priests should put an end to the notorious misconduct of the clergy who were "not able to remain continent," and to distressed consciences (Art. XXIII; Tappert, p. 51). Was not the estate of marriage instituted by God precisely to avoid unchastity? "God's word and command cannot be altered by any human vows or laws" (Tappert, p. 52). The tradition of ecclesiastical celibacy, in any case, had a history of no more than 400 years in Germany. Pope Pius II (1458—64) judged that "while there may well have been some reasons for prohibiting the marriage of clergymen, there were now more important, better, and weightier reasons for permitting them to be married" (Tappert, p. 53).

—The Mass was not abolished. Much care was taken to instruct the faithful about it and teach them to use it properly, "namely, as a comfort for terrified consciences" (Art. XXIV; Tappert, p. 56). German was used along with Latin because "the chief purpose of all ceremonies is to teach the people what they need to know about Christ" (ibid.). Private or venal masses, which were said only for money, were suppressed. "At the same time the abominable error was condemned according to which it was taught that our Lord Christ had by his death made satisfaction only for original sin, and had instituted the Mass as a sacrifice for other sins" (Tappert, p. 58). "The holy sacrament was not instituted to make provision for a sacrifice for sin—for the sacrifice had already taken place—but to awaken our faith and comfort our consciences."[43]

—"According to divine right, therefore, it is the office of the bishop to preach the Gospel, forgive sins, judge doctrine and condemn doctrine that is contrary to the Gospel, and exclude from the Christian community the ungodly whose wicked conduct is manifest. All this is to be done not by human power but by God's Word alone" (Art. XXVIII; Tappert, p. 84). The bishops have abused their charge, by grasping for temporal power or by doctrines or institutions contrary to the Gospel. "It is necessary to preserve the teaching of Christian liberty in Christendom, namely, that bondage to the law is not necessary for justification (Tappert, p. 89). Such errors were introduced into Christendom when the righteousness of faith was no longer taught and preached with clarity and purity" (Tappert, p. 92). The bishops must be required to "relax certain unreasonable burdens which did not exist in the church in former times and which were introduced contrary to the custom of the universal Christian church. Perhaps there was some reason for introducing them, but they are not adapted to our times" (Tappert, p. 93).

Such therefore, in broad outline, was the "program" envisaged in 1530 with a view to bringing the Church back to the purity of the Gospel. The demand of conscience which had led to the ignoring of Rome's interdicts no longer feared to attract public notice before imperial power. It rested chiefly in Scripture and the ancient tradition, in reaction against the innovations of the last centuries. The care to justify dissidence is evident, and there is a recognition that things have gone further than the law of the

Church would allow.[44] But the questions or objections which the Augsburg Confession raised do not take away its character as a witness to the eternal faith. In the circumstances, the signatories could not have had any other intention. The fact that their conception of an evangelical Church shattered the existing framework is explained in the first place by the newness of the questions that had to be resolved without delay. The question of the pope was passed over in silence, but then the Creed doesn't mention it either.[45] And above all, the Augsburg Confession, just like Luther's, in no way renounces one of the essential functions of the Church and of faith, that of denouncing heresy.

As it stood, it was a proposal for the whole Church. The question was—would the bond with Rome remain, even perhaps in the form of a painful dialog? The traditional theologians, also called together at Augsburg, adopted a resolutely hostile and negative attitude.[46] Even in the absence of the dogmatic precision which the Council of Trent expressed only much later, the representatives of the schools could at best concede to the "evangelical" faith only the status of a theological opinion. The disorders and heresies it provoked took any authority away from the Reformers, and the only stance to adopt was to attack everything they put forward. That had already been the position of the editors of the bull *Exsurge Domine* in 1520, with regard to Luther.

As for the Lutherans, they were doubtful about whether the whole Church was ranged on their side. They simply insisted on the liberty to comply with their convictions of conscience. Doubtless they can be reproached for not having taken the trouble to overcome their anti-Roman prejudices sufficiently to understand the viewpoint of the defenders of the papal position. But we have seen that Luther envisaged the disappearance of the Mass, and it seems that the signatories of the Augsburg Confession believed that time would bring about a trend towards their view. Only Melanchthon admitted the necessity of negotiating an agreement. While this corresponded to the desires of Charles V, who wanted to conclude matters by convoking a council, the situation was inevitably heading for a break.

In less than a decade, with the Smalcald Articles (1537), the point of no return was reached. This document,[47] which we owe to the major Lutheran theologians, was requested by the elector of Saxony, who was looking for a basis of discussion indicating what concessions were ruled out and what compromises were possible. In fact, what happened was a confirmation of what had already transpired at Augsburg, namely Luther's intransigence prevailing this time over Melanchthon's conciliatory views. From 1530 Luther saw no possible compromise between Christ and "Belial." He had made a clear judgment that the two pathways were incompatible.[48]

At that time the pope and the Mass became the points where the divergences crystalized. Luther made reference to his 1528 Confession as a standard. The Mass was again rejected as an expiatory sacrifice for sins committed after Baptism and also for the mediatory power it gives to the priest himself, since he celebrates it when he wants to. Luther denounced the Mass as the keystone of the papal system, which maintained a discretionary power over Christ, grace, and the faithful.

> This article concerning the Mass will be the decisive issue in the council. Even if it were possible for the papists to make concessions to us in all other articles, it would not be possible for them to yield on this article. It is as Campegio said in Augsburg: he would suffer himself to be torn to pieces before he would give up the Mass. So by God's help I would suffer myself to be burned to ashes before I would allow a celebrant of the Mass and what he does to be considered equal or superior to my Saviour, Jesus Christ. Accordingly we are and remain eternally divided and opposed the one to the other. The papists are well aware that if the Mass falls, the papacy will fall with it. Before they would permit this to happen, they would put us all to death.[49]

The pope was accused of substituting himself as head of the church, imposing as a necessity for salvation the dogma of papal primacy.[50] The arguments brought forward in support of these radical and frankly polemical views are not without interest, and the religious preoccupation is no pretense. But we cannot escape the impression that towards the end of Luther's life the perspective of the Gospel is clouded by the *rabies theologica*—the anger of controversy. There is no more communication, and the passions, sincere as they are, are not as lofty as the cause which each is defending. Was this the price of a Reformation of the Church by the Gospel—should it be carried out at any price?

The Smalcald Articles were written in the perspective of the council which everyone thought to be on the way. It could hardly be otherwise. While the Anglican schism was final from 1534,[51] there were still not many churches. Calvin was not yet master of Geneva. But the Church was troubled and without remedy. There was no other recourse than a council.

The policy of Charles V, who tried to prevent the final break, was to press for rapprochement and reconciliation, leaving the threat of a military repression of Protestantism to hang suspended all these years. This policy led to religious "colloquies" at Worms, Hagenau, and Ratisbon (1539—41),[52] the only effect of which was to show the incompatibility of the two positions. Participating Catholics were prepared to concede only priestly marriage, communion in both kinds, and eventually acceptance of the plundering of monastic property already lost. But Rome remained inflexible on the marriage of priests.

The failure of the colloquies at least proved the existence of a solid front, united in its refusal to go as far as the Protestants in the remodeling of Catholicism. That resistance came from those who recoiled before the prospect of mutilating and disfiguring tradition. Protestantism did not convince everyone of the harmfulness of what it was rejecting.[53] At the same time there was a feeling that the die was cast and the time had come for lawful authority to settle the matter.

7

The Faith
of the Papal Church

Luther studies have no purpose more important than to contribute to a positive resolution of the debate opened in the 16th century between the papal Church and Luther, the Reformation and Protestantism.[1] Most of the discussions today are pursued in other terms than before, and it would be of no interest to return to stages we have left behind. But everything points to the fact that the Church has still not really finished with Luther.

We have been able to see what appeared to be the basis of the Luther phenomenon: a unique perception, certainly a Biblical one, of the Gospel of Jesus Christ, received in faith, by the mediation of the Word and the grace of the Holy Spirit. It is there first of all that Luther makes an original contribution to our understanding of Christian faith. Whether he was followed or not, wrongly or rightly, the Church has no longer been the same. Beyond the Eucharistic presence, dear to the Catholic faith, Luther awakened the Christian world to the real presence of the Word of God, to which Protestantism is called to be witness.

This represents progress towards a better grasp of Luther's truth. We see in particular that Luther had not agonized all his life in the spiritual states which he tells us about. It was from his thought, nourished by the Bible, not from his moods, that the power of his activity within the Church derived. And the great significance of his life was that he stimulated an evangelical renewal of the late medieval Church. The Augsburg Confession shows how his action took shape and allows us to predict what the Gospel of justification by faith could have brought to the Roman Church since the 16th century. But the Council of Trent showed no openness at all to the viewpoint Luther had outlined, in his own distinctive way, but assuredly on the basis of the Bible. There is thus a place for trying in conclusion to go to the heart of this great debate which has to do less with the memory of Luther than with the cause of the visible unity of Christians as a condition for the manifestation of the Gospel to mankind today.

1. The Verdict of the Council of Trent

With Paul III (1534—49) a new type of pope appeared, resolved to attack head-on the problem of Church reform. He set up a commission which was able to set down, freely and without circumspection, a strong indictment of disorders and abuses at all levels of the Roman institution.[2] Then he set out on the path of a council despite the inconveniences and apprehensions accompanying such a solution.[3] After so many fruitless discussions his only wish was to put an end to the confusion and correct the most glaring abuses.

The council which opened at Trent, in Italy, on 13 Dec. 1545, two months before Luther's death, was an act of faith in the papal Church.[4] The question of the pope himself was definitely settled by unconditional submission to the authority of the Roman pontiff and his legates, which made superfluous all discussion about papal dogma. Full confidence was expressed in the conciliar institution. Thus Catholicism attended (a little late) to its own reformation, on the basis of its tradition and proven methods. Individual efforts of Reformers gave way to the common action of the bishops and the labors of the theologians.

The aim was to provide for the well-being of the Church, which had been undermined by an inward decadence (set out in such tragic detail in the report requested by Paul III) and by a wild and revolutionary reform. The council's business was to restore the authority of the papal and episcopal ministry, to attempt a dogmatic clarification, the necessity of which had been shown by the criticisms and the novelties of the Reformers, and to remedy scandals, discords, and abuses by a more effective reform than that of the Lateran Council. Though the Protestant Reformation was naturally among the foremost preoccupations of the council fathers, it was the Catholic faith which they had in view. The problems they took up were for the most part those raised by Luther and the Augsburg Confession, but the solution was sought in the Catholic interpretation of Scripture, the tradition of the fathers, the popes, and the councils, and the teaching of the theological schools recognized in the Church. The condemnation expressed by the bull *Exsurge Domine* always remained in force, and no one gave any thought to defending Lutheran ideas. Luther himself was not alluded to in the texts. He was consigned to oblivion, and it was still thought that the Protestants would detach themselves from him to return to communion with the Church.

The sessions of the first period dealt with Scripture and tradition, original sin, preaching, justification, the sacraments, episcopal residence, and ecclesiastical discipline. It was not by chance that the problem of authority in the Church was treated as a priority. The Reformers had set up the Scriptural principle in opposition to papal authority and contended for its primacy in matters of faith. The question in that radical form was new, for the authority of Scripture had always been admitted without requiring a limitation of the papal principle. The council's reflection dealt with the relationship of Scripture and tradition; while the unique value of the Scriptural revelation was not questioned, the last word was left to the pope in all disputes.[5]

The decree on original sin takes up the defense of human nature and free will and recognizes in man the power and the responsibility of freely doing good works. The ancient condemnation of Pelagianism was renewed against certain recent theological developments already denounced by Luther. But contrary to Luther, no contradiction was seen between that condemnation and the power of free will to do good.

The story of the long debates on justification is very moving,[6] for it witnesses at one and the same time to a real sensitivity to the problems discovered, thanks to Luther and the Reformation, and to the resistance of the Roman tradition to the ideas which threatened its power over the conscience. Agreement was reached on this declaration by the legate Cervini: "It is said that we are justified by faith because faith is the beginning of man's salvation, the basis and the root of all justification. For without faith it is impossible to please God (Heb. 11:6), to enter into community with the Son of God.'"[7] Luther would have subscribed to that, and it has been said many times that if the Tridentine decrees on justification had been adopted at the Lateran Council, the Reformation would have taken another course. But it took Luther to make the Roman magisterium think about the question![8]

However, the divergences remained numerous and important, notably because the Council of Trent worked in reference to the Aristotelian concept of human nature, whereas Luther described the justification of the person constituted in grace by the adherence of faith to the Word and promise of God.[9] The weight of medieval theology did not allow Trent to accede to Luther's Biblical theology, in which it saw a debased Augustinianism (there would be much to say on the ambiguous relationship of Catholicism to the Augustinian heritage). The Tridentine doctrine of faith is that of scholasticism, which Luther had rejected. He placed faith everywhere; the council was content to put it back "in its place," restoring things to their accepted order.[10]

Trent emerged from the whole matter without too much difficulty on the sacrifice of the Mass. The Mass is "the memorial and representation of the sacrifice of the cross, with the same high priest and the same offering, the two sacrifices differing only by the method of offering."[11] It is the application of the sacrifice of the cross to the remission of sins. While that doctrine let stand the theology and practice denounced by the Reformation, the Mass after Trent became a focus of religious fervor for the priests and the spiritual elite (while the common people often went along with it). The surprising thing is that Luther could believe and make others believe that it was a "horror."

The work of the Council of Trent, on which I cannot dwell very long, was marked less by originality than by a refinement of Church teaching.[12] The objections of the Reformers were not received as such. The procedure was to discuss controversial questions among people convinced that Catholic truth remained unchanged and that it was only a matter of better explaining and formulating "what has been believed by everyone, everywhere, and always." Everything that the Reformation had denied was reaffirmed and justified: free will and the merit of good works, the seven sacraments, the sacrifice of the Mass, the power of priestly orders, transubstantiation and the cult of the Holy Sacrament, the liturgy in Latin, monastic vows, and the intercession of the saints. Doctrines which did not conform were labeled as heresies by a long series of "anathemas."

With the closing of the council in 1563, the Roman Church reached the end, as far as it was concerned, of the crisis inaugurated by Luther's appearance. It took firmly in hand its dogma, its believers, and most of all its clergy.[13] The Protestant peril was effectively circumscribed, its development checked in Catholic areas. The beginnings of a splendid renewal were put into effect, and a reform of wide scope was undertaken. Abuses, to be sure, would not disappear so soon, and only in the long term would the council be accepted everywhere. But the whole Church would align itself progressively with the rule of faith and the Tridentine discipline.

The two notable effects of this council, which were to determine for a long time the new religious situation in the West, were the break of the Roman Church with everything, near or far, which evoked memories of Protestantism; and the advent of "Tridentine" Catholicism, freed from the burden of a reform which was out of control, and marked by strict discipline and a rigid orthodoxy. This new Catholic orthodoxy is one of the tangible fruits of the 16th-century crisis. It offered the image of a Church solidly anchored in its hierarchy, its dogma, and its cult. In the circumstances of a struggle which offered no other outcome at the moment, it represented the best possible situation, and we must credit some responsible Catholics for knowing how to preserve a type of Christianity which the Protestants abandoned. Inevitably, it came to the point where everyone had to take sides: either to be Catholic in the sense newly defined by Trent, or to be lost to the Catholic faith. That strategy made possible the rapid elimination of the assumption (not very probable) that the Roman faith would dissolve into Protestantism. Trent proved that Catholicism could remain perfectly viable instead of being "reformed" in the sense indicated by Luther. Besides, time has not decided in favor of Luther, either on the pope, or on the Mass, or on vows.[14] The papal principle in particular was able to affirm itself as the ultimate recourse against doctrinal chaos: the Council of Trent owed everything to the will of a few popes. Moreover, discussion of the questions raised by the Reformation in the light of traditional doctrine was imperative. That discussion was not to be found in Luther. We need to know just what arguments the Church, whose integrity had been questioned by Luther, had up its sleeve in response to Protestant ideas. Without a knowledge of these answers, we cannot understand Luther's thought or Protestantism.[15]

For the participants, to be sure, the Council of Trent appeared more than once to be a useless proceeding and even a defeat. The European powers sabotaged it as their interests dictated, and there was no assurance that Rome would follow through on the decisions, including those taken under duress. The aim of union with that part of the Church which had become Protestant came up against a growing hardening of attitude, as everyone perceived that differing conceptions of the Church were in confrontation with each other: papal and clerical on one side, Biblical and communal or national on the other.

Success came from many currents of renewal faithful to Rome, and of these the Jesuit order founded in 1534 remains the symbol. This Catholic reform provided the men who were needed for the council and who would ensure the application of reforming principles. Catholicism of the 16th and 17th centuries presents a curious paradox, of a host of saints and great churchmen face to face with a situation whose lamentable character their efforts only corrected in a very feeble way.

The fortunate result of the council and the strong decisions taken by the popes ensured, nevertheless, that things would be rectified. Thus everything was looking up from the point of view of the life and the future of Catholicism. Hence the triumphal feeling of a Church once again become sure of itself, which the extravagance and audacity of baroque art still evokes for us.

The great problem of the centuries which followed was, in fact, Catholic anti-Protestantism. Trent is mainly responsible for it, even if it was less anti-Protestant than anxious for orthodoxy. In recovering the clear sense of its identity against the Reformation, Catholicism could not avoid becoming a Counter-Reformation,[16] and that so much less because in the last period of the council Calvinism took over from Lutheranism and threatened to take France away from the Church, which had already lost Germany. In England the advent of Elizabeth had annihilated the hopes raised by the bloody Catholic reaction of Mary Tudor. Everything combined at this time to put the Roman faith on the defensive. On the other hand, the knowledge of having reestablished the full Catholic truth maintained the illusion that Protestantism would not last and that the heresy would in the end be reabsorbed. That was the calm certainty of Bossuet in the 17th century. It explains the violent reactions like those of Mary Tudor or the revocation of the Edict of Nantes by Louis XIV. If such a supposition were verified, if the Roman point of view had prevailed, everything would certainly be in agreement today. But in fact Protestantism is still there. The evangelical impulse has lost nothing of its mysterious fruitfulness, and it is impossible to represent the Reformation as a futile event. The Gospel of justification by faith in the Word of God, rejected by Rome, has been able to set up churches on all sides and to lead into faith peoples who would otherwise not have been evangelized. For without Luther and the Reformation, the Church would have stayed with the Lateran Council, and the report submitted to Paul III shows that it was scarcely ready to do what the Reformers achieved at the same time by relying on the Gospel.[17]

Thus for centuries we have been left with two rival solutions between which the Church of Reformation times was split. The religious history of the Christian West became one of two closed worlds, each firm in its own sense of right, and choosing to know nothing about the other, while slandering it at the same time and heaping up treatises of self-justification. These centuries have been a golden age for polemic and apologetic, of verbal rivalry which could degenerate into bloody conflicts: There were Protestant martyrs right down to the French Revolution. Proselytism made missions beyond Europe flourish while European society was fed up with religion and turned towards rationalism. It was an uncertain situation, unresolved, yet in its way productive to a considerable extent.[18] The crisis had at least produced two fruitful formulations of Christian life.[19] But today we still accept the Church divided into Catholicism and Protestantism. Divided Christianity has lost out to secularization. Too preoccupied with the past, the churches have been unable to see new questions. The Gospel has been supplanted in historic Christianity by a messianism more in touch with reality: Marxism.

A thaw began at the beginning of the 20th century, with the ecumenical movement, born in a Protestant setting out of the shame of sensitive consciences in the face of persistent division. Rome at first could see in it only a new form of Protestant subversion. But she could not remain insensitive to that awakening of an awareness of the visible Church which Luther had not had, yet which was very close to her own. Since Vatican II the rapprochement progressed and, symptomatically, in the former terms: While the Protestant world, heir to the Gospel, opened itself to the demands of the Church which it had disregarded since Luther, the Roman Church discovered a new evangelical pathway. We have thus returned to the problem with which we began before the break, but in a new form.

Now the division has remained no less insurmountable, and ecumenism marks time, so much so that, in concluding this section on Trent, it is brought home to us that the council could only bequeath us a poorly handled problem still waiting for a better solution. Catholicism's response to Luther's faith represents an attempt that could not go as far as the situation demanded.

2. From Trent to Vatican II: The Non-Gospel in the Church

It cannot be too greatly regretted that Rome was not grasped by the question of the Gospel from the moment it was raised by Luther.[20] Thus was lost the only acceptable response to the problem whose urgency was unceasingly accentuated by the course of events. If it was no longer in the papacy's power to slow up the change which suddenly occurred around 1520, it had the best chance of positively influencing the future of the Church by itself taking in hand an evangelical reform, for which Luther's ideas were arousing so much support. It should have avoided giving historical permanence to the rejection at Worms. In acting as it did, it allowed what could have remained a salutary pressure on Rome and the pope to harden into an antipapal revolt. The break between the dynamic force which carried Luther along and the Church to which his preaching of the Gospel was directed—a break which was the act of the Roman magisterium, whatever were Luther's wrong attitudes, faults, and errors—caused the irresistible force of faith in the Christ of justification to overflow into blind violence. It did so because it was deprived of its proper focus, the traditional Church, which alone had the power to stem the tide of impetuosity.

Was it so difficult to discern the lucid diagnosis made by Luther and the Augsburg Confession on the state of the Church, despite the unjust criticism, the polemic, and the arbitrary innovations? Among the people faith in merits and in the intercession of the saints was, in fact, supplanting faith in the benefits of Christ. The new sense of a personal and living relationship to the Risen One, "the sole priest of our souls," which came to light with Luther responded to a genuine need.[21] Theology no longer showed forth the Biblical promises; the Word of God was stifled by the doctrines of men, and faith was turning into superstition. The abundance of priests and monks in no way overcame the poverty of evangelical content in the Christian life and in preaching. Scholasticism, moreover, had dried up the teaching about faith. Since Julius II the papacy was making war to consolidate its temporal power in Italy. It was a far cry from the Gospel.

The Reformation showed that the weak point of the Church lay in its relationship to the Gospel. It prospered or declined in terms of this relationship, which is the savor in the salt (Matt. 5:13). But the Gospel has never won the day in the Church.

The Council of Trent did not really grasp this point. It cannot be denied that it had what amounted to a sincere evangelical concern, but it created for a long time a cold-war Catholicism, authoritarian and tyrannical over the conscience, obsessed by heresy. In the shadows of the dogmatic Iron Curtain intended to prevent Catholics from yielding to the allure of the Protestant sirens (Scripture alone, faith alone, the Word of God) the Roman power after Trent jealously watched over faith and morals, through the Inquisition, the Holy Office, the Index, papal nuncios, not to mention the priests. The "anathemas" made it possible to disqualify as heretical every divergence, every sign of opposition. The free creative expression of Catholic truth was tolerated only in strict conformity with orthodoxy and the official ideology. Research was suspect. The cult of the Holy Sacrament maintained among the common people devotion to the papal throne. Anti-Protestantism did not shrink from persecution: The revocation of the Edict of Nantes (1685) with its persecution aimed at extorting the "final" conversions is the eloquent symbol of the sectarianism and fanaticism of a religion of fear and intimidation, which many today feel to their confusion was less sure of itself than could have been thought possible.[22]

Moreover, the vitality of this Catholicism was sapped. The Church did not recover from the amputation of such an important part of itself, and not the least devout part. Protestant evangelism continued the awakening of the "New Devotion" which was already touching the fringes of hardened ecclesiastical structures.[23] Values which had borne fruit in Protestantism but had become suspect in Catholic circles, though originating there, were not to be seen—heartfelt faith, Christian freedom, Biblical piety, and the study of the Scriptures at school or in the family.[24] The Law stifled the Gospel, the discipline of works led to a disregard for the holiness of faith and gave rise to legalism, doubt, and often much hypocrisy. The Church of Rome boasted of its "intact" faith, but the parish clergy were left with an audience of children whose perseverance was not assured and women who occupied themselves during the Mass by telling their rosaries.

It was this Church which "lost the working class" in the 19th century, according to Pius XI. While the excesses of capitalism stimulated the rise of Marxism, the papacy looked for a remedy for the evils of the age in a new stiffening of doctrine (the Syllabus), devotion to the pope, and Marian piety. Today Christians look to socialism for the hope for a better world which they no longer expect from the Church.

The Catholic faith was certainly able to preserve its position and never failed to awaken a goodly number of believers to the Gospel. From this point of view it bears comparison with any other strand of Christianity, for things were no longer always rosy in Protestant parishes. But even assuming the best, there still remained the problem of patterns of thought and action that were strangers to the Gospel, thought officially maintained by the Church from the time of the Crusades.

It would be a mistake to be shocked by this. From New Testament times it is clear that the Gospel will find its greatest obstacles in the Church, for conversion to the Word of God is so much more a way of crucifixion than has been recognized. Protestantism itself has not been able to maintain the level that it criticized Rome for not attaining. The Church is no less "sinful and righteous" than its members. Despite its sanctity and infallibility, it remains always in need of reform. Luther's originality was to discern that reformation is not first of all a matter of correcting abuses or adaptation. The problem is always basically the obsession with the Law to the detriment of the Gospel. The Church cannot boast of its zeal and its virtues. What draws our faith to it is its commitment to the Gospel, and primarily in relation to itself. It was evidence of this that the Christians of the Reformation despaired of receiving from papal Rome.

Catholicism needed time to awaken to the questions posed by the development of the Church under the influence of the feudal mentality and of Aristotelian scholasticism. The demand for a reform in the *head* as in the members indicated that the trouble came from the top. Medieval and Renaissance Rome, thirsty for power and money, and prisoner of its own pleasures, could not willingly countenance the unsettling impact of the Gospel. It would need the pressure of events. In particular, there was little hope that the papacy would take up what Leo X called a monkish quarrel, for it had learned to distrust evangelical radicalism, which stirred up in turn new religious orders and more or less revolutionary movements of dissidence (Waldensians, Savonarola). A council that had not paid proper attention to the questions which the Luther of the indulgences was raising had just broken up. A condemnation of his ideas appeared all the more justified because they raised doubts about the purity of his motives, and because many were interpreting them in an anti-Roman sense. The test of strength which followed gave to the claim of the Gospel the appearance of a pretext. As far as the Roman curia was concerned, it was the authority of the pope that was under attack. The deplorable turn taken by the affair thrust its logic on the situation, which had to be played out to the end.

The Council of Trent took place in circumstances that left no choice but to reestablish as a priority the cohesion of the Church around the pope and purity of doctrine. It sought to rely on tradition. But the concern to preserve the "revealed deposit" could not but prevent recognition of the contribution of the new Biblical understanding and the promise of God for a renewal of the Gospel and a liberating critique of the Church. Trent had the methods, conceptions, and prejudices of the theology of the day, and the Protestants did not know how to seize the opportunity that was offered them to come there to plead the cause of evangelical faith.

The result could have been foreseen given the state of Catholicism, that is to say, an exercise of hierarchical authority consistent with its mission, a reform which represented progress on its former negligence, and more important, a strong attempt to reinforce orthodoxy, which is characteristic of the papal function. That was all that the Roman institution was able to derive from the questions arising out of Luther's discovery, after conflict had entered into the situation. And the blame for this conflict may be found more in the heedlessness of Leo X than in the monk's revolt.

The Council of Trent was unable to perceive the change from one age to another which individual appropriation of the Word of God would translate into the pathway openly taken by Luther: The Christian came of age and became conscious of his liberty before God. The rallying to the Scriptural principle was also the awakening of the sense of the universality of the Gospel, clearly perceptible in the Lutheran idea of the Church as "without frontiers" rather than "invisible." That represented a protest against the development of the papacy, since the break with the Eastern Church, into the governing factor in the Western politico-religious system. The discovery was made that the inspired texts did not confirm the dogmas and institutions of the medieval papacy and that they spoke of realities which had long disappeared from the consciousness of the Church.

In excluding the Protestants and what they represented, Catholicism became incapable of confronting such problems. The opening of the Church to the world, a world subject to ceaseless change, was jeopardized for centuries. Trent wagered on Renaissance humanism, choosing Erasmus against Luther without seeing that the canonization of free will and the ideal of individual perfection was a choice for the elite and a principle of alienation from the masses. The missions transplanted among various people that ideology of post-Tridentine Catholic Europe, often in defiance of all evangelical liberty (as in the condemnation of the Chinese rite).

A famous engraving by Lucas Cranach illustrates the gulf which Catholicism has never been able to overcome: at the left Catholic man, oppressed by the Law and aided in heaven by the intercession of the saints. Protestant man, by contrast, has regard only for Christ, represented by the bronze serpent, the Virgin Birth, the Crucifixion, the victorious Lamb, and receives every grace directly from the cross.

The problem, undoubtedly, was too new for anyone to take its measure in the space of a generation or two. Too many things had to be taken up again, as was shown by Luther's confession of faith at the end of his *Confession Concerning Christ's Supper*, by the Augsburg Confession, and by the few paragraphs on the work of the Council of Trent. It was a difficult task which no one has really mastered, some drawing from the Gospel exaggerated conclusions, others stiffening the principle of the hierarchical institution. It needed a longer experience of what the demands of the Gospel entail for a Church which had developed for centuries in another spirit altogether, and a period of waiting to see the Protestant communions give proof of their vitality. The Church of Rome had to take cognizance of the distortion and impoverishment which the total division of the Reformation entailed for it. The myth of a Catholicism unchangeable in the face of cultural change had to vanish. Trent could only be a first response, calling for a sequel.

It was only with Vatican II that Catholicism began to open itself freely to the critique of the Gospel. Pope Pius XII had still continued to hold back the inquiries which were called forth here and there by the demands of a world that was rapidly changing (Teilhard de Chardin, worker-priests). His successor, the evangelical John XXIII, better placed than Luther, was able to do what the Reformer had dreamed of: to have the Church under its own impetus enter the pathway of a return to the Word of God, by giving attention to the Bible, evangelical poverty, and the humble obedience of faith (Rom. 1:5). This fact has not escaped notice in Protestant circles and has left a lasting impression.

With a new consciousness of the Gospel. Vatican II applied itself to a broad self-examination about the Church and her mission,[25] and developed a renewed conception of the Church as people of God,[26] with emphasis on the common priesthood of the baptized. That idea, close to the community of believers of Luther and the Augsburg Confession, has made it possible more clearly to mark the servant character of the hierarchical ministry and has created a new spirit. The Church has taken on the aspect of the "humble and poor servant in the process of ridding itself of the royal finery with which the covetousness and guile of men— including Christians—had clothed it, effectively stifling the voice of the Gospel."[27] The sense of evangelical poverty has brought a reaction against "Constantinian" (in fact Roman-Germanic and Tridentine) triumphalism, and a spectacular change of style in the clergy. Papal absolutism has been tempered by the recognition of the proper mission of the bishops. The Word of God has regained ground over the doctrines of men in a way that has not been seen for a long time. The celebration of the liturgy in the language of the people has once more given back a solid base to evangelization (was it necessary to wait four centuries after Luther to stop saying Mass in Latin?) and has favored a renewal of preaching and catechizing. Concern about mission, first of all in Christian lands, that is in the Church, has involved throwing institutions and the clergy into an examination of the concept of mission. High society, which honored the priest as a leading figure, now turns away from him, for he is no longer seen as an agent of the establishment. At the same time Vatican II defined a Catholic doctrine of ecumenism with an openness unthought-of before. One would have to go far back into the past to find a comparable awareness of what had become clear to Luther, the knowledge that the Church is nothing without the Gospel.

The confusion after the Council is explained, as in the 16th century, by the explosion of the Gospel into a Gospel-starved situation. Conversion to the Gospel does not occur by itself today, any more than formerly, and it is not without its problems. It is clear that every move towards a recovery of the Gospel reverberates profoundly within the structures of the Church. Clericalism comes under indictment once more, and with it the pursuit of the sacred for its own sake, doctrinal abstractions, the monarchical style of the papacy (which clearly does not stem from the early Church), and a conception of the Church which is more juridical than communal. Some groups look for the Gospel without the Church, but the lesson of the Reformation has not been lost: This time it is within the Church that the evangelical renewal of the Catholic faith is being accomplished.

That transformation runs foul of some still important after-effects of the Counter-Reformation. Movements more Catholic than the pope condemn the changes brought in by the demands of poverty and evangelical liberty or by the necessities of mission. Everything that recalls Luther, near or far, is assimilated to the ideas condemned at Trent. In the name of the integrity of faith, life is arrested at a period already past, confusing tradition and the letter, ideals and ideology. The facile slogan of "Protestantization" is bandied about. However, there has never been the least danger that Rome would become Protestant, and we now see why. On the contrary, today's resistance to the Council under the pretext of stopping heresy and disorder proves that the Counter-Reformation's long-drawn-out delaying tactics are continuing to damage the Church.

What kind of reform? That question, which was the question of many sincere Christians, called for a response which neither Protestantism nor the Counter-Reformation has provided: the former, because effecting a reformation of the Roman Church without and outside Rome was out of the question; the latter, because the problem of the Gospel in the Church was passed over too quickly. Vatican II's change of direction allows us to recognize what kind of reform was at stake from the beginning: an evangelical reform carried out by Rome itself, seeing that it would not accept Lutheranism. But, on the other hand, the often risky upheavals of the Reformers show that the Church of the 16th century could not practically take up the process of reform without a doctrinal preliminary. This was Trent's objective, and everything depended on that. The second opportunity that Vatican II represented was able to benefit from the Tridentine clarification to go more deeply into the matter. It had to wait so long only because of the old anti-Protestant obsession. There had to be another historic turning point, the transition to the atomic age, which once more reshaped the given politico-social realities within which Christians have to translate the eternal message of the Gospel.

Moreover, Vatican II opened a new period of debate between Catholicism and Protestantism for it created an alternative to the disappointing ecumenical discussions as they existed then. These discussions, derivative of the whole problem which had been distorted from the beginning by the condemnation of Luther, were bogged down every bit as much as the fruitless colloquies prior to the Council of Trent. The doctrinal definitions of Trent and of Protestant orthodoxy allow no concessions,[28] and the contentious dogmatics between the Churches are even less negotiable today than then. There is nothing to be expected from a revision of dogma. One cannot imagine Rome going back on Trent in order to model itself on Luther.[29]

But in fact the dogmatic formulas are not in themselves obstacles to unity. They are irreplaceable, for they allow each one to know what he is as a Christian and what he owes to his own tradition. The difficulty is not dogmatic formulae as such, but rather the lack of an element capable of liberating their productive potential beyond confessional boundaries in the same way as it is already at work within them. Catholicism was given such a liberator in Vatican II. If we consider the decisive role the papal opposition to the Reformation has played so far, Rome's sudden change in its awareness of the Gospel can only appear as the element that has always been lacking. It gives the lie to the notion that the Roman tradition has totally lost the meaning of the Gospel or any capacity to imbibe new views, as Luther and the Reformers believed. It can be the turning point for unity, for it indicates that the Catholic Church can defend the same dogmas on the basis which served for the elaboration of Protestant dogmatics.

The Roman synod on evangelization and Paul VI's exhortation *Evangelii nuntiandi* (1974—75) have shown a little more of what Catholicism can do itself, in its own style and without denying anything of its tradition or its dogmatic experience,[30] to answer the questions which the Reformers discerned and which have reappeared with an astounding consistency because they cannot be stifled for long. This postconciliar experience is the principal subject of all Catholic literature today. Concern for the Church and for humanity joins forces with the fervor of witness to Jesus

Christ. What is lacking is a greater comprehension of the mechanisms—political or sociological, psychological and also ideological—that shape the opposition between the institution and the Gospel.

Our study of Luther's faith allows us to understand in what respect this often confused research is a new form of the battle against the "non-Gospel" in the Church. While the perspective of the Law no longer has as much place in the consciousness of Catholicism, it appears every bit as omnipresent in the way ecclesiastical power is conceived and exercised. The authoritative prohibition of the Mass of St. Pius V and the occupation by commandos of the Church of St. Nicholas of Chardonnet are eloquent demonstrations of the difficulty churchmen have in putting their confidence in the instrumentality of the Gospel. Jesus could have called to the rescue more than a dozen legions of angels when He was arrested (Matt. 26:53). Ecclesiastical politics often still uses the methods of earthly powers in pursuing the objectives of Jesus, a practice against which many people across the world rise in revolt. The price to be paid for this stepping outside the ways of the Gospel is heavy, for man's disappointment with the Church leads him most often to atheism.

Conciliar Catholicism still seems scarcely conscious of what is at stake. It exerts itself in every way to respond to the problems of humanity and of the world in order to convert others. But it still has a long way to go itself. It will take time for Scripture to be accorded the place that belongs to it in the teaching of the magisterium in preference to the comforting repetition of traditional texts perpetuating formulae born out of violent situations. Legislation is spelled out interminably, as if the great problem were not that people today are expecting the Church to know what it has to say for itself as the Church of Christ.

At the synod on evangelization the representative of South America declared that "Latin America is a people essentially Marian." While declaring that our light "is called Christ," he added that this light "appeared and shone through Mary."[31] Is that form of discourse about faith still adapted to the needs of popular religion, the problems of social justice, or the abandonment of religious practices which is so universal in the most Catholic continent of the world no less than in the others? One cannot deviate with impunity from the pure apostolic preaching. It is to the Word of God that the faithful must be tied in a time when the results of the Church's word become less and less convincing. "Blessed . . . are those who hear the Word of God and keep it!" (Luke 11:27).

After the experience of the Council of Trent and its consequences it is unthinkable that the heart of the Church's preaching could be anything other than the Gospel of justification by faith, despite the condemnations of other times or the views of such exegetes as O. Kuss and G. Bornkamm. Luther had found in this formula "a dogma which had effectively safeguarded orthodox faith and practice in apostolic times."[32] In his time he was opposed by the morality of free will and works. Today individualism is blamed, or the Lutherans' lack of social and political zeal.

> For a long time, the polemic against the spiritual stance of the Reformation developed on two fronts: Catholicism interpreted justification by faith in the sense of an under-estimation of man's possibilities and as the reduction of salvation to a purely inward dimension which does not change personal behaviour; humanism and atheism, on the other hand, doubtless encouraged by certain individual or collective examples of Protestants, have frequently seen in it a principle of social irresponsibility and the source of a morality of defeat, gloom and renunciation accompanied in the background by a secular activity of enrichment and austerity favouring the birth of capitalism.[33]

Salvation is also justice in the world, certainly, and it is true that Luther's reformation was not a social reform. But it is basically to the Bible (and not only in St. Paul) that Luther went to look for his teaching. It is in the light of the Bible that he invited the Christian to submit himself to grace, to recognize in faith the absoluteness of God—the mercy of the saving God as a remedy against fear and as the source of liberty. His convictions are those of the eternal faith.[34] It is on this level that the struggle of the Reformation developed. For it is in the privacy of personal freedom that the reality for which Christ died is settled: that God should be God.

We must hope that Catholicism will discover more clearly the priority of the struggle for the Gospel in the Church over all other objectives of conciliar reform. On this path it can travel fraternally beside Protestants and witness in a way plausible in their eyes to dogmas of which it feels itself to be the guardian. This is a task altogether different from accommodating the past or wanting to reconcile the irreconcilable. The method of unity is to build on the base which has always been lacking before.

The obstacle will in every case remain the resistance of men—churchmen, but not only churchmen—to the Word of God. If Luther lacked the qualities of transparent sanctity displayed by some of the great saints of his age, he remains nevertheless the man who led the Church back to the only struggle which is truly her own. The fact that he did it in his own way, "unilaterally" (according to Lortz), does not take away from him the merit of having discerned such a problem and undertaken the action which governed everything that followed. He belongs to the universal Church because he personifies, perhaps like no other man, the cause of the Gospel in the Church.

His writings retain their value not only for the historian of theology but as a critical analysis of Catholicism on a host of questions that have hardly changed in four centuries. But above all Luther can, in incomparable fashion, show in the Gospel the precious pearl for which everything else is freely surrendered.

Obdurate dogmatism detects in what he calls "evangelism" something empty and suspect. But who does not see the artificial character of the opposition which some want to make between "belief in Jesus Christ" and faith in orthodoxy?[35] Faith is in Jesus Christ alone. He is our Truth, our Way, and our Life.

We know only too well the point of no return. It remains for us to say where we want to go.

3. Liberating the Gospel Within the Church

The cause of the Gospel in the Church is today more pressing than ever, for the Gospel is in jeopardy not in the world but first of all in Christian circles.

Investigations alert us to the decline of faith. But faith comes from preaching (Rom. 10:17). If Christians do not believe, it is because sermons are not fulfilling their function. "'Everyone who calls upon the name of the Lord will be saved.' But how are men to call upon him in whom they have not believed? And how are they to believe in him of whom they have never heard? And how are they to hear without a preacher?" (Rom. 10:13-14).

Stripped of value by its obsolete style, or by the pursuit of novelties which do nothing for anyone, Christian discourse succumbs too often to the terrorism of the experts. All those who speak on the air or write in the press, the professionals of publicity and selling techniques, seem scarcely bothered at all by the discoveries of psychoanalysis, structuralism, materialistic exegesis, and so on. But one hardly dares speak of the Gospel or clearly announce justification by faith in Christ.

The Church must find once more the dual form of discourse which is indispensable to her transmission of the message which is hers and which she alone can deliver: the prophetic and apostolic message which condemns and consoles, which encourages and frees. The Christ who is present in His Word must be liberated.

Justice within the world originates more than is thought in the righteousness of God, despite all the reproaches brought against Luther. Slogans like "the Church of the poor" or "the poor servant-Church" call for a theology of the cross, to dismantle power within the Church. For it is power which everywhere produces poverty and upholds injustice. Justification as "God's act within history" (Casalis) is born of the powerlessness of the cross. The Church has no other "power" than the Word of the Gospel.

The time has come also for the exodus of the churches from confessional securities towards the promised land of evangelical communion. We shall discover just how much the Christian tribes are *together* the people of God. Our generation is nearer to the realization of the promises than those who have gone before. The past should not immobilize us. Faith is what unites rather than divides us. It is time to bring to an end a thousand years of history, to throw off the narrowness and self-sufficiency which has marked our confessional allegiances, and deliberately to turn ourselves towards the future.

Luther will always be the business of specialists. But the attempt to make his most accessible writings known will be imperative, so that he will perennially remain one of our best witnesses to the apostolic message. He had the genius of the *viva vox evangelii*, the living voice of the Gospel. He knew, as no other man did, how to address the Christian about that which alone makes him truly Christian. He rediscovered the secret of the message of faith addressed to the individual in order to convert him and make him a believer. With a sure sense of the one thing needful he staked everything on personal faith in Christ, which we receive from God. The greatest shortcoming in the Church always concerns its attachment to Christ.

Faith in Christ reveals that God, by virtue of his promise, is present in the Christian life through his Son and Spirit. He fashions the heart and very being of the believer according to his law and pardons his sins. The preaching of the Gospel declares this work of grace openly to all, and arouses in the heart living faith in the divine promise. This message is the substance of the first Reformer's reflection and teaching, as this book has tried to show. One can be disconcerted by the many practical applications Luther draws from it, scandalized by the positions he takes up, his mistakes in doctrine and language, his contradictions. But who has not learned to distinguish in every human life between the essential impulse and everything else? Luther lived only to plead within the Church for a new union with Christ.

Catholicism at the end of the 20th century, after Vatican II, is perhaps for the first time able to grasp the providential significance of the vocation of a Luther—called as he was by circumstances to make himself the advocate of the Gospel within the Church, disregarding all obstacles and objections—and finally to draw out from that Gospel the real lessons for the future of the Church and the common faith.

In this ongoing debate there was an urgent need for a Christian perspective which dissociates itself from the Church when that Church ceases to be seen as the pure creation of the Gospel. For 20 years that has been the entire justification for my Luther studies, which have become, as far as I am concerned, the concrete expression of the ministry of the Gospel within the Church.

Paris, Epiphany 1978

Notes

Introduction

1. Translator's note: The author refers here to "l'affaire d'Ecône," using the name of the remote Swiss seminary where this movement originated. As this terminology is unfamiliar to English readers, I have translated these references by using the name of the leader of the dissident movement, Archbishop Marcel Lefebvre (b. 1905).
2. This confessional language, which I use here deliberately, conveys the reality of our divisions and can disappear only with them.
3. Translator's note: This book appeared as No. 27 of a series of books dealing with key theological issues, under the general theme *Le point théologique* (Editions Beauchesne, Paris).
4. Cf. the annual bibliography of the *Lutherjahrbuch*, published since 1919, now at Göttingen.
5. Cardinal Willebrands' address at Evian. See Daniel Olivier, *Le procès Luther* (Paris, Fayard, 1971), pp. 216—18.
6. Cf. Richard Stauffer, *Luther as Seen by Catholics* (Richmond, John Knox, 1967).
7. At the Diet of Augsburg (1530) John Eck listed more than 400, following the example of the pope himself, who had denounced without explanation 41 of Luther's theses in the bull *Exsurge Domine* (15 June 1520).
8. Joseph Lortz, *The Reformation in Germany*, 2 vols. (New York, Herder, 1968), I, 218; cf. Erwin Iserloh, "Luther in Contemporary Catholic Thought," *Concilium*, Vol. 4, No. 2 (April 1966), pp. 4—9.
9. Otto H. Pesch, "L'état actual de l'entente," *Concilium*, 118 (1976), p. 147. (Translator's note: As far as I can determine, this volume of *Concilium*, devoted to Luther, has not been translated into English.)
10. Cf. W. Michaelis, "Les controverses autour de la levée de l'excommunication de Luther," *Concilium*, 118 (1976), pp. 123—40.
11. Hubert Jedin, cited by Pesch, ibid., p. 155.
12. Vignaux introduced me to the experience of reading Luther in the light of 14th—15th-century theology. Fr. Congar was responsible for my entry to the "Lortz school" at the Institute of European History, Mainz.
13. The Luther of my previous book, *Le procès Luther (1517—21)* (Paris, 1971); trans. *The Trial of Luther* (St. Louis, Concordia, 1978), benefited from the picture I had gained of him through his writings. In a trial like this, the accused necessarily has the best role. Some of my Catholic colleagues took an adverse view of this book, with a trace of meanness which I am not the first to point out. The public, however, was not deceived by it.

Chapter 1

1. The history of the last few centuries—politics, ideology, and thought—would have been totally different if Luther had retracted at Worms. His reformation

169

eliminated from history the possibility of a modern age still under Roman sway and experiencing the unity of faith.

2. Cf. Jean Delumeau in *2000 ans de christianisme*, 5 (1976), p. 5.

3. Cf. Pierre Chaunu, *Le temps des réformes* (Paris, 1975).

4. Jacques Maritain, *Three Reformers: Luther, Descartes, Rousseau* (London, 1944).

5. "The Reformation, far more than a revolt against Catholic faith, was its culmination and its full flowering." E. G. Léonard, *A History of Protestantism*, 2 vols. (London, Nelson, 1965), I, 4.

6. "The Reformation was caused by the disintegration of the basic principles and basic forms upon which the Middle Ages were built." Joseph Lortz, *The Reformation in Germany* (New York, 1968), I, 8.

7. Delumeau, op. cit., pp. 5 and 17. Cf. also by Delumeau, *Naissance et affirmation de la Réforme* (Paris, 1965), and *Catholicism Between Luther and Voltaire* (London, 1977), chs. 4 and 5.

8. The Church of Rome was able to train the generation of the Reformation towards this exclusive passion for faith, without which Luther's message would have fallen on deaf ears. The abuses were no worse than in other times, and they were not the kind of abuses which motivated the assault on the doctrinal authority of the pope. Their importance lay in the fact that that Church, at the point where its very being was at stake, was not responding sufficiently to religious needs.

9. Cf. R. Esnault, *Luther et le monachisme aujourd'hui* (1964).

10. C. V. Gheorgiou describes the climate in which Luther grew up very well in *La jeunesse du Dr. Luther* (1965).

11. Translators note: These early lectures are to be found in the American Edition of *Luther's Works*, as follows: Psalms, vols. 10—11; Romans, vol. 25; Galatians, vol. 27; and Hebrews, vol. 29.

12. Tradition has it that he posted his theses on the door of the Castle Church in Wittenberg, where, on All Saints' Day, relics were venerated to gain indulgences. The *95 Theses* have been made into a declaration of war on the Roman Church: In the culture of the time a challenge of this kind was the occasion for a public act of provocation. But E. Iserloh has shown that Luther never mentions the event of the posting. In 1517 it had not come to a revolt against the pope. His theses against scholastic theology (4 Sept. 1517; LW 31, pp. 9—16) had had no echo in public opinion. How could he imagine that those which followed would arouse the crowds? A Luther in revolt would have imitated the *Letters of Obscure Men* (1515—17), the anti-Roman pamphlet which emerged from humanist circles.

    The public got to know of the *95 Theses* through a leak. The printers scented a good issue. In a few weeks the theses were everywhere. Iserloh has at least made the point that a damper should be put on the tradition—for him legendary—of the posting. 31 Oct. 1517 remains the birthday of the Reformation because of the letter addressed that day by Luther to the Archbishop of Mainz, which set in motion the Roman proceedings against Luther (LW, 48, pp. 43—49).

    [See E. Iserloh, *The Theses Were Not Posted* (London, Chapman, 1961), translated from the second German edition, for Iserloh's argument and a bibliography of major contributions to the debate. K. Aland, in *Martin Luther's 95 Theses* (St. Louis, Concordia, 1967), has assembled all the key documentary evidence bearing on the issue.]

13. D. Olivier, *The Trial of Luther* (St. Louis, Concordia, 1978).

14. LW, 46, pp. 49—55; cf. F. Engels, *The Peasant War in Germany* (English translation, London, 1927). This work, written in 1850, opened up the Marxist

"trial" of Luther, who was judged guilty for not being free of the political and social prejudices of his class.

15. This marriage has scandalized Catholics. But it was in the first instance the vicar-general Staupitz who released Luther from his vows in Oct. 1518, to protect him from coming under the sanction of the Augustinian order. Before the crisis Luther seemed never to have thought of leaving the monastery (WA TR, 4, p. 440, No. 4707, July 1539). Katharine von Bora was one of those frequent cases of young girls put into convents by their families.

16. He was sent to Rome, in the company of a colleague, to bring grievances against Staupitz, but the mission was unsuccessful and on his return he rallied to Staupitz's defense. This journey left him with unedifying memories of papal Rome. At Heidelberg Luther was commissioned as vice-provincial, to which post he had been elected in 1515. See Heidelberg Disputation theses in LW 31, 39—70. Luther's account of the Augsburg proceedings, where he made his first refusal to retract, is to be found in LW 31, 259—92.

17. On Luther's portraits cf. E. G. Schwiebert, *Luther and His Times* (1951), pp. 573 ff. Luther was of medium height. In 1519 he was only skin and bone. He had a clear voice and a piercing ("demonic") glance, fluent speech, great learning, and he knew the Bible by heart. He could be caustic, but was generally even-tempered, affable, and gregarious.

18. The religious orders are one of the Church's sources of living strength. The Savonarola episode indicated that reform would come from the monastic stream (there were many monks among the Reformers) and that it would be revolutionary. Florence was the home of the future Pope Leo X, who had to flee the Dominican's dictatorship. When Luther appeared, 30 years later, Leo X saw in him the spark which threatened the Church with a new conflagration.

19. "The humanist reading of Scripture was not a sufficient condition for the beginnings of the Reformation. A religious revolution can only be born out of deeper waters. The beginnings of the outbreak and the breakup presupposed something more and better than Erasmian knowledge, or even a questioning of the basis of dogma and the institutional structure of the visible Church—it required the anguish of salvation, it needed more than reformers, a 'prophet.'" (Chaunu, p. 362). Cf. Léonard, I, 8—26.

20. Pierre Imbart de la Tour, *Les origines de la Réforme*, 3 (1914), p. 32.

21. Franz Xaver Kiefl, "Martin Luthers Religiöse Psyche" in *Hochland* 15.1 (1917—18), pp. 7—28.

22. From the Roman point of view the indulgence affair appeared like a resurgence of the Hussite heresy (see above, n. 18). At the Leipzig debate (1519) John Eck obliged Luther to recognize that he was taking up the ideas of Hus, Wyclif's heir.

23. Translator's note: For an account of the manuscript's history see LW, 25. pp. xii—xiii, or *Library of Christian Classics*, XV (Philadelphia, 1961), xxiii—xxiv.

24. Heinrich Denifle, *Luther und Luthertum in der ersten Entwicklung quellenmässig dargestellt*, 2 vols. (Mainz, 1904/9), completed after the author's death by P. Weiss, O.P. A partial English translation, *Luther and Lutherdom*, was published in Somerset, Ohio (1911), and a French translation of the entire first part was done by J. Paquier, *Luther et le Luthéranisme*, 4 vols. (Paris 1910—16). Cf. K. A. Meissinger, *Der katholische Luther* (1952), pp. 276—81; L. Febvre, *Un destin: Martin Luther* (1968), p. 14.

25. Hartmann Grisar, *Luther*, 3 vols. (Freiburg/Breisgau, 1911—12). Grisar initiated a "moderate" stance, in tone if not in content, in Luther interpretation in Catholic circles. The quality of his documentation gained him a large following. We owe to him the popularization of the (apocryphal) story (cf.

Meissinger, pp. 303—304) that Luther discovered the Gospel in the privy. He also raised the question of the Reformer's mental balance. Translator's note: Grisar's work was translated by E. Lamond (London, Kegan Paul, 1913). A one volume version produced by Grisar in 1926 was translated as *Martin Luther: His Life and Work* (New York: Herder, 1930).

26. F. X. Kiefl, op. cit.; Richard Stauffer, *Luther as Seen by Catholics* (Richmond, John Knox, 1967), ch. 4.

27. Cf. Y. Congar, *Chrétiens en dialogue* (1964), pp. 123—39.

28. Lortz speaks of the causality, responsibility, and collective fault of all Catholics in the Reformation drama, *How the Reformation Came* (New York, Herder, 1964), pp. 107 ff.

29. Catholic orthodoxy was defined by the Councils of Trent and Vatican (I & II). Before these three councils many questions were matters of dispute, which is difficult to imagine today.

30. Lortz, *The Reformation in Germany*, I, 217—18.

31. Often Luther's works were not even used. The priest Johann Dobneck (Cochlaeus) (1479—1552) had published in 1549 a polemical summary of Luther's deeds: *Commentaria de actis et scriptis Martini Lutheri*. A. Herte showed that Catholic books from the 16th century to our own time were inspired by this work. See A. Herte, *Das katholische Lutherbild im Bann der Lutherkommentare des Cochlaeus*, 3 vols. (1943).

32. Cf. Y. Congar, *Une vie pour la vérité: Jean Puyo interroge le P. Congar* (1975), p. 59.

33. Forgetfulness of Luther in Protestantism today expresses the feeling that the Reformer's teaching is no longer adapted to our problems. Catholics, who know from close hand the Catholicism of which Luther speaks (Jared Wicks, *Man Yearning for Grace* [1968], pp. vi ff.), find him less dated than the Protestant public. They seek a dialog with his writings from a point of view which is still that of the undivided Church. Cf. J. Wicks (ed.), *Catholic Scholars Dialogue with Luther* (Chicago, 1970), including works of Lortz, Iserloh, Pesch, Hacker, McSorley, Manns; O. H. Pesch, "Luther 1967" in *Martin Luther: 450th Anniversary of the Reformation* (1967), pp. 15 ff.

34. The matter of Luther's violence and grossness has to be judged in historical context. It went beyond what one would expect of a prophet devoted to a sacred cause. But this epoch understood such extremes.

35. See, e.g., the diverse views of H. Strohl, *Luther jusqu'en 1520* (pp. 23—42); E. H. Erikson (*Young Man Luther* [New York, 1958], ch. 3); P. Weijenborg (*Antonianum* 31 [1956], pp. 247—300); T. Süss (PL 5 [1957], pp. 284—95); J. Lortz (*The Reformation in Germany*, I, 179 ff.); L. Cristiani (*Revue des questions historiques*, 48, Vol. 51, p. 14).

36. The authenticity of this account is not in doubt. Cf. C. Schubart, *Die Berichte über Luthers Tod und Begräbnis* (Weimar, 1917), and C.R.S. Lenz in ARG, 66 (1975), pp. 79—92. On the Catholic side the legend that Luther hanged himself was rejected by Grisar, *Luther*, III, 851—55.

37. Heresy—"truth gone mad"—is a denaturing of faith. The real point is that every alteration of the givenness of faith brings about the corruption of the whole faith. Heresy is always more than particular errors. In Luther's time this doctrine was abused to disqualify all opposition to the power of the clergy. It was enough to declare someone suspect of heresy to put them in difficulties. Luther had to defend himself against prosecution for heresy well before his statements or his writings gave material for an action justified by the facts. One aspect of the question of heresy was that, in condemning a heretic, the Church tended to close itself to the truths on which his ideas were based.

38. Theses 62 and 68 (LW, 31 p. 31). An indulgence is an amnesty by the Church for punishments for sins. Luther saw them as a caricature of God's grace.

39. J. Lortz, *Die Reformation als religiöses Anliegen heute* (1948); trans. *The Reformation: A Problem for Today* (Westminster, Md.: Newman, 1964).

40. Notably E. Iserloh. Cf. Otto H. Pesch, "L'état actuel de l'entente," *Concilium*, 118 (1976), p. 155.

41. Translator's note: At this point I have omitted, as not relevant to English readers, a few sentences in which the author discusses his own French translations. See Translator's Preface.

Chapter 2

1. Luther struggled throughout his life against distortions of his doctrine by his followers: Melanchthon, who understood justification by faith in juridical fashion ("forensically"); the Anabaptists, who rebaptized adults, because the newborn are incapable of an act of personal faith; Agricola, who affirmed that faith suppressed the obligation of the Law, etc. Cf. the works of Léonard, Lortz, Iserloh, Edwards (see Bibliography).

2. LW, 35, pp. 117—24; WA, 10, I (1), pp. 8—18. This heading is Luther's, but the subheadings are the author's.

3. In the Vulgate the books of Scripture were accompanied by introductions, mostly by Jerome, who was also the translator into Latin. If we can believe Luther about this, scarcely any distinction was made between the statements of the Bible itself and the comments of the authors of these introductions. These prologues had falsified the meaning of the Gospel among the people. See Luther's *Preface to the New Testament*, LW, 35, pp. 359—411.

4. Precepts and examples have always been taken from the teaching and life of Christ. Luther is going to show that Christ is not another Moses (the Law!) and that he is more to us than the saints, who are also preached to us as examples.

5. This mode also applies to those who, even while being sincere, are not truly Christians. They deceive themselves about their good intentions. The Pharisees in the Gospel whom Christ treated as hypocrites (Matt. 23:13-33) also professed to be above all reproach.

6. The Christian's identification with Christ plays an essential role in Luther's doctrine of justification. It results from faith in the Word and explains how we can be justified and please God. God sees in us no more than His own Son. Catholic theology rests on the idea of a "grace" which communicates to the soul a divine disposition which penetrates it, is attached to it, raises it to a supernatural state, and makes it worthy of the friendship of God and an inheritor of eternal glory. The idea is the same. But where the Lutheran was addressed about Jesus Christ, the Catholic had to content himself with abstractions.

7. The word "apostle" comes from the Greek *apostolos*, "one who is sent."

8. In *The Freedom of a Christian* (1520) Luther explains that the good works of the Christian are the fruits of faith. "The Christian does not live in himself but in Christ and his neighbor: in Christ by faith and in his neighbor by love" (WA, 7, 38.6-8; cf. LW, 31, pp. 364 ff.).

9. The pope, in whom Luther saw the opponent of the Gospel, the Antichrist. He reproached him for imposing on theology students the study of papal decretals in place of the Gospel. The Church was encumbered with doctrines and practices which concealed from the faithful the content of the Scriptures. Erasmus criticized this situation as much as Luther did.

10. The best commentary on the *Brief Instruction* is this group of sermons of which it forms the introduction. Translator's note: The Gospel sermons from this series are translated in LW 52. The complete sermons were included in J.

N. Lenker's translation of Luther's works early this century (Minneapolis, Luther Press, 1908 ff.).

11. *Sermon on the Epistle Lesson for the First Sunday in Advent* (Rom. 13:11-14), WA, 10, I (2), 7.4-17.

Chapter 3

1. Luther rejected transubstantiation as an explanation of the Real Presence because it was a recent doctrine (13th century) and not drawn from Scripture.
2. Henri Strohl, *Luther jusqu'en 1520*, p. 73.
3. Luther's youth is known especially through his numerous autobiographical references. These "glances backward" are late (up to 30 years after the event), occasional (Table Talk), and slanted, for Luther interpreted his "papist" youth in a polemical way. His confidences have to be carefully interpreted, and some authors do not always show evidence of a necessary critical sense in this regard; details on which the evidence leaves some doubt are presented as established facts. For the most reliable information see C. V. Gheorgiou, *La jeunesse du Dr. Luther*, and the great biographies by Köstlin, Scheel, Boehmer, Febvre, Villoslada. (See Bibliography.)
4. Cf. Pierre Chaunu, *Le temps des réformes* (Paris, 1975), pp. 181 ff.; J. Huizinga, *The Waning of the Middle Ages* (Penguin, 1955); Jean Delumeau, *Naissance . . . ,* pp. 48 ff.
5. Cf. above, ch. 1, n. 35.
6. Strohl, *Luther jusqu'en 1520*, pp. 52—53 and context. Denifle did not believe Luther's account of his monastic life; but Luther had no need to invent what he stated so often and so consistently. However, the old Luther did hav a tendency to dramatize the crisis, and did not distinguish stages and dates. But his pathos is not without all content, even if he did give birth to the now abandoned "Luther legend."
7. He had to admit that he remained inclined towards evil. Do we need to recall that, in the Augustinian tradition, "concupiscence" is not only lust and that in the Gospel "impurity" is not defined by adolescent "autoeroticism," as has long been taught to seminarians? Luther said at least once that as a monk, he had not known great temptations of the flesh (LW 54, 15). Investigations into his shortcoming with regard to chastity are scarcely conclusive, in the absence of sufficiently authentic and explicit evidence. Cf. E. H. Erikson, *Young Man Luther*, pp. 162—63.
8. Erikson, chs. 2 and 5.
9. Attempts to put in truer perspective the idealized image of Luther long entertained in Protestantism have turned to an excess in the other direction— the idea of the "fallen monk" (see ch. 1 above). Denifle's hostility leads him to perspicacious insights but also into reckless conclusions. He sets over against Luther in an unqualified way the texts of the tradition, of the liturgy, and the law (Augustinian constitutions, the Missal, etc.). But the Church documents explain only in part the reality of the lives of individuals and groups. Denifle should have looked more closely at the Catholicism of Luther's generation rather than that of the books.
10. While teaching the existence of minor faults, Catholicism subordinated entry to heaven to the complete achievement of purification in the purifying fire of purgatory. Sin thus always has a very serious character because it absolutely closes access to heaven. In itself, it belongs only in hell. No compromise is possible between holiness and evil. Luther could have found a way out of his dilemma in the distinctions of the moralists, but he had to go to the real depths of the problem.
11. *De spiritu et littera*, VIII, 14; MPL, 44, 208.

12. In this connection Luther freely cites Gen. 4:3-5. Cain and his brother Abel each offered a sacrifice. God approved Abel and his offering but not Cain and his. The difference lay in the attitudes of the two brothers. Cf. Gen. 4:7.

13. Imbart de la Tour excels in depicting Catholic "moralism," *Origines de la Réforme*, 3 (1914), pp. 33—42. These pages are typical of the way Catholicism has often refuted Luther—and they show the deficiencies of these refutations. We need only to read the quotations given by Imbart in context to see that he leaves out the real point of the discussion by which Luther explains in each case what he wants to say.

14. Luther's idea of God is the enemy of all complacency. His sense of righteousness prevented him from believing that God accommodates himself to our imperfections. Following St. Augustine, he took the view that if sins are to be pardoned daily, the Christian's sanctity always remains in the shadows. God alone is holy.

15. The historian of medieval theology knows the importance of the debates opened up by Duns Scotus' "voluntarism." Cf. P. Vignaux, *De Saint Anselme à Luther* (Paris, 1976), e.g. pp. 237—43. Luther strongly assimilated the influence of this conception of God, in particular by way of the conclusions which 14th- and 15th-century nominalism drew out for the doctrine of individual salvation.

16. Strohl, *Luther jusqu'en 1520*, p. 65.

17. R. Dalbiez, *L'angoisse de Luther*, pp. 57, 215; see below, ch. 4, section 3.

18. Luther opposed the Law to the Gospel, and saw his youthful faith as having been falsified by a conception of the Law which negated the Gospel's new life. He had seen Rom. 1:17 in terms of the rigor of the Law. Later he put Church lawyers in the same bag as the scholastic "sophists." Yet he professed to take literally Christ's affirmation that "not an iota, not a dot" will pass from the Law (Mt. 5:18), and depicted the Law as an executioner authorized to put Christ to death as guilty of the sins of men. Cf. *Commentary on Galatians* 3:13 (LW, 26, pp. 276 ff.).

19. Dalbiez rejects every mystical explanation. For him, Luther seeks only to escape from suicide. But how can we believe a man to be ill and irresponsible whom his colleagues, between 1510 and 1515, sent on a mission to Rome, made a doctor of theology at 29 years of age, and elected a provincial superior?

20. Strohl, *Luther jusqu'en 1520*, pp. 64 ff., makes a good study of this point.

21. The picture of a monk obsessed with scruples is based on an uncritical reading of the *Table Talk*, in which Luther (or his editors) showed themselves implacable about the monastic system.

22. The successive writings show that he held to the teachings he had received until he found the means of replacing those which he judged unacceptable. The convictions with which he began sometimes prevented him for a long time from turning to account those discoveries for which he lacked a principle of coherence that would allow him to turn them into genuine dogmas.

23. "Temptation." Luther meant by this the temptation to despair of God, from the fact that one can never be sure of pleasing him. Cf. E. Vogelsang, *Die Anfänge von Luthers Christologie* (1929), pp. 124—25.

24. H. Bandt, *Luthers Lehre vom verborgenen Gott* (1958).

25. Cf. Theses 4 and 24 of the Heidelberg Disputation (LW, 31, pp. 44 and 55).

26. H. Bornkamm, *Luthers Gestalt und Wirkungen* (1975), pp. 136—43.

27. Strohl, *Luther jusqu'en 1520*, pp. 121; cf. Chaunu, pp. 396 ff.

28. It was on this occasion that Luther called them "swine theologians." The whole passage is full of indignation for the damage wrought in the Church by the insipidness of the doctrine of sin.

29. One of his first initiatives was the publication of the *German Theology* (1516 and 1518), Bornkamm, loc. cit.

30. The doctrine that affirmed that God necessarily grants grace to the one who does what is in him. Luther's judgment was that man in himself had no possibility of doing other than evil. He took a theological, not a moral point of view of it. Cf. Theses 13 and 16 of the Heidelberg Disputation (LW, 31, pp. 48—51).

31. Chaunu, p. 423.

32. Denifle benefited from his discovery of Luther's lectures on Romans. Before him the history of the young Luther was known mainly through late witnesses, and this did nothing to stimulate the study of the Reformation discovery.

33. B. Lohse (ed.), *Der Durchbruch der reformatorischen Erkenntnis bei Luther* (Darmstadt, 1968).

34. Cf. the account given by Pesch in Lohse, pp. 445—505.

35. At Wittenberg they were preoccupied with bringing together the authentic writings on the origins of the Reformation, to allow Lutherans to reply to their opponents. Luther's writings and those which established the sequence of events were edited. The volume published in 1545 classified the writings of Luther beginning with the theses on indulgences and covered the first two years of the movement. What Luther wrote during his "papist" period was consigned to oblivion. It was difficult for the intended public to interpret it. Luther himself put his readers on guard against his remnants of papism. This censured part of his work occupies many volumes in the Weimar Edition.

36. Luther saw an opposition between the Gospel, which is the declaration of mercy, and the idea of righteousness, which is entirely the opposite; righteousness does not forgive. See the text that follows. In Luther's *Lectures on Genesis*, a little earlier than the Preface, we read: "Every time I read this passage, I always wished that God had never revealed the Gospel" (LW, 5, p. 158).

37. Luther and his contemporaries took literally the affirmations of the Bible, which explains the role played by the authority of Scripture in the difficulty (WA TR 5.5553). This selection seems to indicate that scholasticism had educated Luther to see the retributive justice of God in all the texts of the Vulgate or the liturgy where he found the words *iustitia Dei*. Other texts showed him the perspective of the Gospel. But then came Rom. 1:17: "In the Gospel the righteousness of God is revealed."

38. *De spiritu et littera*, IX, 15 (MPL, 44, 209). Luther recognized that Augustine's doctrine was not exactly his own, proof that his citation was due entirely to Augustine's sentence on the meaning of Rom. 1:17.

39. Neither in the preface, nor anywhere else, has Luther left a memorial like that in which Pascal recorded and dated the experience of his conversion of 23 Nov. 1654.

40. Cf. the extract from Grisar in Lohse, pp. 49—52.

41. My view on this matter is that of a small number of authors, notably Bizer and Kurz (each of whom has his own reasons) and, from the Catholic side, Grisar and more recently Wicks, who declares that from 1518 Luther made salvation depend solely on the certainty of faith. (*Man Yearning for Grace*, Wiesbaden, 1967). Cf. Otto H. Pesch, "L'état actual de l'entente," *Concilium*, 118 (1976). K. Aland fixes the Reformation discovery in the second half of February 1518 (Pesch, p. 483). It is striking to find in the commentary on Ps. 5:9 (WA, 5, 144), which dates from the period 1518—19, the essence of the Preface's account.

42. The fact that the debate is centered on Rom. 1:17 is doubtless the explanation for the mention of the *Lectures on Romans*. But the Preface does not specifically draw attention to this course of lectures, which was not to be

published in the Reformer's complete works. (The first edition ever published was that of Ficker, in 1908).

43. Could Cajetan have been behind the crystallization of Luther's reforming thought by challenging him to explain in the name of the pope the basis of his doctrinal position? Luther would then have grasped that his concept of justification by faith, based on Scripture, allowed him and gave him the obligation to resist every demand for a retraction.

44. The question of the Reformation discovery is a theme of the old Luther, which is why I hold to the Preface. The texts scarcely allow us to return to the event of which they speak. Their content, never sufficiently precise, perhaps allows us to say that the texts of 1517 say more than those of 1516 and that before 1518 Luther explains Rom. 1:17 without insisting on the problem of active righteousness or the agonizing interpretation which it would have led him to give to Paul's formulation. But is the effective progress of his thought really around Rom. 1:17? My impression is that Luther came to sum up all his quest by this text which had become more and more significant in his eyes.

45. At least intellectually. We shall see that "anxiety" was still a difficulty throughout his life.

46. Chaunu, p. 417.

47. Luther was carried along by the intellectual movement (humanist and Augustinian) at the University of Wittenberg, of which he was at first the most brilliant representative (cf. the works of Grane, Weier, and Oberman, and the old work of K. Bauer: Bibliography). Moreover, Luther's fathering of the Reformation is disputed by the partisans of Zwingli. But though Zwingli would have developed something even without Luther, we may doubt that the Swiss reform would have found such a favorable reception if its public had not been abreast of the events taking place in Germany, and had not had in hand the writings of Luther, which Froben at Basel had already begun to disperse throughout Europe.

48. Nathan Söderblom. Cf. PL, 5 (1957), 1, p. 53.

49. G. Rupp at the Helsinki Congress, 1966, in *The Church, Mysticism, Sanctification, and the Natural in Luther's Thought* (Philadelphia, Fortress, 1967), pp. 9—19.

50. Cf. Joseph Lortz, *The Reformation in Germany* (New York, Herder, 1968), I, 268.

51. Cf. Imbart de la Tour, op. cit., 3, p. 63, n. 2.

Chapter 4

1. The *Lectures on Romans* are available in English in LW, 25 (ed. H. Oswald) and in Library of Christian Classics, XV (ed. W. Pauck).

2. *Preface to the Epistle of St. Paul to the Romans* (LW, 35, p. 370).

3. LW, 35, pp. 365—80. Translator's note: This heading is Luther's but all the headings within the quoted material are the author's.

4. See above, ch. 2, n. 3.

5. *Unglaube:* incredulity, unbelief, lack of faith, absence of faith, nonfaith, refusal to believe, doubt, etc. It has to do very precisely here with resistance to the Word of God. The difference between it and faith, which is unreserved acceptance of the Word (the gift of Christ), is as radical as between day and night, good and evil. There are no intermediate states. The perspective is not psychological but logical and existential, also Biblical (cf. St. Paul, St. John). One either believes or does not believe.

6. Adam and Eve began by doubting the words of God before eating the forbidden fruit. Sin thus began in unbelief.

7. Luther thought, along with many others, that Paul spoke of himself in Rom.

7:14 ff. The Jerusalem Bible says, on the contrary, that it refers to man under the rule of sin, before justification. But the text has interest only if the sinner of whom Paul speaks is the apostle himself, after justification. Cf. the article of Y. Congar in RSPT, 60 (1976), p. 643, n. 9.

8. Not that faith has the power to "procure" the Holy Spirit. The gift of faith accompanies the effusion of the Spirit, who has no place without faith: "Did you receive the Spirit by works of the law, or by hearing with faith?" (Gal. 3:2). Cf. Rom. 5:5; Gal. 3:14; etc.

9. It was with these feelings that Luther went to Worms the year before. A century earlier John Hus answered the emperor's summons, armed like Luther with a safe-conduct. His "heresy" was not upheld, and he was burned immediately, in contempt of the safe-conduct. At Worms history was in everyone's memory.

10. It is faith which God counts as righteousness; cf. Rom. 4:22. Righteousness is, at one and the same time, being freed from sin and rendering each what is due him.

11. Without faith, that is, in unbelief, every attitude, no matter how correct, lacks the necessary disposition before God. The whole problem of religion is letting God be God. Cf. P.S. Watson, Let God Be God (London, 1970).

12. Heresy and hatred are attitudes of the spirit, but they depend on the flesh.

13. In the matter of faith Luther recognized the authority of no author outside the Biblical writers. He himself was thus obliged to provide the proof of his assertions. He was reproached for his "pride." But he was not wrong to recall that the Church fathers cannot entirely be relied on.

14. Nature without grace here means humanity without Christ, as in Rom. 1—3; cf. 1:18-32.

15. The law of God is a grace which makes us do his will. But for the man disposed to evil, the sinner, it reveals his faults, provoking rebellion and new transgressions. Luther attributes great importance to this teaching of Romans 7, and for the same reason as Paul: The Law should lead the man whose life is not in order to the Savior. See below, Romans ch. 6.

16. "Without merit," for a sinner is beyond the state of meriting the righteousness of God.

17. The righteousness of faith is precisely that which ensures that the Law and the works of the Law will never be attained.

18. God overlooks our sin and does not condemn us, for he wants to take account of faith, which is as much trust in him as it is a struggle against the old man. In the margin it reads: "Faith engages in a ceaseless struggle against sin" (WA DB, 7, p. 19). The whole text is against the idea of an easygoing faith.

   The Lutheran dynamic of faith postulates the persistence of sin. The Catholic conception of the state of grace envisages the soul as coming out of the state of sin. It seems that, in bringing back the problem of sin to morality, we lose the dynamic line which Luther was able to spot in the Bible, as we see here. Cf. D. Olivier, "Péché, Pénitence. Critiques et nouveautés chez Luther et les Réformateurs du XVIe siècle" in Le supplement, 120/121 (March 1977), pp. 75—109.

19. There are formulas of this kind which lead us to say that Luther teaches the "total corruption" of human nature (like a rotten apple). But Luther's consistent view, which we are in the process of reading, is reminiscent of the "enemy" who becomes a friendly foreigner in time of war with his country. Man is at war with God. He is an "enemy" by nature. Whatever his qualities and good feelings, he cannot but conduct himself as an enemy of Christ and his cross. St. Paul says the same.

20. 2 Cor. 3:13-16; cf. Rom. 11:6-8. Moses was the symbol of the Law, opposed to

Christ. But Luther knew the true significance of Moses' teaching, forgotten by the Jews in the New Testament.

21. Luther does not miss the opportunity of pointing out that the Romans of his own time could well apply to themselves what Paul wrote of their distant precursors.

22. R. Garcia-Villoslada speaks (following Lagrange and Lyonnet) of a "Paulinism out of orbit" (*paulinismo desorbitado*) in *Martin Lutero* 1, ch. 8, p. 357. By contrast a view favorable to Luther is seen in J. Lortz, "L'epistle aux Romains dans l'exegèse de Luther" in *Da Tarso a Roma* (Milan, 1961), pp. 78—107.

23. G. Lindbeck, "Critique de l'Église et doctrine de la justification," *Concilium*, 118 (1976), pp. 32—34; Congar, RSPT, 60 (1976), p. 645, n. 27.

24. Johannes Janssen takes this view in his *History of the German People at the Close of the Middle Ages*, 17 vols. (London, Kegan Paul, 1896—1925). Catholics believed in the deep-seated immorality of Luther and his doctrine. Apart from his marriage to a nun, there was his advice to Melanchthon in 1521 to "sin boldly," provided that he believed, and his statement that "if the wife refuses, let the serving-maid come" (Grisar, *Luther*, II, 505). But in the first case, the context shows that there was no encouragement to vice, and in the second, the point is that marriage is broken by the refusal of conjugal rights. In the case of the permission given to the Landgrave Philip of Hesse in 1540 to contract a second marriage without dissolving the first (cf. Delumeau, pp. 105—106), Luther was acting in the role of a confessor with the problem of putting Philip in a situation where he would no longer be sinning, though he lived in marital relationship with two women. Political reasons ruled out a divorce with the first wife. A solution was for ecclesiastical authority to define for the particular occasion the licitness of two marriages simultaneously in force. The incident did not reflect credit on the Reformers (Luther, Melanchthon, and Bucer), who were guilty of abusing the power of the keys and of servility before a powerful defender of the Reformation. It witnesses to the Lutheran sensitivity to the demands of the conscience (concerned only for the avoidance of sin) and to a certain arbitrariness in matters of objective morality. Morality was preserved in that the prince married his second wife according to the rules, but the Church has never authorized polygamy.

25. See the studies in Vilmos Vajta (ed.), *Luther and Melanchthon* (Philadelphia, 1961; papers of the Second International Congress for Luther Research). It was clear that Luther in no way reduced justification to such an elementary schema.

26. His conception of grace as a "divine disposition" made him uninterested in habitual or sanctifying grace (a disposition in man which makes him acceptable to God) or present grace (God's help to do good), ideas which he did not find in that form in the Scriptures.

27. Cf. Strohl, *Luther jusqu'en 1520*, pp. 10—11.

28. Roland Dalbiez, *L'angoisse de Luther: Essai psychologique* (Paris, 1974). Cf. A. Greiner, PL 24 (1976), pp. 54—56; Y. Congar, "Sur l'angoisse de Luther," RSPT, 60 (1976), pp. 638—48. I cannot find fault with Congar's critique and am borrowing some details from it.

29. Paul J. Reiter, *Martin Luthers Umwelt, Charakter und Psychose*, 2 vols. (Copenhagen, 1937/1941). Reiter rules out other illnesses attributed to Luther: syphilis, alcoholism, schizophrenia, epilepsy, neurasthenia. Cf. Armand Iselin, "Les maladies de Luther," *Fraternité évangelique* (July-Aug. 1945); H. Bornkamm, *Luther: Gestalt und Wirkungen* (1975), pp. 11—12.

30. Dalbiez acknowledges that he has not read Reiter, and he does not talk about Erikson's *Young Man Luther*. Both Erikson and Dalbiez analyze the well-known phenomenon of Luther's obscenity. It can be admitted that the "anal"

factor is more marked in the Reformer than in others. Reiter counted 12 "crises" in Luther's life (depression, anger, etc.); cf. Congar, p. 638. Dr. Lamache, however, while declaring Luther "completely irresponsible in the religious domain," in no way questions that "in daily life he bore himself as a normal man" (Dalbiez, p. 9).

Luther's psychosis was tied to his religious experience. Dalbiez's conclusions, rejected by many on confessional grounds, may be refuted by theological argumentation. Luther's anxiety was found among many saints (Augustine, Theresa of the Infant Jesus, etc.). It does not in itself decide the issue of the validity of their doctrine. Dalbiez, moreover, attributes a decisive importance to his theological demonstration. As for Luther's "irresponsibility" in the religious domain, it can be judged from the writings reproduced in this book.

31. Special faith is distinguished from general faith: It is not enough to believe in general in the mysteries of the faith; each should also believe that salvation concerns him especially. Luther effectively insisted on this meaning.

32. Cf. Congar, RSPT, 60, p. 648.

33. See the discussion in E. W. Kohls, "Die Lutherforschung im deutschen Sprachbereich seit 1970," Lj (1977), pp. 29—33.

34. Jacques-Bénigne Bossuet (1627—1704), *Histoire des variations des églises Protestantes* (1688), available in many editions, several in English. Dalbiez refers to Book I, No. 7—8. He cites hardly any other Luther scholars outside Bossuet, except Denifle, Grisar, Cristiani, and Paquier.

35. "Extrinsic" justification is the righteousness imputed by God from outside. It is laid over our sinful reality. In ourselves, we remain sinners. The benefit of imputation is only acquired by the one who believes with total certainty in his own justification. That special faith makes man justified "solely by the fact that he believes in his own justification" (p. 18). Necessary guilt is the idea that man cannot avoid being guilty whatever he does because of his natural temptation to concupiscence, which Peter Lombard and others make into sins. I am limiting the discussion to special faith, which is my subject.

36. Translator's note: The reference is to the noted French psychotherapist Emile Coué (1857—1926), remembered for his method of curing by optimistic autosuggestion.

37. The question of free will was, along with the problem of the pope and the Mass, the decisive difference between Catholicism and Protestantism. The conflict arises from what tradition holds about the value before God of man's spiritual efforts, which Luther tries to exclude from the theology of justification. Catholicism's stubborn resistance to that exclusiveness, and Luther's attempt to prove that when the Christian counts on himself he stops counting on Christ, must *both* be retained. The stakes on both sides are high, but they are not the same. Each has its weak points: Catholicism is exposed to Pelagianism, while Lutheranism is insufficiently motivated to attack the problems of morality at their basis. Cf. James Preus, "La discussion luthérienne sur Luther," *Concilium*, 118 (1976), pp. 92—93.

38. The problem posed by these texts justifies the psychological inquiries on condition that they are interpreted in line with our whole knowledge of Luther. Now the psychological evidence about Luther is made up of a limited number of authentic fragments (a few lines) of occasional confidences reported by others (*Table Talk*) and some isolated facts. There is nothing comparable to Luther's writings about faith, of which we have an embarrassment of riches and which show a balance which psychological investigation is mistaken in not taking into account.

39. Congar enlarges the overly narrow base of Dalbiez's idea. He shows that the data newly put forward by Dalbiez's book allow us to sharpen the debate, not to modify it in a radical way.

40. *Proceedings at Augsburg*, LW 31, pp. 270—71.
41. Ibid., p. 272.
42. Ibid.
43. Delumeau, pp. 289—95, has an adequate discussion of the debate.
44. C. V. Gheorgiou, *La jeunesse du Dr. Luther*, pp. 4 ff.

Chapter 5

1. We have just seen the example of Dalbiez. Another typical instance is the article by M. Clavel, "La nuit de Luther," in the *Nouvel Observateur* 89 (Nov. 1975).
2. Ian D. Kingston Siggins, *Martin Luther's Doctrine of Christ* (Yale, 1970), p. 1; cf. WA, 45, 511.4 (1537).
3. M. Lienhard, *Luther: témoin de Jesus Christ* (Paris, 1973). The expression "faith in Christ" (*fides Christi*) was, like the formula "righteousness of God," among those by which Luther summed up his thought. Cf. Augustine, *De spiritu et littera*, IX, 15 (MPL 44, 209).
4. Cf. E. Wolf, "What Did Luther Really Want?" *Concilium*, Vol. 4, No. 2 (April 1966), p. 13.
5. It appears that purification is worked by Christ, who is personally present in the life of the Christian, thanks to faith. The one who has no faith, the unbeliever, is deprived of that presence and action.
6. "Sermon on the Epistle for Christmas Day" (Heb. 1:1-12). Translator's note: As the sermon is not translated in the American Edition, I have based this translation on the Weimar Edition (WA 10, I (1), pp. 160—62). An English version was published earlier this century, translated by J. N. Lenker: *Luther's Epistle Sermons*, Vol. 1 (Minneapolis: Luther Press, 1908), pp. 166—93.
7. Studies like those of F. Refoulé, "Jesus dans la culture contemporaine" in *Les quatre fleuves* 4 (1975), pp. 6—28, or H. Bourgeois *Libérer Jesus: Christologies actuelles* (Paris, 1977), prove, however, that interest in Christ has not slackened. Cf. Luther's sermons on the Passion of Christ (Lent 1518), WA 1, 336 ff.; Lienhard, pp. 99 ff.
8. This echoes Anselm's theory of redemption, which dominated Catholic theology in the Middle Ages and is still one of the marks of the Germanization of the church. See Joseph Lortz, *History of the Church* (Milwaukee, 1948), Pt. II.
9. In reference to Luther's prologue to his first commentary on the Psalms, Congar remarks (*Chrétiens en dialogue*, pp. 645—46, n. 28): "The ecclesiological allegory is indeed Augustinian. The tropology is specifically that of Luther." From the beginning of his career Luther searched the Scriptures first of all for what concerns Christ (literal-prophetic sense) and what concerns the Christian (tropological sense).
10. On the exegetical method of the young Luther see the works of the Catholics A. Brandenburg, *Gericht und Evangelium* (1960), and J. Vercruyse, *Fidelis populus* (1968), both of which depend on the studies of G. Ebeling. (See Bibliography.)
11. Translator's note: The author uses the standard French version of *The Freedom of a Christian* as the basis for his extended quotation here. This version was a translation of Luther's own German version, rather than the earlier Latin version which is translated in the American Edition (LW, 31, pp. 333—77, our selection pp. 351 f.). The two differ substantially in wording, though their essential thought is identical. In order to present the exact passage which Olivier uses, I have translated the passage direct from the Weimar Edition (WA, 7, 25.26—26.12), borrowing occasional phrases from the English translation of B. L. Woolf in *Reformation Writings of Martin Luther* (London, 1952), I, pp. 363—64.

12. D. Olivier, "Les deux sermons sur la double et triple justice" in *Oecumenica* (1968), pp. 39—69; W. von Loewenich, *Duplex iustitia*, 1972; Lienhard, pp. 114 ff.

13. Luther spoke of Mary in terms of Christ and the Christian. In WA, 5, 624.28 ff. in reference to the virgin birth he compares Christ to honey which has everything from the flower (through the bee) without damaging the flower's integrity. His commentary on the Magnificat (trans. LW 21) has been reedited by a Catholic publisher. See also H. Düfel, *Luthers Stellung zur Marienverehrung* (1968).

14. For Luther's exposition of his view of transubstantiation see *The Babylonian Captivity of the Church* (1520), LW 36, and *Confession Concerning Christ's Supper* (1528), LW 37.

15. *An Exposition of the Lord's Prayer for Simple Laymen*, LW 42, p. 59.

16. The ecumenical movement has brought Protestantism a eucharistic renewal. "The first Christians would never have had the idea of celebrating worship without the meal of the real presence of Christ. It was a command of Christ: 'Do this in memory of me!' Who is there who should not obey? Frequent Communion is a sign of a Church bound to Christ" (Evangelical Lutheran Church of France; Paris, 1974).

17. *On the Councils and Churches* (1539), LW 41; cf. WA, 50, 582 ff.

18. For the theology of the Church's ministry in Luther cf. W. Stein, *Das kirchliche Amt bei Luther* (1975), or my essay "Les deux visages du prêtre: Les chances d'une crise" (Paris, 1971).

19. Y. Congar judges that Luther does not allow the need for seeing merit in the human freedom of Christ: "Regards et réflexions sur la Christologie de Luther" in his book, *Chrétiens en dialogue* (1964), pp. 453—89. Lienhard, op. cit., often returns to this question.

20. Doctrines in dispute between Catholics and Protestants are not mentioned in the Creed (the pope, transubstantiation, etc.). Luther allowed the Creed without any discussion (though there was a difficulty with "I believe in the Catholic Church").

21. The Lutheran tradition tied the merit of Christ to the obedience of his whole person. *Formula of Concord* (1577), II, 3. In speaking with the same insistence as Catholicism of the merits of Christ, Lutheranism does not generally say altogether the same thing. Cf. Lienhard, pp. 93—94 and passim.

22. Lienhard, pp. 120—28. Cf. Paul Althaus, *The Theology of Martin Luther* (Philadelphia, Fortress, 1966), ch. 5; W. von Loewenich, *Luther's Theology of the Cross* (Belfast, Christian Journals Limited, 1976), passim.

23. A psychologizing reading of the passages in which Luther develops this point leans towards the view of "morbid culpability." Most often it is a matter of a strictly theological reasoning which appeals to many passages of Scripture. Cf. Heidelberg Disputation, Thesis 4; LW, 31, 44.

24. WA, 5, 603 ff.; Lienhard, pp. 122 ff.

25. The remark is Luther's own in this context.

26. The idea that Christ is stripped of his divinity for us. Cf. Lienhard, p. 398, who explains the misunderstanding by reference to Luther.

27. J. Moltmann, *The Crucified God: The Cross of Christ as the Foundation and Criticism of Christian Theology* (London, 1974).

28. Cf. R. Mokrosch, "Politique et société dans la théologie de Luther," *Concilium* 118 (1976), pp. 35—47; P. Althaus, *The Ethics of Luther* (Philadelphia, Fortress, 1972); J. Heckel, *Lex charitatis* (2nd ed., 1973); H. Bornkamm, *Luthers Lehre von den zwei Reichen im Zusammenhang seiner Theologie* (3rd ed., 1969). The texts cited in the next chapter give the essence of Luther's ethics and those of the Augsburg Confession. In my article "Personne chrétien,

personne social: Luther et la vocation" in *Le supplement* 123 (Nov. 1977), pp. 489—506, I have attempted a presentation of this debate, for which there is no room here.
29. Heidelberg Disputation, Thesis 28. Siggins (pp. 80—84) shows the development of the theme throughout Luther's life.

Chapter 6

1. Because it touches the conscience and, through that, the structure of a society still unquestionably religious.
2. Luther's refusal to retract at Worms set off a crisis in which problems of Church and society were intermingled. Political factors were often more determinative than doctrinal questions, for the princes were more disposed to reform than the bishops. There are also, of course, other Reformers. Yet Luther's Gospel lay at the source of the dynamism and expansive power of early Protestantism. It was he alone who pronounced the "no" at Worms. Cf. Delumeau, *Naissance* . . . , pp. 257—80.
3. Taking things this way from the standpoint of the Roman Church and thus of its language seems to me to be justified by the need to push beyond the ecumenical balance sheet which Brandenburg, for example, sets up in *Martin Luther gegenwärtig* (1968), pp. 43—62.
4. Historians who think too much importance is given to Luther do not always seem to have read his writings closely, or they forget that his contemporaries fought to get their hands on them, while many other writers of the 16th century have only been discovered by modern scholarship. The radical novelty of the doctrine of justification by faith should not be obscured by studies developed today on the "Prereformation" and the nonreligious factors in the Reformation. Every explanation which minimizes the influence of Luther's doctrine flies in the face of historical truth.
5. Letter to Albrecht of Mainz, LW, 48, pp. 43—49.
6. Has Catholicism ever understood what Luther, the Reformation, and Protestantism represent for it—as expressions of the question of the Gospel posed to a Church which gives the greatest place to the Law?
7. From the Protestant point of view, there was no departure of the Reformers from the Church, rather the liberation of the Church from the Babylonian Captivity of the papacy.
8. *Confession Concerning Christ's Supper*, Pt. III; LW, 37, 360—72 (WA 26, 499 ff.). The context was Luther's attack on those who falsified the doctrines of Baptism and the Eucharist. The subheadings are ours.
9. Luther and his generation expected the end of the world. The Last Judgment was thus imminent. According to 2 Thess. 2:3-12 the last days would see the appearance of the Antichrist, whom the Reformers saw incarnated in the papacy of their time.
10. Heresies in regard to the Trinity, of the third and fourth centuries.
11. Confession of Christ and his grace leads to a rejection of free will. The struggle on this issue between Luther and Erasmus in 1525 was the decisive turning point of the Reformation from the standpoint of ideas. The debate went to the heart of the matter, the conception of man which underlies every theology of sin and grace. Luther saw in Catholicism's affirmation of the freedom to choose good over evil a negation of Christ's grace. If man can manage his own conversion to God, he can finally dispense with Christ. The *Confession* uses a schema borrowed from feudalism, that the servants of a Lord or prince are identified with his cause. Original sin makes us vassals of Satan, sin, and death, whom Christ must attack and reduce to his will.
12. Lutheran theology took Catholic theology of sin and works for Pelagianism.

That accusation follows logically from Luther's neo-Augustinianism. In bringing back the conflict to the controversy between Augustine and the Pelagian heresy, the Reformation put itself in the position of strength and gave itself the leading role. What was lacking, despite everything, with Luther was the decisive point: why Augustine and a thousand years of Christian faith after him had recognized in man an effective role in his salvation, while rejecting Pelagianism. Catholic theology of Reformation times was open to semi-Pelagian ideas condemned at the Council of Trent. Luther had not invented the problem, but he did not fully justify his radical solution. (See the works of Pesch and McSorley, Bibliography.)

13. Cf. Matt. 24:24.
14. 1 Tim. 2:5.
15. This passage expresses the basis of Luther's radicalism.
16. Luther defines the Church by its members (the believers) and its Head (Christ). The ministry of clergy comes afterwards. The papal Church is not to be confused with the Church of Christ. The pope is on the human level the head of a particular Church; only Christ is the head of the Universal Church (*On the Papacy at Rome*, LW 39). Cf. J. Vercruysse, *Fidelis populus* (1968); Scott Hendrix, "Luther et la papauté," *Concilium*, 118 (1976), pp. 49—60.
17. A rigorist sect which refused pardon to those who fell into sin after absolution.
18. *Gebetbüchlein*, pub. 1522; LW, 43, pp. 11—45 (WA 10, II pp. 331—501).
19. Luther pretended not to know anything of the ancient and impressive tradition of prayers for the dead, arguing from the silence of Scripture. The abolition by the Reformation of such practices born of feeling and popular piety was an unprecedented act of violence to the Church, to realism, and good sense. In Luther's case it was based on his concern for the unquestioned authority of Scripture.
20. Did Luther here mean to speak of *Anfechtung*, or indicate that he was not ignorant of what was written about purgatory?
21. Cf. the beginning of Luther's exposition of ordination in the *Babylonian Captivity*, LW 36, pp. 106 ff.
22. In one phrase we here have Luther's three grievances against the Mass: money, sacrifice, meritorious work. On the first point, there were abuses, but Luther's picture of the Church as riddled with simony was too simple. On sacrifice, Luther reproached himself for having crucified Christ through his Masses, while the conception of the meritorious value of the Mass left too much to human initiative. We shall return to these points.
23. Was this a reference to youthful errors, prior to Luther's entry to the monastery? Most similar declarations (WA, 58, I, pp. 17 ff.), however, concern a monastic life, the search for justification by works, and lack of faith in God's mercy.
24. Leonard, I, ch. 3. In 1529 a protestation of Lutheran princes and cities brought the term "Protestant" into usage. It was a protest against the questioning of the first achievements of the Reformation. Attachment to the Gospel was by this time no longer Luther's business alone.
25. The first two were burnt alive at Antwerp in 1523. The punishment of Berquin took place in Paris on 16 April 1529. On the French martyrs see R. J. Lovy, *Les origines de la réforme francaise* (1959).
26. De la Brosse, *Latran V et Trente*, p. 171, speaks of "aversion." The papacy was concerned not to let partisans of conciliar theory, who were not all Lutherans, reopen the chronic question of primacy.
27. The text was edited by Melanchthon (under direction from a distance by Luther, who was forbidden to travel to Augsburg, because of the Worms edict). On the divergence between Luther and his lieutenant cf. W. Maurer, *Historischer Kommentar zur Confessio Augustana*, I (1976), and P. Manns, *Ökum. Rundschau*, 29 (Oct. 1977), pp. 426—50.

Translator's note: The Latin and German versions of the confession are not identical in detail. Both are translated into English in Theodore G. Tappert (ed.), *The Book of Concord* (Philadelphia, 1959), pp. 23—96. Citations in the text are from this edition and, where not otherwise given, may be found by reference to the article indicated. The critical edition is *Die Bekenntnisschriften der evangelisch-lutherischen Kirche* (1930; 5th ed. Göttingen, 1973).

28. In respect to both doctrine and abuses, true Christianity is defined by going back to the sources. The Reformation responded to the need for finding a surer religious basis in a Church which characteristically dealt with problems on the basis of recent matters.

29. Incapacity for believing in God is the proof *par excellence* of original sin.

30. German: *angeborne Seuch* (infection). Latin: *morbus seu vitium originis* (concupiscence).

31. German: *opfer*. Latin: *hostia*. This vocabulary is directed against the Mass.

32. In this passage the Anabaptists and other "enthusiasts" are condemned. They pretend to know the Holy Spirit without the instruments intended by God for this purpose, and they rely on subjective dispositions.

33. Cf. MPL 17, 195 (Ambrosiaster).

34. German: *die Versammlung aller Glaubigen*. Latin: *congregatio sanctorum*. Another passage brings together the two ideas: community of saints and true believers.

35. The rites and festivals which can be allowed without sin are preserved. But it should not be believed that the cult as such is necessary for salvation. Everything said and done in this sense is contrary to the Gospel.

36. J. Hamer, "Les pécheurs dans l'Eglise" in *Festgabe Lortz*, I, 193—288.

37. It is maintained that no one should exercise ministry in the Church without having "a regular call" (Art. XIV).

38. Art. XIII. Zwingli made the sacraments signs of recognition between Christians: insignias.

39. The Augsburg Confession does not discuss sacraments in general, but notes only important points such as Baptism and the Real Presence, and emphasizes the proper use of the sacraments to build up faith in God's promises. This entailed defense of the signs, which Luther believed to be in decay. This held true for the practices of withholding the cup from the laity and of baptizing by daubing the child's forehead with water on the fingertips, which evoked Christ's plunging into the Jordan River only in a very distant way.

40. This is followed by a resumé of Luther's doctrine with reference to Augustine, notably to the *De spiritu et littera*. The absence of the Gospel from the Church, as far as the Reformation is concerned, derives from attributing efficacy to the merit of works, which brings with it a real negligence in the proclamation of faith and certainly an alteration in the consciousness of God.

41. Tappert, pp. 44—45. Cf. Augustine, MPL, 34, 2055; 40, 1025. The true knowledge of God is accessible only to faith. See E. Wolf, "Martin Luther: Das Evangelium und die Religion" in *Peregrinatio*, 1 (1954), pp. 9—29. (That controversy caused much ink to flow in the 20th century, in the debate between Karl Barth and Emil Brunner.)

42. Art. XXII. The suppression of the tabernacle is a consequence of the same idea. For Luther it does not have the meaning of negating the Real Presence.

43. Tappert, p. 59. We can here see clearly that opposition to the sacrifice of the Mass attacks, on the one hand, the idea that the sacrifice of Christ had value only in respect to original sin, which made necessary other sacrifices for present sins; and, on the other hand, the existence of another expiatory sacrifice for sins after the one offered once for all by Christ. Theology lays itself open to the

objections of the Reformers, even if the ideas objected to are taken in an acceptable sense.

E. Iserloh, *Der Kampf um die Messe in den ersten Jahren der Auseinandersetzung mit Luther* (Münster, 1952), and E. Jamoulle in NRTh, 67 (1945), 513—31.

44. After the break in negotiations at Augsburg (summer/autumn 1530) Melanchthon published a substantial Apology for the Augsburg Confession, in which he showed at length that the ancient Church had known and practiced what the Lutherans were asking for (Tappert, pp. 97—285).

45. The silences of the Augsburg Confession are not necessarily negations. The aim of tracing the essential line of an evangelical reform leads it to accentuate the differences: Not all questions require fresh definition. Silence on the pope was to avoid putting the papacy in question in the emperor's presence, and in any case, Melanchthon was not as hostile as Luther to the pope. On transubstantiation it was judged sufficient to declare agreement with Rome on the Real Presence (Art. X).

46. A Confutation was drafted. CR, 28, cols. 81—184, 189—240.

47. Tappert, pp. 287—318. Cf. T. McDonough, *The Law and the Gospel in Luther* (1963).

48. Cf. P. Manns, op. cit.

49. Smalcald Articles, Pt. II, Art. II; Tappert, p. 294.

50. Luther's exposition has to be supplemented by Melanchthon's Treatise on the Power and Primacy of the Pope; Tappert, pp. 319—35.

51. It was difficult to say whether his despotism or his matrimonial and religious problems predominated with Henry VIII. But with the advent of Elizabeth I (1558, excommunicated 1570) it becomes clear that the Reformation has taken place.

52. Cf. P. Fraenkel in *Oecumenica* (1968), pp. 70—116.

53. Luther himself sometimes had questions. The reverberations of his message made him say that the very stones would have cried out if the followers of the Gospel had kept silence (Luke 19:40). Yet he thought that if he had it to do all over again he would have done it differently, or not at all. The consequences of his actions frightened him, and he was conscious of many errors (not those for which Rome reproached him). At other times he was sustained by the knowledge that God had led him (WA, 58, 47 ff.).

Chapter 7

1. The Fifth International Congress for Luther Research (Lund, August 1977) included a "disputation," between the Lutheran Eric W. Gritsch and the Catholic A. Brandenburg, on Luther's present significance. There I found the major ideas for this chapter. But where Brandenburg envisaged a reception of Luther by the Catholic Church, the first question seems to me to be that Catholicism should be seized by the problem of the Gospel in the Church. This is what Luther asks, and he certainly has nothing to lose by it.

2. De la Brosse, *Latran V et Trente*, pp. 433—44.

3. The Lateran Council had been held less than 30 years ago. Protestantism had again put forward conciliar theories against papal primacy. The existence of the (Protestant) Schmalkaldic League had the effect of discounting hopes of leading the Protestants to negotiate without first defeating them in battle.

4. For the history of the Council of Trent cf. H. Jedin, *Geschichte des Konzils von Trent*, trans. *History of the Council of Trent*, 2 vols. (London, Nelson, 1957). De la Brosse gives a good account of the first period, 1545—47. See also Delumeau, *Catholicism Between Luther and Voltaire*, ch. 1; *Nouvelle histoire de l'Eglise*, III, 125—86.

5. That faith in the living magisterium of the Church defines Catholicism. Vatican I (1869—70) would proclaim papal infallibility. Protestantism attributes every bit as much to the Holy Spirit the grace of infallibility in the interpretation of revelation. But instead of seeing in the successor of Peter the privileged depository of this gift granted to the whole Church, it ties it to Scripture itself and sees it distributed within the community of the faithful. Cf. the discussion in B. Sesboue, *L'Evangile dans l'Eglise* (1975).

6. De la Brosse, pp. 284—305.

7. Ibid., p. 299.

8. For the debate on justification through the ages see H. Küng, *Justification* (London, Burns & Oates, 1964).

9. For the conception of the person in Luther see G. Ebeling, *Luther: An Introduction to His Thought* (London, Collins, 1970); W. Joest, *Ontologie der Person bei Luther* (1967), P. Hacker, "Martin Luther's Notion of Faith" in J. Wicks (ed.), *Catholic Scholars Dialogue with Luther* (Chicago, 1970).

10. According to Ch. Baumgartner, *La grace du Christ*, 2nd ed. (Paris, 1963), pp. 105—20, faith according to Trent prepares for justification (p. 112) and is found in the train of righteousness; it is not the cause of it.

11. *Nouvelle histoire de L'Eglise*, III, 181; cf. above ch. 6, n. 43.

12. Catholicism recoils from implicating "the Church" as such in the errors and faults of its history. It is thus more free to criticize churchmen and theologians once they are no longer in power.

13. By the institution of seminaries. Delumeau, *Catholicism Between Luther and Voltaire*, pp. 31 ff. The Reformation, for its part, placed the emphasis on schools of preaching.

14. Protestant theologians can judge that the Reformers' objections preserve all their force. But who would want to take the offensive on these points in the terms of Luther's confession of faith? Catholicism is only maintaining the heritage of the ancient undivided Church.

15. Catholic doctrine remains the point of departure and necessary reference point of Protestant theological systems. J. Pelikan, *Obedient Rebels: Catholic Substance and Protestant Principle in Luther's Reformation* (New York, 1964), expresses the wish that these two aspects be united. For the Catholic, Protestantism is generally more convincing as a critique than as a continuation of tradition; cf. Paul Tillich, *The Protestant Era* (London, 1951) and other writings. The Reformers appealed to Scripture, ancient tradition, and a more personal awareness of faith and grace. They intended to reject only inventions and corruptions and to assure the true continuity of the Church, but Protestantism today finds in Catholicism many reasons for correcting the excessive radicalism of the suppressions carried out in the 16th century.

16. Because the Tridentine reform had nothing in common with a program like that of the Augsburg Confession, historians speak of two Reformations in the 16th century though, for the Protestant, the Catholic reformation brought nothing new. The new aspect of the crisis was quite certainly the awakening of conscience to the Gospel of justification by faith. Trent saw in the Reformation only a providential punishment for the negligence of the hierarchy. But if everything boiled down to inadequacies happily overcome, would not the Church sooner or later have recovered her unity?

17. The defenders of orthodoxy did not allow themselves to be disturbed by such a small matter. That the Protestants were Christians and were right about the facts did not in their view change the fact that they were in error. The strict logic of such an attitude precluded the question of whether Rome had incorrectly understood the problems.

18. The need to demonstrate, on one side as on the other, that one was in continuity

with the Church provided the impulse for study of the Bible, patristics, and church history.

19. J. Delumeau, *Le christianisme va-t-il mourir?* (Paris 1977) and the works already cited.

20. There was no reason to adopt all the views of the Wittenberg monk. His theology, which was still in part mixed up with that of his university, was novel and corresponded to concerns not shared at Rome. Even if it was necessary to make concessions in relation to indulgences, the injury would not have been irreparable and merited better than the trifling critique of a Prierias or an Eck.

21. The Middle Ages sacralized everything. The Lutheran faith consecrated the person.

22. Protestant antipapism ("No Popery!") is no better. But it is not really a question of deciding which of the two streams of Christianity can claim to be better than the other.

23. H. A. Oberman, *Masters of the Reformation* (Cambridge, 1981), p. 7.

24. The Scriptural principle could have been seen at Trent as a development of dogma. The Church has never had the experience of the real fruitfulness of the Scriptures, as in Protestantism. The Bible is one of the true foundations of the Church.

25. Sesboue, Lindbeck. Fr. Sesboue scarcely considers the problem of the non-Gospel in the Church.

26. M. Vidal, *L'Eglise peuple de Dieu dans l'histoire des hommes* (1975).

27. G. Casalis, cited by F. Refoule, "Deux réformes." *Études théol. et religieuses,* 1—2 (1968), p. 80. Cf. A. Ganoczy, *Calvin et Vatican II: L'Eglise servante* (1968).

28. Fraternization between individuals has not advanced Church union by one step. The fact that it takes place changes nothing in law.

29. The doctrine of Trent nevertheless allows a large margin of interpretation which the Counter-Reformation would not have conceded. Cf. A. Dulles, *La foie, la dogme et les chrétiens* (1975).

30. Paul VI, "Annoncer l'Evangile aux hommes de notre temps" (Paris, 1976). Texts of the 1974 synod: *L'Eglise des cinq continents,* ed. J. Potin and C. C. Ehlinger (Paris, 1975).

31. *L'Eglise des cinq continents,* pp. 68—78.

32. Eric W. Gritsch at the Lund Congress.

33. G. Casalis, *Protestantism* (1976), pp. 22—23.

34. The incompatibility of Luther's faith with the Catholic faith defined at Trent is not the real obstacle. All the difficulty has come from the false starting point; Trent's exclusiveness clearly was valid only in this perspective which no longer applies.

35. Cf. Jean Guitton, "Orthodoxie," *Le Monde,* 26 Oct. 1977.

Bibliographical Suggestions

Part I. Basic Works

A. Interpretation

Pierre Chaunu, *Le temps des réformes* (Paris, Fayard, 1973).

Jean Delumeau, *Naissance et affirmation de la Réforme*, 3rd ed. (Paris, Pr. Univ. de France, 1973).

Lucien Febvre, *Un destin: Martin Luther*, 4th ed. (Paris, Pr. Univ. de France, 1968); trans. *Martin Luther: A Destiny* (New York, Dutton, 1929).

Émile G. Léonard, *Histoire générale du protestantisme* (Paris, Pr. Univ. de France, 1961); trans. *A History of Protestantism* (London, Nelson, 1965).

Joseph Lortz, *Die Reformation in Deutschland* (Freiburg, Herder, 1939/40); trans. *The Reformation in Germany* (New York, Herder, 1968).

Henri Strohl, *Luther jusqu'en 1520*, 2nd ed. (Paris, Pr. Univ. de France, 1962).

B. Cyclopedia Articles on Luther

Catholicisme (1975) (F. Frost).

Dictionnaire de spiritualité (J. Wicks).

Dictionnaire de théologie catholique (Paris, 1903) (J. Paquier).

Die Religion in Geschichte und Gegenwart, 3rd ed. (1957—65) (H. Bornkamm on biography, G. Ebeling on doctrine).

C. Periodicals (publications of French Protestantism marked*)

Archiv für Reformationsgeschichte (Gütersloh).

*Bulletin de la Société d'Histoire du Protestantisme Francais** (Paris).

*Études théologiques et religieuses** (Montpellier).

Lutherjahrbuch (Göttingen).

*Positions Luthériennes** (Paris).

Revue d'histoire ecclésiastique (Louvain).

*Revue d'histoire et de philosophie religieuses** (Strasbourg/Paris).

Revue des sciences philosophiques et théologiques (Paris).

D. Reference

Kurt Aland, *Hilfsbuch zum Lutherstudium*, 3rd ed. (Witten, Luther-Verlag, 1970).

E. *Bibliography and Historiography*

Walter Beyna, *Das moderne katholische Lutherbild* (Essen, Ludgerus, 1969).

Harold J. Grimm, *The Reformation Era* (New York, Macmillan, 1965).

Hans Gerhard Koch, *Luthers Reformation in kommunistischer Sicht* (Stuttgart, Quell, 1967).

Lewis W. Spitz, *The Reformation: Basic Interpretations* (Boston, Heath, 1972).

Richard Stauffer, *Le catholicisme à la découverte de Luther* (Neuchâtel, Delachaux, 1966); trans. *Luther as Seen by Catholics* (Richmond, Va., John Knox, 1967).

Gerhard Philip Wolf, *Das neuere französische Lutherbild* (Wiesbaden, Steiner, 1974).

Also: Léonard, Lortz (above, I A), *Lutherjahrbuch* (above, I C).

Part II. History of the Church and the Reformation

A. *Collective Works*

Deux mille ans de Christianisme, Vol. 5 (Paris, 1976).

Histoire de L'Eglise (A. Fliche and V. Martin), Vol. 16. *La crise religieuse du XVIe siècle* (ed. E. DeMoreau, P. Jourda, and P. Janelle) (1950).

Kleine Reformationsgeschichte (Freiburg, Herder, 1969) (J. Lortz and E. Iserloh).

Nouvel histoire de L'Église, Vol. 3. *Réforme et Contre-Réforme* (ed. H. Tuchle, C. A. Bouman, and J. LeBrun) (1968).

Ökumenische Kirchengeschichte, Vol. 2. *Mittelalter und Reformation* (Munich, 1973).

B. *Individual Works*

Henri Daniel-Rops, *L'Église de la Renaissance et de la Réforme* (Paris, Fayard, 1967); trans. *The Protestant Reformation* (New York, Dutton, 1961).

Helmar Junghans, *Die Reformation in Augenzeugenberichten*, 2nd ed. (Düsseldorf, Rauch, 1967).

Joseph Lortz, *Geschichte der Kirche in ideengeschichtlicher Betrachtung*, 21st ed. (Münster, Aschendorff, 1964); trans. from 4th/5th ed., *History of the Church* (Milwaukee, Bruce, 1948).

Rene-Jacques Lovy, *Les origines de la réforme francais* (Paris, Lib. Protestante, 1959).

Marcel Pacaut, *Histoire de la papauté, de l'origine au concile de Trent* (Paris, Fayard, 1976).

Lewis W. Spitz, *The Renaissance and Reformation Movements* (St. Louis, Concordia, 1981).

Part III. Biography

A. *French*

Georges Casalis, *Luther et l'Église confessante* (Paris, iv Ed. du Sevil, 1970).

Frantz Funck-Brentano, *Luther* (London, Cape, 1936).

Albert Greiner, *Luther: Essai biographique*, 2nd ed. (Geneva, Labor et Fides, 1970).
Rene-Jacques Lovy, *Luther* (Paris, Univ. de France, 1964).

B. *German*

Heinrich Boehmer, *Der junge Luther* (Gotha, Flamberg, 1925); trans. *Martin Luther, Road to Reformation* (Philadelphia, Muhlenberg, 1946).
Heinrich Fausel, *D. Martin Luther, Leben und Werk* (Munich, Siebenstern, 1966).
Richard Friedenthal, *Luther, Sein Leben und seine Zeit* (Munich, Piper, 1967).
Hartmann Grisar, *Luther* (Freiburg, Herder, 1911—12); trans. *Luther* (London, Kegan Paul, 1913—17).
Julius Köstlin, *Luthers Leben* (Leipzig, 1882); trans. *Life of Luther* (New York, Scribners, 1927).
———, (with G. Kawerau), *Martin Luther, Sein Leben und seine Schriften*, 5th ed. (Berlin, Duncker, 1903).
Franz Lau, *Luther*, 2nd ed. (Berlin, de Gruyter, 1966); trans. *Luther* (Philadelphia, Westminster, 1963).
Karl Meissinger, *Der katholische Luther* (Munich, Lehnen, 1952).
Otto Scheel, *Martin Luther, Vom Katholizismus zur Reformation*, new ed. (Tübingen, Mohr, 1921—30).
———, *Dokumente zu Luthers Entwicklung*, 2nd ed. (Tübingen, Mohr, 1929).

C. *English*

Roland H. Bainton, *Here I Stand: A Life of Martin Luther* (New York, Abingdon, 1950).
E. Gordon Rupp, *Luther's Progress to the Diet of Worms* (London, SCM, 1951).
Ernest G. Schwiebert, *Luther and His Times: The Reformation from a New Perspective* (St. Louis, Concordia, 1950).
John M. Todd, *Martin Luther: A Biographical Study* (London, Burns and Oates, 1964).

D. *Spanish*

Ricardo Garcia-Villoslada, *Martin Lutero* (Madrid, Ed. Catolica, 1973).

Part IV. Theology

Paul Althaus, *Die Theologie Martin Luthers*, 2nd ed. (Gütersloh, Gerd Mohn, 1963); trans. *The Theology of Martin Luther* (Philadelphia, Fortress, 1966).
Martin Bogdahn, *Die Rechfertigungslehre Luthers im Urteil der neueren katholischen Theologie* (Göttingen, Vandenhoeck, 1971).
Louis Bouyer, *Du Protestantisme a l'Église*, 3rd ed. (Paris, Ed. Cerf. 1959).
Charles Boyer, *Luther: Sa doctrine* (Rome, Gregorian Univ., 1970).
Albert Brandenburg, *Martin Luther gegenwärtig* (Munich, Schöningh, 1969).

Leo Chestov, *Sola Fide, Luther et L'Eglise* (Paris, Pr. Univ. de France,

Leo ... ther et Saint Augustin* in *Augustinus magister*

Ger ... *Evangelisch Evangelienauslegung* (Munich, Kaiser,
194...

———, ... *Denken*, 2nd e. ———ingen, Mohr,
1974); trans. *Luther: An Introduction to His Thought* (London,
Collins, 1970).

Mark U. Edwards, *Luther and the False Brethren* (Palo Alto, Stanford,
1975).

Leif Grane, *Modus loquendi theologicus: Luthers Kampf um die
Erneuerung der Theologie* (Leyden, Brill, 1975).

Maurice Gravier, *Luther et l'opinion public* (Paris, Aubler, 1942).

Albert Greiner, *Martin Luther, ou l'hymne à la grace* (Paris, Plon, 1966).

Walter Koehler, *Katholizismus und Reformation* (Giessen, Töpelmann,
1905).

Marc Lienhard, *Luther, témoin de Jésus Christ* (Paris, Ed. Cerf., 1973).

Walther von Loewenich, *Luthers theologia crucis*, 5th ed. (Munich
Kaiser, 1967); trans. *Luther's Theology of the Cross* (Belfast, Christian
Journals Limited, 1976).

Thomas McDonough, *The Law and the Gospel in Luther* (London,
Oxford University Press, 1963).

Harry McSorley, *Luther: Right or Wrong?* (New York, Newman, and
Minneapolis, Augsburg, 1969).

Roger Mehl, *La théologie protestante* (Paris, Pr. Univ. de France, 1965).

Heiko A. Oberman, *Werden und Wertung der Reformation* (Tübingen,
Mohr, 1977); trans. *Masters of the Reformation* (Cambridge, Cambridge University Press, 1981).

Otto H. Pesch, *Theologie der Rechtfertigung bei M. Luther und Th. von
Aquin* (Mainz, Matthias Grünewald, 1967).

Stephan Pfürtner, *Angoisse et certitude du salut: Luther et saint Thomas
au delà des oppositions traditionelles* (Paris, Centurion, 1967).

Richard Stauffer, *La Réforme*, 2nd ed. (Paris, Pr. Univ. de France, 1974).

Wolfgang Stein, *Das kirchliche Amt bei Luther* (Wiesbaden, Steiner,
1974).

Henri Strohl, *Luther, sa vie et sa pensée* (Strasbourg, Oberlin, 1953).

Theobald Süss, *Luther* (Paris, Pr. Univ. de France, 1969).

Philip Watson, *Let God Be God* (London, Epworth, 1947).

Reinhold Weier, *Das Theologieverständnis Martin Luthers* (Paderborn,
Bonifacius, 1976).

Jared Wicks, *Man Yearning for Grace* (Washington, Corpus, 1968).